UPGRADE

UPGRADE

TAKING
YOUR WORK
AND LIFE FROM
ORDINARY TO
EXTRAORDINARY

RANA FLORIDA

Mc
Graw
Hill
Education

New York Chicago San Francisco Athens London Madrid Mexico City
Milan New Delhi Singapore Sydney Toronto

1 2 3 4 5 6 7 8 9 0   DOC/DOC   1 8 7 6 5 4 3

ISBN: 978-0-07-182721-8
MHID: 0-07-182721-8

e-ISBN: 978-0-07-182722-5
e-MHID: 0-07-182272-6

McGraw-Hill books are available at special quantity discounts to use as premiums and sales promotions, or for use in corporate training programs. To contact a representative, please visit the Contact Us page at www.mhprofessional.com.

Library of Congress Cataloging-in-Publication Data

Florida, Rana.
  Upgrade : taking your work and life from ordinary to extraordinary / by Rana Florida.
     pages cm
  ISBN-13: 978-0-07-182721-8 (alk. paper)
  ISBN-10: 0-07-182721-8 (alk. paper)
  1. Self-actualization (Psychology) 2. Success. I. Title.
  BF637.S4F59 2014
  158—dc23
                              2013010960

This book is printed on acid-free paper.

For Richard

CONTENTS

What do you want to do with your life? So why aren't you doing it?

Find your passion. If you can't get paid for your passion, do it on the side. If you don't have a passion, do things that make you happy. It's that simple.

Creativity is everywhere and in every person. Fitting into the status quo is out. Thinking differently is in. Learn to tap, harness, and unleash your creative potential.

Guard your schedule and protect your time from the negative, bored, and filler people in your world. Think of everything as a time management tool and use technology to your advantage.

ACKNOWLEDGMENTS

As with all of our work, the writing of this book was accomplished with the contributions of insightful collaborators. The book first came to life in the interviews I conducted for my column "Your Start-Up Life." *Huffington Post* editor Danielle Crittenden Frum gave me the chance for my voice to be heard. Her enthusiasm and support are a rarity in the media business, where ideas are shot down quickly. The senior blog editors at the *Huffington Post* are lightning quick in responding to my inquiries and featuring my posts, including Erin Ruberry in D.C. and Stuart Whatley in New York.

I am grateful to all the people who took the time to answer my questions, including Andre Agassi, Mario Batali, Tim Brown, Amanda Burden, Tory Burch, Mark Cuban, Richard M. Daley, Peter Diamandis, Jamie Drummond, Nelly Furtado, Zaha Hadid, Tony Hsieh, Ricardo Illy, Carter Kustera, Tomas Maier, Peter Marino, Dr. John Noseworthy, Governor Martin O'Malley, Bruce Nussbaum, Wayne Pacelle, Dan Pink, Ryan Prince, Sir Ken Robinson, Mera Rubell, Kenny Scharf, David Stark, Don Tapscott, Frank Toskan, Ali Velshi, and Jean-Georges Vongerichten.

Several are good friends, some are collaborators, and all are great inspirations to me. I learned a great deal from each and every one of them.

I want to thank my literary agent Zach Schisgal, who made this book a reality. An editor for decades at Random House, Simon & Schuster, and HarperCollins, he reached out to me after reading my columns to see if I was interested in writing a business advice book. He helped shape my ideas and the proposal from the get-go, serving as both agent and editor, fine-tuning my work along the way.

Thanks also to the team at McGraw-Hill who believed in me, including senior editor Stephanie Frerich, whose comments were always positive and really kept me motivated to keep working harder; director of marketing Stacey Ashton, who believes women can have a strong voice in media and business; and associate publisher Mary Glenn, as well as editor Casey Ebro, senior marketing manager Courtney Fischer, senior publicity manager Ann Pryor, and senior editing supervisor Scott Kurtz, and senior production supervisor Cheryl Hudson.

I'd also like to thank my dedicated team members north of the border in Toronto, who have been instrumental in marketing the book in Canada, including Claudia Hawkins, Laryssa Hulcio, Todd McLeish, and Amanda Reynolds at McGraw-Hill, as well as Angelina Chapin at the *Huffington Post*.

My own team at the Creative Class Group was instrumental. My sister, Reham Alexander director of events and operations at the Creative Class Group, is the hardworking mother of my two amazing nephews. Her speed and efficiency at driving things forward and keeping the business running are awe-inspiring; her help in lining up interview subjects for my columns was invaluable. Steven Pedigo, director of everything, pitches in everywhere, assisting me with all of my *Huffington Post* columns and the research that goes into them. Steven and Reham manage our clients, the media, and the rest of our team—all the while keeping me laughing. Arthur Goldwag is a force to be reckoned with; we were very lucky to find him. While writing his own books, he helps

Richard with all of his writing and somehow manages to find the time to support my work at the *Huffington Post* and with this book. He takes my words and makes them better! He, too, works at lightning speed, and his intelligence and insights are amazing. I'd also like to thank our CCG support team, including Bradley Glonka, Gonzalo De la Pena Andreu, Vicky McGill, and Ann Cunningham.

I have an amazingly supportive family. My dad, Zak Kozouz, whose memory will always be alive, taught us a great deal by his example. At the young age of 18, with just $120 in his pocket, he set out for a new land where he didn't know a soul and proved his favorite adage, "You can do anything if you put your mind to it." My mom, Ruth Kozouz, taught us the value of family and friendships—and the importance of believing in ourselves.

My siblings Reham Alexander, Ruba Alexander, Leena Hosler, Tarig Kozouz, and Ramiz Kozouz have made me appreciate the importance of a firm foundation. My in-laws Dean Alexander, Adam Hosler, Anastasia Kozouz, Christina Kozouz, and Rob and Ginny Florida are wonderful extensions to my family. Our growing brood, some of them toothless, some of them bald, and all of them short—13 nieces and nephews under the age of 12 in total (and a newcomer on the way)— have a healthy and positive outlook on life; their laughter and energy are infectious. I hope that by the time Sophia, Luca, and Tessa Florida; the bros Markis and Adiev Alexander; Christian, Melia, and Sophia Hosler; and Zackary, Zaiden, Isaac, and Lukas Kozouz enter the workforce, many of the practices and principles I write about in these pages will have been put in place to make their world a more engaged and interesting one. I hope they will continue to explore, discover, and learn with the same awe and excitement they have now and that the social structures and organizations we have built will not have squelched it out of them.

As always, I save the best for last: my partner in work and in love, Richard. Every day is a new experience and adventure with him, a true joyride. A professor through and through, he always keeps me growing and learning; he has helped shape my thinking in countless ways. He is my best friend, my soul mate, and the love of my life. Because of him, I am living the life I always dreamed of, my upgraded life.

LIST OF INTERVIEWS

The interviews contained in this book draw upon my Huffington Post columns and were conducted with the following individuals:

Andre Agassi, Tennis Star
"Perhaps the biggest worldwide star in [tennis's] history" (*BBC*), Andre Agassi is an eight-time Grand Slam champion and one of a handful of singles players to achieve a career Grand Slam. His Andre Agassi Foundation for Education has raised almost $177 million for its mission of transforming public education in the United States.

Mario Batali, Chef and Restaurateur
Über-chef, television star, cookbook writer, and restaurateur Mario Batali began his career in a pizza parlor. Today his culinary empire has outposts in New York, Los Angeles, Las Vegas, Hong Kong, Connecticut, and Singapore. Since 2008, the Mario Batali Foundation has been working to educate and empower children all over the world.

Tim Brown, CEO of IDEO

A board member of the Mayo Innovation Advisory Council and the Advisory Council of Acumen Fund, a nonprofit global venture fund focused on improving the lives of the poor, Tim Brown has been with IDEO since its inception and has advised Fortune 100 companies such as Microsoft, PepsiCo, and Procter & Gamble. He is a participant at the World Economic Forum at Davos, a speaker at TED, and a frequent contributor to the *Harvard Business Review, The Economist*, and many other publications. His work can be seen at the Axis Gallery in Tokyo, the Design Museum in London, and the Museum of Modern Art in New York; he is the author of the book *Change by Design*.

Tory Burch, Fashion Designer

Fashion designer and businesswoman Tory Burch worked at *Harper's Bazaar* magazine, Vera Wang, and Polo Ralph Lauren before launching her own fashion label, TRB by Tory Burch. There are now 69 Tory Burch stores worldwide, and her fashion line is carried in over 1,000 department stores.

Amanda Burden, Chair of New York City Planning Commission

Amanda Burden has reshaped New York City for the better, introducing top-notch new architecture into neighborhoods while preserving their historic character, expanding the city's parks and green spaces, and spearheading game-changing projects such as the New York City High Line. *Vanity Fair* called her "arguably the most influential figure in New York City government, next to Mayor Bloomberg."

Mark Cuban, Media Maven and Owner of the Dallas Mavericks

The owner of the Dallas Mavericks, Landmark Theaters, and Magnolia Entertainment and a star of TV's *The Shark Tank*, Mark Cuban made his first millions when he founded and sold MicroSolutions. He cofounded Broadcast.com and became a billionaire when it was sold to Yahoo!

Richard M. Daley, Former Mayor of Chicago
Elected six times and serving 22 years, Richard M. Daley was Chicago's longest-serving mayor. Millennium Park—a once abandoned railroad yard that is now a green space alive with art, music, and people—is perhaps his greatest public works achievement. He is counsel to Katten Muchin Rosenman LLP, a managing principal of Tur Partners LLC, and a distinguished senior fellow at the Harris School of Public Policy at the University of Chicago.

Peter Diamandis, Founder of X Prize and Singularity University
Chairman and CEO of the X Prize Foundation, Peter Diamandis has founded, cofounded, and served in leadership positions at the International Space University, International MicroSpace, Inc., Constellation Communications, the Zero Gravity Corporation (Zero-G), Angel Technologies Corporation, Space Adventures, Ltd., the BlastOff! Corporation, the Rocket Racking League, Singularity University, and Planetary Resources, Inc. Diamandis received an MS in aeronautics and astronautics from MIT and an MD from Harvard Medical School. He is the author of the *New York Times* bestseller *Abundance: The Future Is Better Than You Think.*

Jamie Drummond, Cofounder (with Bono) of ONE
The cofounder with Bono and Bobbie Shriver of DATA (Debt, Aids, Trade, Africa) in 2002 and ONE in 2004, Drummond also worked at Christian Aid and was the global strategist for Jubilee 2000 Drop the Debt. ONE fights extreme poverty and preventable diseases by raising public awareness and lobbying political leaders to support effective policies.

Nelly Furtado, Singer
Platinum-selling singer, songwriter, producer, dancer, and actress, Nelly Furtado saw her career take off in 2001. She has won more than 50 international prizes and honors, including a Grammy, a Latin Grammy, and 10 Juno Awards. Active in a number of philanthropies, in 2011 she announced that she was donating $1 million to the Free the Children charity.

Zaha Hadid, Architect
Hadid is one of *Forbes* magazine's World's 100 Most Powerful Women and *Time*'s 100 People Who Most Affect Our World. The principal of her own architecture practice and a professor at the University of Applied Arts, Vienna, Hadid has been involved in projects that include the Guangzhou Opera House in China, the BMW Central Building in Leipzig, the Rosenthal Center for Contemporary Art in Cincinnati, and a boot for Lacoste. In 2004 she became the first Arab and the first woman to win the Pritzker Prize, architecture's Nobel Prize.

Tony Hsieh, Entrepreneur, Author, and CEO of Zappos.com
After graduating from Harvard with a degree in computer science, Tony Hsieh founded LinkExchange and sold it to Microsoft for $265 million. Still in his twenties, he cofounded the venture capital firm Venture Frogs, through which he invested in the online shoe seller Zappos. After he became the firm's CEO, he sold it to Amazon for $1.2 billion. The author of the bestselling book *Delivering Happiness*, he lives in Las Vegas, which he is seeking to transform into a creative center.

Ricardo Illy, Former Politician and CEO of Illy Caffé
Chairman of Gruppo Illy S.p.A. and vice chairman of Illycaffè s.p.a., Ricardo Illy first joined his family's firm in 1977. In 1993, he was elected mayor of Trieste, and he was later elected to the Italian Parliament. He has also served as president of the Friuli–Venezia Giulia region.

Carter Kustera, Artist and Product Designer
Carter Kustera's illustrations and paintings have been exhibited in numerous galleries and museums nationally and internationally and were included twice in the prestigious Venice Biennale. His latest commercial venture, "Portraits with Carter Kustera," is a web-based as well as an iPhone and iPad collaboration with the media company AOL.

Tomas Maier, Creative Director at Bottega Veneta
Born in Germany to a family of architects and educated at a progressive Waldorf school, Maier trained at the Chambre Syndicale de la Haute Couture in Paris and worked with leading fashion and luxury goods houses such as Sonia Rykiel, Revillon, and Hermès before starting his own private label. In 2001, he became the creative director of the luxury brand Bottega Veneta.

Peter Marino, Architect
After apprenticing with I. M. Pei and George Nelson, Peter Marino struck out on his own, designing the New York apartments of luminaries such as Andy Warhol, Yves Saint Laurent, and Gianni and Marella Agnelli. Marino is notorious for his personal style—he dresses like a biker—but his designs, including the Fendi stores in New York and Rome, the Luis Vuitton stores in Singapore and Hong Kong, the Chanel boutiques in Paris and New York, Los Angeles's Barney's, and New York's Christian Dior, are notable for their understated elegance.

Dr. John Noseworthy, CEO of the Mayo Clinic
A former chairman of the Department of Neurology at the Mayo Clinic, where he has practiced since 1990, and editor-in-chief of *Neurology*, the journal of the American Academy of Neurology, Dr. John Noseworthy rose to president and CEO of the Mayo Clinic in 2009. He completed his neurology training at Dalhousie University in Halifax, Nova Scotia, and was a research fellow at Harvard Medical School.

Bruce Nussbaum, Professor of Innovation and Design,
Parsons School of Design
A member of the Council on Foreign Relations, Nussbaum is the founder of the Innovation & Design online channel and *IN: Inside Innovation*, a quarterly innovation magazine, and blogs at Fast Company and *Harvard Business Review*. As assistant managing editor of *BusinessWeek*, he oversaw the magazine's World's Most Innovative Companies survey. His newest book is *Creative Intelligence: Harnessing the Power to Create, Connect, and Inspire* (HarperBusiness, 2013).

Martin O'Malley, Governor of Maryland
The sixty-first governor of Maryland and a two-term mayor of Baltimore, O'Malley is frequently touted as a potential candidate for president in 2016. *Esquire* magazine named O'Malley "The Best Young Mayor in the Country," and a few years later, in 2005, *Time* magazine named him one of America's "Top 5 Big City Mayors." A husband and father of four, he is also a talented musician who still finds time to perform in a Celtic rock band.

Wayne Pacelle, CEO of the Humane Society of the United States
After graduating with degrees in history and environmental studies from Yale University, Pacelle cofounded the nonprofit Humane Society Legislative Fund, which lobbies for animal welfare legislation, and the nonpartisan PAC Humane USA, which supports candidates of any party who stand for animal protection. He has worked with the Humane Society since 1994 and was named its president and CEO in 2004.

Dan Pink, New York Times Bestselling Author of To Sell Is Human
A graduate of the Yale Law School, a former speechwriter for Vice President Al Gore, and an aide to former Labor Secretary Robert Reich, Dan Pink is a leading author and lecturer on business, technology, and creativity. Among his *New York Times* bestselling books are *Free Agent Nation, A Whole New Mind,* and *Drive.*

Ryan Prince, Vice Chairman, Realstar Group, International
Previously a cofounder of the venture capital firm iGabriel, Prince established Realstar's London office in 2002, where he spearheaded the investment group's entry into the British healthcare sector and its acquisition of a £1 billion hotel portfolio and more recently a number of residential and student accommodation properties. Realstar is a privately owned company with over $5 billion in assets under management. It is an owner and operator of multifamily properties and has interests in hospitality assets and brands, sports and entertainment venues, and healthcare facilities.

Sir Ken Robinson, Expert on Education and Creativity
Professor emeritus of education at the University of Warwick, Ken Robinson works with governments in Europe, Asia, and the United States, and with international agencies, Fortune 500 companies, and some of the world's leading cultural organizations on issues pertaining to education and creativity. He is the bestselling author of *The Element: How Finding Your Passion Changes Everything*, and his TED Talks have been viewed more than 25 million times and seen by an estimated 250 million people in over 150 countries.

Mera Rubell, Art Collector
Together with her husband, Don, Mera Rubell built not just a business empire (they own a number of boutique hotels in Miami Beach, Baltimore, and Washington, D.C.) but one of the most important private contemporary art collections in the world. Housed in a former Drug Enforcement Agency facility, the Rubells' 45,000-square-foot museum and residence pioneered the development of galleries and artists in the Wynwood neighborhood of Miami. The Rubell Family Collection includes works by Jean-Michel Basquiat, Keith Haring, Damien Hirst, Jeff Koons, Cindy Sherman, and Andy Warhol.

Kenny Scharf, Artist
After training at the New York School of Visual Arts, Kenny Scharf burst onto the art scene in New York in the 1980s, where he straddled the worlds of graffiti, pop art, and fine art. He was a close friend to and collaborator with Keith Haring, and today his work can be seen in top museums and galleries around the world, including MOCA Los Angeles, the Waddington Gallery in London, the Vincent Van Gogh Museum in Amsterdam, and the Gagosian Gallery in Beverly Hills.

David Stark, President and Creative Director, David Stark
Design and Production
David Stark, a New York–based event producer, stages innovative and imaginative events for a host of high-wattage celebrity clients such as Beyoncé Knowles and Martha Stewart, and for Target, West Elm, Condé Nast, and other top corporations. He has orchestrated fund-raising galas for the nation's most prominent cultural organizations, including the Whitney Museum of American Art and the Metropolitan Opera. He is a frequent guest on *E! News, The Today Show,* and *The View,* and his work on decor, party planning, decorating, and gardening has been featured in *The New York Times*, *ELLE Decor*, *House Beautiful*, and many other publications.

Don Tapscott, Author of Wikinomics
Don Tapscott is an adjunct professor at the Rotman School of Management, University of Toronto, and is currently listed by Thinkers50 as one of the top 10 living management thinkers. He is the author or coauthor of 15 widely read books about technology and new media in business and society, including *Paradigm Shift*, *The Digital Economy*, *Growing Up Digital*, *The Naked Corporation*, and *Wikinomics*.

Frank Toskan, Founder of MAC Cosmetics

Toskan was a makeup artist when he founded MAC Cosmetics with his partner, Frank Angelo, in 1984. Not only is MAC well known for setting the bar high for its humanitarian work, it also pioneered cause-related marketing, standing up for animal rights, encouraging recycling, helping children, and more. It was also one of the first companies to courageously feature a drag queen (RuPaul) front and center in its ad campaigns during the AIDS crisis. Since selling the company to Estée Lauder in 1998, Toskan has devoted his time to his philanthropies.

Ali Velshi, CNN Chief Business Correspondent

Ali Velshi is CNN's chief business correspondent, the anchor of *Your Money,* and a cohost of CNN International's *World Business Today.* Velshi frequently reports on breaking news events and politics, and has created many in-depth personal profiles. His guests have included White House advisors, CEOs, musicians, and activists. He was honored with a National Headliner Award for Business and Consumer Reporting in 2010. As I write this book, Ali announced that he will be joining Al Jazeera America as a future host.

Jean-Georges Vongerichten, Chef and Restaurateur

A master chef who pioneered the fusion of Asian and classic French cuisine, Vongerichten is a James Beard Award–winning cookbook author, the host of cooking shows on TV, and the owner or co-owner of 30-plus restaurants in locales as far-flung as Doha, Paris, Mexico City, London, Bora Bora, and Shanghai. He has earned a galaxy of Michelin stars and other accolades.

INTRODUCTION

You know your life is changing when you're headed to Siberia for Valentine's Day.

I had just taken on the job of CEO of the Creative Class Group and had booked my new husband to speak at a meeting of a major Russian economic development organization in Krasnoyarsk Krai, Siberia, where he and I would be spending February 14.

It might not be Paris, I thought as I started the preparations for our departure, but at least it would be an adventure. Or maybe it was a bit too daring at that: reports of the orange snow that was blanketing the region were disquieting (at first it was thought to have been caused by industrial pollution; scientists later determined that it was the result of a sandstorm in Kazakhstan) not to mention that the weather forecast was for temperatures of 29 degrees below zero. But as apprehensive as I was, I couldn't have begun to imagine all the twists and turns that lay ahead.

First there was the nine-hour delay in Moscow while we waited for the minister who had kindly invited us to ride with him on his private jet to show up with his entourage at the airport. Then there was the five-hour flight to Krasnoyarsk Krai. The seats faced one another, which made it difficult to ignore our fellow passengers, who smoked incessantly, drank vast quantities of Scotch, and conversed loudly with one another in Russian. When we arrived at the hotel, our room wasn't ready and we were left to wait for another three dreary hours in the lobby. Then, when we were finally sent upstairs, it turned out that our room already had an occupant: a large and highly irritated naked man who chased us down the hallway screaming Russian epithets because we'd "'broken in" to his room. The *New York Times* thought this story was so funny that it featured me on the front page of the business section with the headline "On Adventure's Trail, Some Endings Bring a Blush."[1]

Our 26-hour return trip was the following day. It turned out to be equally challenging, as the hostess who was supposed to escort us to the airport had gone AWOL after we had all attended a raucous bonfire party on the ski slopes the evening before, leaving us with a non-English-speaking substitute at 5 a.m. who couldn't understand us when we tried to tell him which airport to take us to. When we fortunately got to the right one, we were left clutching our luggage on the icy stairs to the plane's first-class section. When they finally let us in, it was only so that we could be sent back outside to walk through the howling wind to the back of the plane, even though we had paid a non-English-speaking attendant 600 rubles for an "upgrade," the one word he understood. There we stood in the early morning blackness, shivering in the freezing cold for what felt like hours before they let us into the last row of the coach section. There was no room left in the overheads for our luggage, our seats did not recline, and the washrooms were right behind us.

We spent the whole five-hour flight with our carry-ons on our laps, and when we arrived at the international airport in Moscow, there was another long delay. Smoking was permitted in every part of the airport at that time; there was no fresh air to breathe anywhere—not at the gates, the lounge, the restaurants, or even the restrooms.

When we made it home to Washington, D.C., at long last and my head crashed onto my familiar pillow, my last waking thought was this: This is not how my father commuted to work. I grew up with five siblings in a bucolic suburb north of Detroit. My mother stayed home with the kids while my engineer father held the same 9 to 5 job for years and returned home on time every night to have dinner, help us with our homework, and watch the 11 o'clock local newscast. The routine was the same: familiar, safe, and comfortable.

My parents—first-generation immigrants from Jordan—drilled the importance of education into my three sisters, my two brothers, and me. Nothing less than straight A's would do if we were ever going to get ahead; all of us were expected to go on to college and then graduate school to become doctors or lawyers.

Since I was not interested in either profession, I went to business school without a clue as to what I would end up doing. I just knew that once I graduated, I would get a high-level corporate job. I wasn't disappointed, either. In due course I landed a senior position at a Fortune 500 company just outside of Washington, D.C. I was super excited by my six-figure salary with its terrific bonuses; I imagined that I was well on my way to becoming one of those CMOs who were bringing home half a million a year or more by their early thirties.

Not only was the pay great, I had finally landed a job I really enjoyed. I had a big budget, a great team, and wonderful colleagues. However, after just a year, my husband's work started to get a lot of attention beyond the usual suspects of mayors and city officials.

My husband, Richard, was a well-respected but not widely known academic until 2002, when he published his internationally bestselling book *The Rise of the Creative Class*. By identifying the ways in which creativity was changing our ways of living and working—and showing how companies, cities, and individuals could make those changes work to their advantage—he not only made a permanent mark on his field, he became—and remains—a highly sought-after speaker, editor, and advisor. *TIME* magazine called him an urban development expert, *Fast Company* dubbed him a pioneering cartographer, the *Sunday Times* called him one of the most respected academics in the world, and British Prime Minister David Cameron called him a guru, and Bono even name-dropped him to President Clinton. Mayors, city leaders, governors, and prime ministers from around the world invite him to speak, consult, and advise on economic development, growth, and prosperity.

It isn't often that big companies and major brands such as Johnson & Johnson, Hitachi, Microsoft, Bacardi Dewar's, Absolut, and Citigroup beat a path to a college professor's door, but that was what was happening. Apple's Power Mac G5 was branding itself as the "power tool for the Creative Class," Banana Republic was promoting urban style for the Creative Class, and the U.S. CEO of Fiat and the president of Smart Car USA were both focusing their branding efforts as the car of choice for the Creative Class. Nokia, Samsung, Adobe, and Epson were launching new products that were aimed at the Creative Class as well.

With my business and marketing skills, Richard thought I could help build something. But it wasn't until an ad agency representing BMW called and said it wanted to create an entire television and print advertising campaign based on his work that I started to appreciate the opportunity we had.

Still, I hesitated. I knew next to nothing about the economic development of cities, Richard's core area of expertise, and then there were all those nights I'd spent cramming for the GMATs and my courses in business school and the hundreds of hours of volunteer work and internships I'd done. After training my whole life for a corporate job, I had finally arrived. I was managing a $2 million budget. I couldn't fathom giving up my nice office and big paycheck and bonuses, my full staff, and my much-coveted board position to work from home on a shoestring. The whole proposition seemed like a huge gamble not just professionally but personally too, as we had only recently become engaged. Living together and working together seemed like a very risky venture.

After much anguish and many discussions, I took the leap and became CEO of the Creative Class Group. Once I'd given up the cushy job, I had to reprogram myself completely to make the transition into start-up mode. There was no human resources department to help me with employee relations, no help line to call for tech support, no finance department to balance the budgets, no graphic design department, and no assistants for scheduling and administrative duties. I was my own one-stop shop. I had given up job security and a steady paycheck, but I regained control of my time and schedule.

My husband's research documents the ways in which creativity has emerged as the defining feature of economic life, the font from which new technologies and new industries flow. Our creative economy, he says, has ushered in new ways of working—and a whole new way of life. As CEO of the Creative Class Group, I found myself confirming these theories in the field as my team and I reinvented ourselves on an almost daily basis.

Whereas my father left at the same time for work every day and drove just a few miles to his office, I now found myself traveling to Tokyo, Melbourne, Abu Dhabi, Seoul, Poznan, Maastricht, Shanghai, London, Barcelona, and everywhere in between. Increasingly, so were my friends in all sorts of other industries, from tech and fashion to finance, architecture, advertising, publishing, and business. My father's weekends were the downtime he devoted to us kids, whereas, I found myself with no downtime at all.

It's that way still. We take conference calls with Middle Eastern clients at 8 a.m. and Asian clients at 10 p.m. and work on the go with shoddy Internet connections on trains, in the back of taxicabs, on planes and in airports, and in hotel lobbies, restaurants, coffee shops, the gym, and even the beach or the neighborhood park. My team and

I set up live videoconferences whose participants are in as far-flung locales as Islamabad, Pakistan, and the Congolese jungle. Our clients run the gamut from the United Nations to the *Financial Times* to IBM and across industries from healthcare to education to media and the arts. Nothing is constant, and we are almost always on the move.

Many of my friends think we just book speeches. Speech making is a core focus, of course. Richard and other experts on our team give presentations on creativity, place-making, and economic development for our clients, and Richard delivers countless keynote addresses to political, professional, and academic associations; business and real estate conferences; and meetings of art and cultural organizations and other nonprofits. But speeches are only a small part of what our company does.

Working with a vast number of clients around the world and across industries, we realized early on that it wouldn't make sense to have a fixed menu of services; instead, we customize every project to meet our clients' needs. This taught me the importance of flexibility, of being able to adapt to different situations across constantly changing contexts. It was vastly different from my first job in corporate America, in which I was an executive in an advertising agency whose major client was Chrysler and that delivered a set suite of products and services. The real joy of my role today is the constant challenge, the learning and discovery.

Our projects have run the gamut from helping BMW's advertising agency launch the Idea Class print and television campaign to designing a workshop to teach Bacardi Dewar's marketers and public relations executives how to better understand and appeal to the Creative Class. We've brainstormed strategies to revitalize Las Vegas's downtown with the CEO of Zappos, his strategic team, and city leaders and economic development officials. We've provided architectural and urban planning feedback for the city of Halifax's landmark Central Library Project, and we led a yearlong community engagement project with a major real estate developer and the mayor and city leadership of Noosa, Australia.

As part of Starwood's Le Méridien cultural curator team, we helped rethink the guest lobby experience and were its key data engine for locational choice investments. We worked with Philips in Amsterdam to devise a brand new Livable Cities Award in partnership with CNN, a contest that attracted more than 450 inspirational proposals from 29 different countries and culminated in an awards ceremony in the Rijksmuseum, famous for its Rembrandt collection. We advised Pinewood Studios, one of the world's largest film and television production facilities, on the impact of the United Kingdom's creative clusters on the regional economy. We've helped clients with smaller budgets advance their agendas as well, conducting workshops and undertaking research. We worked with the U.S. Department of Labor and the recruiting firm Monster Government Solutions to craft a regional talent attraction strategy.

We decided early on not to box ourselves in. We had a data engine, research, and expertise to share. How we delivered it—whether as a half-day workshop, a yearlong engagement, a *charette*, a strategy report, a contest, a new program, a media campaign, or an online tool kit—would be tailored to the client's needs and resources. Each project was vastly different in scope, size, and deliverables.

Not once did we say, "No, we don't do that," or, "Sorry, we don't offer that." We took each opportunity as an adventure, a challenge to expand the business model and grow professionally. Often, after conference calls and meetings with potential clients, we'd gather and say, "What did we just promise we could deliver? We've never done that!" Then we'd laugh and say, "We'll figure it out," and, "Whoa, do we have some work to do!"

Not only did we learn and grow, but we had some amazing personal experiences along the way. A client in Australia who also happened to be an Olympic swimmer gave us surfboarding lessons. A mayor showcased his harmonica talents for us, and we formed lasting friendships over client dinners in Barcelona and on location with CNN. Once we held a press conference on a beach while dressed in shorts and flip-flops.

As massive as the shift from my father's world was, it was easy to understand and accept; what was startling to me was that in just the short span of time between the rise of Gen X and the advent of the Millennials, our work styles and lifestyles changed even more. Whereas I was taught to go to graduate school, fit in, excel, and get a corporate job, wearing a suit every day except on casual Fridays, people just a few years younger than I was were seeking jobs at tech firms not because all of a sudden they had an interest in technology but because those firms were worlds away from typical formal corporations. They let workers be themselves and offered work environments that were less rigid, more open, and more creative and innovative.

Why was this happening? What did I need to know? I wanted to understand this new paradigm. Immersed as I was in this brave new world of work, business, play, and life, I decided to launch a business advice column, "Your Start-Up Life," in the *Huffington Post*. My three sisters and I had doled out personal advice for over a decade in a column that ran in several newspapers and on Fox News in Detroit. But this time, I wanted to talk with successful entrepreneurs, creative thinkers, and innovative leaders. I needed answers to the questions I was asking myself. Perhaps I could learn from others who had successfully navigated this shift.

I set out to interview not just traditional business leaders, Fortune 100 executives, managers, and CEOs but also a rocket scientist, a neurologist, a famous graffiti artist, politicians, tech billionaires, fashion designers, a Grammy Award–winning musician, a star athlete, philanthropists, celebrity chefs, starchitects, bestselling authors, and media personalities. I wanted a diverse set of inputs to find out if it is as interesting for them to negotiate the confluence of work, life, and play as it's been for me. How do they do it? What makes some businesses or individuals or leaders succeed and others fail? Why do so many people hate their jobs while others love what they do? What makes them enjoy their work? What new sets of skills are needed for this new way of working and living? Is it timing, luck, the team they put into place, the right financing? Why can some people incorporate this success into their personal lives as well as they do? What makes them tick? Where do they find their inspiration? How do they lead, motivate, and collaborate? What I found was that their perspectives were remarkably similar and that the principles that guide them apply to everyone's life.

Our employers are also in a major transition period. Some will trap you in a dead-end, mind-numbing job in a fishbowl cubicle—I've endured my fair share of this kind of misery myself—but others provide enriched and engaged campuses or lofts where you are encouraged to be yourself and celebrate your diversity. Bring your children, your dog, or your mom or grandparents to the office. Ride your bike to work; take the Wi-Fi–equipped company bus. Some leaders recognize the need for work-life balance and give you the freedom to manage your workload and schedule, whereas others hover over you like a prison warden, watch the clock to make sure you're keeping traditional hours, or, worse yet, deny your vacation requests and force you to devote your off hours to corporate retreats and team-building exercises.

Many of us get caught up, as I did, in the linear path of life—college, graduate school, career, and family—which keeps us on the hedonic treadmill of unfulfilling work, suffering through long commutes and living from paycheck to paycheck. When we look around, we see that our friends' lives have been upgraded. They are raking it in as iPad DJs or launching profitable start-ups in their garages; driving electric cars or fast cars and riding expensive carbon fiber bikes; and going off on exotic safaris through Africa, jungle adventures in Costa Rica, or party weekends in Reykjavik whenever they want and without having to seek approval for the time off from a boss. It can drive us crazy.

Why isn't that my life? we ask. As a funny man once joked, "What's worse than not getting what you want? Someone else getting it!"

Maybe you did everything right. You went to school, got great grades, and got a good job. But the American dream has shifted seemingly overnight. It seems the rug was pulled out from under us. While you put in late hours at the office to slowly climb the ranks, you look around and see others rolling out of bed whenever they want, buying front-row tickets to the Jay-Z concert or Yankee or Miami Heat games, working from the comfort of their homes or the fun of the local coffee shop on their state-of-the-art Apple device. They are constantly buying the latest pumped-up kicks, the season's expensive designer bag, the newest red-soled shoe, or the coolest pair of new skinny jeans. They have access to a network of top professionals, including celebrity doctors, architects, and designers.

Worse yet, our popular culture rewards those who are willing to make spectacles of themselves with multimillion-dollar book deals, high appearance fees, and reality shows. Whether it is Snooki from *Jersey Shore* urinating on herself on the dance floor, someone who actually calls himself Mike the Situation spending all his time at the tanning salon or pumping iron at the gym, or the *Real Housewives* of any city getting into hair-pulling, name-calling, table-turning drama, this is the type of circus freak show our society rewards. Not the doctors making breakthroughs in cancer research, not the schoolteachers who spend hours educating our children every day while struggling to make ends meet, and not the midlevel manager putting in 60-hour work weeks.

The rapper 50 cent, who was shot nine times, saw this same struggle. His mother was a drug dealer so he was sent to live with his grandparents. He noticed that his mother had financial freedom while his grandparents struggled to make ends meet by making an honest living. So he decided to start dealing drugs too, until he was fortunate enough to discover his passion for music. Later, he went on to sell 32 million records. In 2004 he invested in Vitamin Water; when Coca-Cola bought it, he made an estimated $60 million from the deal. But most of us are not destined to be reality TV stars, drug dealers-turned-rappers-turned-multimillionare business execs. Many of us are enslaved within a mind-numbing system of constant drudgery, while others are living the new global dream.

If they don't have a reality show, they must have had a trust fund, you tell yourself. It would be selfish and reckless of me to try to break out of my box; I have a family to support, a mortgate, massive student loans to pay off. I can't afford to take that risk. But still, you want in. You want a piece of the new creative economy, the happiness economy, or the purpose-driven career path. You want to make a difference, have a vision, set a course for your life.

The whole paradigm of work is changing, and many of us are still stuck under the thumb of the boss in our life when what we want is to *be* the boss of our own life. We crave the freedom to manage our own time, to be valued for who we are. We want a career that encourages risk and excitement, growth and personal development, learning and exploration.

Do you really have to stifle your inner child, who is dying to come out and play in this dynamic new world? Is stultification the price of security? Is it asking too much of your family to risk trying for more? Our parents went to work every day too, but when they looked around, everyone was in the same box, following the same well-worn paths. Now there are those who pave their own paths and create their own futures—and those who are bound by the old system with its old rules.

For much of my adult life I've had a foot in both of these worlds. While I was mining Stephen Covey's *7 Habits of Highly Effective People* for advice on how to get ahead, I was also feeding my soul with Jack Kerouac's *On the Road*. On the one hand, *Good to Great, Who Moved My Cheese?, Made to Stick,* and *Drive*; on the other, *The Unbearable Lightness of Being, Tropic of Cancer, The Fountainhead,* and *Catcher in the Rye.*

Maybe in a generation or two our working and our thinking, feeling lives will be seamlessly joined and equally fulfilling, but for now, most of us must navigate back and forth between them.

I know I've done that. I've worked in 1950s-style Organization Man corporations as an employee/prison inmate with the watchful boss/warden monitoring my every move and counting the minutes I take for lunch breaks. In my new role, I've toured them as a consultant. I've observed their environments, workspaces, and policies with a keen eye; I've studied the ways they work and collaborate, consuming every fine detail. And I've been an insider in the brave new world of creativity. Through my personal and professional network and through my column, I have had the incredible good fortune to meet a number of extraordinarily successful people who do what they love—from Chicago's longest-serving mayor, Richard Daley, to *über*-chef Mario Batali, from the entrepreneur Tony Hsieh to the tennis star Andre Agassi and the award-winning singer Nelly Furtado, and so many more. Some are friends, and some have been collaborators. In our conversations, many of which began over long dinners, I've asked them: How do you do it? In our turbulent times, when the only constant is instability, how have you managed to make things work so well?

Amazingly, their advice was remarkably consistent. What I heard over and over again, though in different words, different voices, and different contexts, were seven key principles that enabled them to lead successful and fulfilled lives:

1. **ENVISION YOUR FUTURE.** The majority of my interview subjects knew fairly early on what they wanted to do and set a course to get there. Even if their first job was not in the industry they wanted to be in, they used it to take away lessons and reinforce their vision of the future. They set a path and pushed forward despite the objections of naysayers and the inevitable setbacks they endured along the way. It's never too late to start living your upgraded life.

2. **FIND YOUR PASSION.** There are two camps here. A few lucky people actually get paid to do the things for which they have a great passion. Then there are the rest of us, who need to do something else to earn our paychecks. Either way, it's essential that you identify what makes you happy and find a way to incorporate it into your life through your career or your free time. This gives your life purpose and meaning.

3. **GET CREATIVE.** No longer is it acceptable to go along with the status quo. Creativity drives our economy forward. Successful leaders understand that creativity requires diversity and bring together people who represent a wide range of perspectives and ways of doing things. Find your inner creativity and unleash it.

4. **PROTECT YOUR TIME.** Time is more important than money and possessions. It's the one thing you can never get back and something you can't buy, barter, or borrow. Once it's gone, it's gone for good. Those who succeed protect their time fiercely and selfishly.

5. **COLLABORATE.** No one can do it all. Successful people know their own strengths and accept their weaknesses. Finding partners or teammates who can complement your skills will maximize results.

6. **TAKE RISKS.** Most successful leaders, thinkers, and innovators are not afraid to take risks. Facebook's motto is "Move fast and break things." Curiosity is stifled in a risk-free environment. Many new discoveries and breakthroughs are realized through trial and error. Our society needs to encourage more risk taking.

7. **EMBRACE FAILURE.** True pioneers embrace failure as part of the learning process. Be it at work or school, we need to create environments where people feel safe to fail. Think of failure as a time to grow, regroup, reflect, reinvent, and ultimately push forward in new directions. Sometimes failure is just the beginning, not the end.

There are tons of self-help books for health and fitness and a gazillion books on weight loss and fashion and home makeovers but not a lot of expert advice on how to optimize and upgrade your personal and professional life. I didn't learn this in business school either. My MBA courses focused on financial spreadsheets and long-form mathematical equations for classes such as statistics and economics. Management consultants stalk the business world, offering strategies on design thinking, vertical integration, cross-platform synergy, integrative thinking, and the like, and their theories are often heavy and impenetrable. *Upgrade* gathers the best of what I've learned from entrepreneurs and creative leaders. It presents their philosophies not in the abstract but in simple and actionable terms that readers can put to good effect in their professional or their personal lives from day 1.

Our lives are changing faster than we can understand. The lines between work, life, and play are growing blurrier all the time. Old churches, firehouses, theaters, and libraries are being transformed into new workplaces. Stay-at-home moms and dads are launching start-ups during play dates; the recession has compelled many displaced salarymen to throw caution to the wind and chart their own ways. It seems as if everyone is opening cupcake shops or dog bakeries, and people are curating their own content by spinning off books, online videos, TV shows, and blogs and hosting Google chats and events. Streets and neighborhoods are lined with live/work spaces where ex-marketing VPs run surf shops, ex-directors of finance handcraft skateboards, and one-time media buyers sell outdoor adventures or open organic dry cleaners.

Creativity is all around us, not just in high tech and biotech but in our everyday lives. Just take a look at our new family units: women delaying motherhood or going about it solo, unmarried men and women raising families. Thanks to new technologies, same-sex couples now have the opportunity to have their own children. Our traditional expectations have been fundamentally transformed.

On a simpler level, check out how dramatically our grocery store shelves have changed from our parents' supermarkets. Staples such as milk, cheese, soaps, and bread now come in all varieties, from vegan and gluten-free, to organic, to preservative- and animal cruelty–free. We have our choice of artisanal cheeses, soy desserts, kale- and quinoa-infused snacks, and almond and rice milks.

Someone has to think up, make, sell, and distribute all these things. Juice bars, nail bars, and wine bars are on every corner. Food trucks and merchandising trucks in all varieties have hit the streets. Pop-up restaurants and retailers come and go, allowing new ideas and products to be tested in the marketplace quickly and without a huge investment.

We no longer live in the separate silos of home, office, and vacation time. People are Skypeing and FaceTiming clients from parks, from home, and from airport gates. Creativity is everywhere, and it reflects the way we live, work, and play. The most successful among us design and integrate every facet of their lives. These individuals have strong visions and strong voices and build flair, resilience, and confidence into their plans. When the path swerves, they turn too, and they never take their eyes off the goal.

Upgrade plumbs my own varied experiences and includes personal and professional advice from leading thinkers to help you optimize your businesses, careers, and personal lives. Its approach is not just for big businesses or entrepreneurs. It is a guide for anyone who dreams of changing his or her life from ordinary to extraordinary—who wants to have fun, be productive, and, just as important, give back. We have one shot to live the life we want to live. Why not do our best to optimize it now? You've been sitting in the coach class for too long; it's time for your upgrade. So settle back, take a sip of that champagne, and enjoy the ride. A whole new destination is awaiting your arrival.

CHAPTER 1

ENVISION YOUR FUTURE

The future depends on what you do today.
—Mahatma Gandhi

What Do You Want to Do with Your Life?

This question seems simple, but it is very difficult. Adults ask it of children all the time because we are so awestruck with the ease with which they answer, their un-self-conscious certainty that they can be whoever or whatever they want to be. I put this to the test by asking my nieces and nephews under age 11. Here's a quick rundown of their answers:

My rambunctious two-year-old nephew Zaiden chimed in first with: "Spiderman!" Then he changed his mind a few seconds later and said, "Poo Poo Man!" When my brother, Tarig, tried to get clarification on this, he said, "Superband!" Three-year-old Zackary, his older and more introspective brother, said, "I want to be a spaceman."

My five-year-old niece Sophia always wanted to be a "glamour girl," but recently she changed her tune to "hospital worker." Seven-year-old Melia wants to be an "artist," and their older brother Christian, eight, wants to be a pro football player. He has a backup plan if that falls through: "I will be president."

The oldest in the bunch, their cousins Adiev, nine, and Markis, eleven, also want to be professional athletes, and each of them has a fallback plan as well. Adiev will settle for being a doctor, and Markis is willing to be a lawyer.

The fact that most of these children will go on to entirely different futures doesn't matter. What does is the fact that they can answer with such confidence and assurance—that they have such a wide-open sense of life's limitless possibilities. Ask adults this question, and most will shrug their shoulders or offer a sarcastic response.

Ask yourself another question: What do you want out of life? Or this: What matters most to you? Most of us will have to stop and think about our answers—if we can come up with any. Why is it that adults have such a hard time with these questions? Why do they make us so anxious? Perhaps because most of us are not fully living the lives we want for ourselves; we envisioned better lives: lives that are more adventurous, fun, exciting, or fulfilling.

The reality is that the majority of us don't think about how we can optimize our lives. Instead of developing a real strategy based on where we want to go in life and why, we just slog through in a state of what I like to call *managed dissatisfaction*. We are doing okay; we are managing to get by but with an underlying tinge of unhappiness. Certain peaks, like an annual vacation, a new car, or a slight promotion at work, lift our spirits for a while, and we ride the peak. But before we know it, the wave has crashed and we are washed up on shore, longing for the next big wave to come through.

My notion of *managed dissatisfaction* is inspired by Herbert Simon's classic theory of *satisficing*. A Nobel Prize-winning economist and a pioneer in artificial intelligence and cognitive psychology who taught at Carnegie Mellon University in Pittsburgh for more than half a century, Simon was one of the world's foremost theorists on decision making. He introduced the concept of *satisficing* (a combination of "satisfy" and "suffice") in 1956 to describe how human beings actually make decisions. Where most economists imply that people make decisions rationally to maximize outcomes, Simon recognized that this is impossible in most circumstances. Most of our decisions, he said, are circumscribed by what he called "bounded rationality." We have limited information and cannot possibly consider every option and alternative; plus, we are influenced by emotion and by our peers. We choose the first solution that works, that *satisfices*, thus sacrificing the best for what's "good enough."

Well, it is never too late to envision an entirely different future—or to actively upgrade your work or life. Anyone can do it, young or old, single or married. You don't have to be a 20-something single person with nothing to lose to start living the life you want to live today. It's not about more money and more time. Imagine finding 10 hours a week you didn't know you had to indulge in something that makes you happy. You'll be surprised, but you can do it. It's about leveraging the resources around you, collaborating, thinking creatively, and protecting your time.

Throughout middle school we are encouraged to dive into different subject areas, to test the waters of our aptitudes and interests, but by the time we reach our junior or senior year of high school, we are expected to have found something to focus on lest we waste valuable time and money in college, spreading ourselves too thin. Some of us follow that linear path from adolescence on, but more than a few of us take enough detours along the way that we never do settle on just one thing.

The Great Recession of 2008 forced the question on many of us. As organizations downsized, declared bankruptcy, or shut down altogether, hundreds of thousands of people whose careers were upended found themselves bitterly reappraising the choices they'd made. The wisest took advantage of the opportunity to rethink and regroup—and to find new and, one hopes, better paths.

But most of us are stuck in our jobs. The only time we can imagine changing our lives is when we finally retire and are free to manage our own time and have enough money to live on. Whether it is traveling more; taking cooking, skiing, or tango classes; or launching a new company, we put all these things off till later in life, and that makes no sense whatsoever. Do you really want to wait until you're 65 to go scuba diving in New Zealand or on a shark-feeding expedition in Tahiti, to take yoga classes in Bali or go backpacking in Fiji? We just don't feel we have the time or resources to risk a stable job to indulge ourselves. But it is ludicrous that we don't do these things now, when we are young and healthy. Why do we set ourselves up to live this way? I'm not saying life should be one big indulgent vacation, but life really doesn't have to be so freaking hard.

Most of us have convinced ourselves that we have to be boxed into the rigid systems our society has imposed on us. If we are not working tirelessly at the office, contributing more than our share at home, or wasting pressure hours in traffic, we feel like we are goofing off and feel guilty about it. If we are among the lucky minority whose employers allow us freedom and flexibility, we are damned by our children's school system, which locks us into the 9-to-5 grind for 18 years. This book will offer simple tips on how you *can* upgrade your work and life now in your everyday routine and with the time and resources you have at your disposal—not just in the two weeks of vacation time you can manage a year or in your granny golden years, when you finally retire.

How to Envision Your Future

Your first step on the road to change starts when you envision your future. Of course there are those among us who know what they want to do—what they are *destined* to do—from a very early age. People with such a clear vision and passion include Mahatma Gandhi, Martin Luther King, and the Dalai Lama; the world is a better place because of them. But most of us have to think long and hard about what we want to do and put a plan in place to make it happen.

A few years ago, my husband and I were invited to dinner at the home of the director of the Art Gallery of Ontario. The guest of honor was the world-renowned architect Frank Gehry, who had just finished his epic redesign and transformation of the museum. A friend who knew him when he was young told us that Gehry was constantly scribbling odd forms, swirls, and shapes on cocktail napkins. At the time, he found this behavior peculiar and odd. It wasn't until many years later that those sketches would be realized in three dimensions, in the shapes of his magnificent buildings, such as the famous Walt Disney Concert Hall in Los Angeles and the Guggenheim Museum Bilbao in Spain, a signature landmark for its city and a must-see for tourists.

Some of us are lucky enough to figure it out from our very first job experience. When I asked the chef Mario Batali how he'd imagined his future, he said, "I worked as a pizza man at a place called Stuff Yer Face in New Brunswick, New Jersey. I loved working with a team, I loved the energy and the adrenaline rush of working toward a common goal with different job responsibilities, and I loved doing it at lightning speed. I hated cleaning the deep fat fryer, but I became very good at it. I knew I wanted to cook professionally after I graduated college, and I took advantage of the luck of finding myself in demand in New York City at a time when the business of food was becoming a national fixation."[1]

Some people have an innate talent that is just dying to get out and that reveals itself in everything they do. Some of us take a more crooked path. But one thing is for certain: the most successful lives are forged by incredible focus.

It's time to focus on you and your life and envision the life you want to lead. Don't let the rest of your life pass you by; spend some time thinking about it. Or maybe ask yourself an easier question: What life would you live if you were given $500 million tomorrow? The very notion gets us excited, and we start daydreaming about all the great things we'd do. I posed this question to 1,000 Facebook friends. The answers that came back were quite different in their specifics, but strategically they were quite similar: pay off bills, take care of family, then work with a charity and do some of the things they've been interested in but never found the time for, such as taking interesting courses, traveling, and indulging in hobbies. Here's one response from Joanne, a 30-something:

What would you do if you were given $500 million?

- *I would improve myself, offer help to the people around me, and be happy.*
- *I would quit my current job. I currently work to live. This would afford me the opportunity to do things I'm passionate about.*
- *I would pay off my mortgage.*
- *I would volunteer and donate money to the arts, the poor, and cancer research.*
- *I would travel—Machu Picchu, Egypt, China, Japan, the UK, Germany, Italy, India, and so on.*
- *I would take a cooking class in the country of origin. I love authentic cooking.*
- *I would get my master's and PhD and teach college business courses.*
- *I would work on my book about my aunts and grandmother and their kids so we wouldn't lose the amazing stories about them and our history.*
- *I would work out and make time to learn how to cook healthier.*

What would your average day look like?

- *Get up.*
- *Work out.*
- *Write/research.*
- *Volunteer at a soup kitchen or library.*
- *Go to a class/teach a class.*
- *Make dinner.*

How would your life be different from what it is now?

- *It would be more fulfilling, healthier, and happier.*
- *I would have more time to work on the things that are important to me and not feel like I'm doing things because I have to.*
- *I would like to help others realize their potential. Nothing is more rewarding than that.*

Another friend and former colleague said: "I would certainly stop working for for-profit companies. I'd first make sure my family's (extended) needs were all taken care of. Pay for their kids' educations, pay off mortgages, set aside money for everyone. I'd spend the rest of my time thinking about how this money could be put to good use to help the world become a better place. I think that would be a combination of donating and starting a nonprofit. I don't think my lifestyle would change all that much, although I would have many more vacations/ family travel."

Others said they'd help children's charities and nonprofits. The funny thing is that the things on these lists that would make their lives more fulfilling don't require a major windfall. It wasn't stuff they wanted but freedom (paying off debt) and the ability to do things that give them a sense of joy, learning, and discovery and that imbue their lives with a sense of purpose and meaning.

It's not *things* that make us happy but experiences, many of which can be incorporated into our lives now. But most of us think that having more money is the key to happiness. In fact the Gallup-Healthways Well-Being Index proves that it's not more money that makes us happier. They surveyed about a thousand U.S. residents, asking a series of questions about their well-being and finding: "Of all the important and interesting findings Dr. Kahneman and Dr. Deaton's research has uncovered, the most reported finding is that people with an annual household income of $75,000 are about as happy as anyone gets." That's the magic number. "More specifically, those with annual household incomes below $75,000 give lower responses to both life evaluation and emotional wellbeing questions. But people with an annual household income of more than $75,000 don't have commensurately higher levels of emotional wellbeing, even though their life evaluation rating continues to increase."[2]

We've made our own choices to strap ourselves down with big mortgage payments, big car leases, insurance plans, and all the additional costs that come with a traditional life. Thus, it's not a pile of money that is the key to an upgraded life. Doing the things you want to do and having the freedom, time, and flexibility to make them happen are the secrets of a rich, fulfilled life.

Wobbling About

When I asked Gehry who he thought the next great architect was, he cited Zaha Hadid. At the time I was not that familiar with her work, and so I did some research and learned that she is a formidably accomplished woman. She has been listed as one of *Forbes* magazine's "World's 100 Most Powerful Women" and *TIME*'s "100 People Who Most Affect Our World." A professor at the University of Applied Arts, Vienna, she has taught at Harvard, the University of Chicago, Columbia, Yale, and many other universities around the world. In 2004 she became both the first woman and the first Arab to receive the Pritzker Prize, architecture's Nobel Prize. Among her many high-profile projects are the National Museum of XXI Century Arts in Rome, the Guangzhou Opera House in China, and the BMW Central Building in Leipzig, Germany.

I was so impressed with her accomplishments that I decided to interview her. When I asked her what advice she had for young people, she answered, "You can't just wobble about," adding, "You have to have some sort of aim. You have to have focus."[3]

Most of us, however, *do* wobble about, and we take detours and sometimes travel long distances toward the wrong destinations. This is the case because we haven't envisioned the future that we really want. Stopping to think about *what* we want to be doing, *who* we want to be doing it with, *where* we want to be doing it, and *why* are essential steps on the way to a happier life.

Damn the Headwinds

When my husband and I were living in Washington, D.C., the then mayor of Baltimore, Martin O'Malley, invited us to dinner in downtown Baltimore. He's a fan of Richard's work and was eager to show us all the new developments along the waterfront. We dined at a lively restaurant, and he shared stories about his city's successes and challenges.

He made a big impression on us then and at a number of his fund-raising events that we attended later. When he addressed his guests, his delivery was as impassioned as it was eloquent; he sounded almost evangelical. During one of those speeches, I turned to Richard and whispered in his ear, "Wow, he really, *really* loves and believes in what he does." Richard agreed, saying, "He could easily be a future president." In fact many pundits are now predicting that he will be a leading Democratic candidate in 2016 or 2020.

Not long after we moved away from D.C., we bumped into him at our hotel when we were in Dublin for an event, and we agreed to stay in touch. When he was elected governor of Maryland, I reached out to him for an interview. I asked him about the links between vision and focus. "There is dignity in all work," he answered. "Your first job will not be your best job. Keep improving your skills, broadening your experience, your knowledge, your ability to think and work with others, and never give up. Damn the headwinds; keep rowing forward."[4] His extraordinary political career—fighting to turn around one of the country's hardest-hit, most crime-ridden cities, rising to a governorship and a possible career in national politics—bears witness to his incredible focus and persistence.

Taking the governor's advice to keep improving your skills throughout your life is critical. Gathering information and knowledge even from your first crummy job will be important later on in upgrading your life.

Live the Life You Really Want to Live

To tell you the truth, Zaha Hadid probably would have called me a wobbler back in the day. It still surprises me when people tell me, "You're living the life you always wanted to live."

You see, I had no idea what I wanted to do in my career when I was young. I talked to career counselors in high school to assess my strengths and weaknesses. One suggested that I become an accountant because I was good at math; another suggested that I become an attorney because I had a linear focus that was useful in debate. Later on, I took the Myers Briggs personality test to see if there was a career that especially fit my ENTJ (extraversion, intuition, thinking, judging) profile. Every time, I came up short. I liked too many different things. I started freaking out that my lack of a vision was going to cost me time and money later on in college if I suddenly did find one and had to change course. It seemed that everyone else knew what his or her major and even minor was going to be.

My older sister, Reham, was going to be a doctor. That was all I heard about when I was growing up. We had a sectioned human brain model that disassembled into five parts that we played with like a Rubik's Cube and a 3B Scientific A10 Plastic Human Skeleton Model "Stan" on a pelvic-mounted 5-foot roller stand in our kitchen to remind us all that this straight A student was going to the University of Michigan to study medicine. Every time I snuck down to the kitchen in the middle of the night for a glass of milk, there was Stan. Wherever he popped up in the dark night, he was a scary and eerie reminder that I needed to find my focus. I had no clue, so I told my parents I was going into "international business." The words had enough credibility to satisfy them and to stave off inquisitive aunts and uncles.

But although I didn't know specifically what I wanted to be when I was growing up, I always had a vision of what I wanted the broad outlines of my life to look like. I knew generally that I wanted to be in business and media. I envisioned a life filled with travel and adventure. I had wanderlust for exploring a lot of different and dynamic cities. I knew I enjoyed spending time with family, friends, and interesting, creative, and smart people from whom I could learn. I loved arts and culture. I really enjoyed food and cooking. I was very much into health and fitness. I liked design, music, fashion, and film. Therefore, I set a path to incorporate all these things into my life personally and professionally, and to a very large extent I did.

Ali Velshi, the anchor of CNN's *Your Money*, wasn't much different from me in that respect. When I turned the tables and interviewed him, he told me, "My life has been full of those proverbial 'left turns' where the outcome is never obvious. But I approached everything I've ever done as an adventure, as if someone, someday, might ask me about it. What ended up happening is I stopped pretending it was an adventure and it actually became one. And I stopped worrying about where it would all end. I couldn't have planned it better."[5]

My sister's path swerved too. She decided to swap medical school for law school. She realized she hated law school after just two months because, "It was too dry and boring; just reading case after boring case." She longed for more adventure, so she applied for a position with the CIA. By the time the CIA contacted her, she was working for a big advertising agency in Chicago. The CIA told her it wanted her for espionage work, given that she was a young female who spoke English, Arabic, and French. Who would make a better spy? But as it turned out, she didn't want that much adventure; she preferred a research job. Ultimately, she found her focus in work that allowed her the flexibility to care for her two young children.

Evaluate Yourself

Too many of us never make such a candid assessment of what we want and need. We put others' needs before our own, whether it's our parents' dreams for us, our significant others' desires, our boss's orders, or our children's needs. The minutiae of daily life also get in the way. The thought that we might change course seems as far-fetched as a fairy tale. In a *New York Times* Personal Health post titled "When Daily Stress Gets in the Way of Life," Jane Brody writes, "For some people, anxiety is a way of life, chronic and life-crippling, constantly leaving them awash in fears that prevent them from making moves that could enrich their lives." The mere thought of a future that is different from the life you are living may cause stress and fear.

Brody cites an interview with the psychologist Dr. Tamar Chansky, who told her how people distract themselves with "extraneous catastrophes." Brody explained, "By 'extraneous,' she means the many stresses that pile up in the course of daily living that don't really deserve so much of our emotional capital—the worrying and fretting we spend on things that won't change or simply don't matter much." We all have distractions, such as a dental appointment, the bills mounting up, the cable repairperson, the battery in the fire alarm that needs to be changed, the car being overdue for an oil change. The mere thought of all those mounting chores can be exhausting.

"If you worry about everything," Brody says, "it will get in the way of what you really need to address." When we pay so much attention to the little things, the pesky things that hog our time and energy, we let life pass us by.

Brody adds, "When faced with serious challenges, it helps to narrow them down to specific things you can do now."

Think about all these things that mount up in your daily life that keep you from living the life you'd like to live. Write down all the things you want to be doing and would be doing if you were given $500 million tomorrow. Write down all the cool things you've decided you're going to do after retirement. Think about all the fun and interesting things you've been putting off in your life because of fear or stress. Write down the kind of life you'd like to live.

"Take some small step today," as Brody puts it. "You never know which step will make a difference. This is much better than not trying to do anything."[6] This small step I've just asked you to take—communicating what it is you want out of life, even if just to yourself—will make a big difference.

What is your vision for the future?

Whatever it is you want to do professionally and personally, write it down. Don't think about your vision for the future as landing that dream job. The reality is, that job barely exists. The goal is to incorporate as many things that you enjoy doing, things that give you happiness and purpose and that put meaning into your daily life.

Author Warren Berger advises CEOs and business executives not to articulate their missions by way of formal statements, about which he says, "Often they're banal pronouncements (like Walmart's, "We save people money so they can live better") or debatable assertions (like Yahoo!'s "Yahoo! is the premier digital media company") that don't offer much help in trying to gauge whether a company is actually living up to a larger goal or purpose." He suggests that we think of mission statements as mission questions, which "zero in on the mission and higher purpose of a company."

"Questions," he says "can provide a reality check on whether or not a business is staying true to what it stands for and aims to achieve. Whether mission questions come from throughout the ranks or are posed by leaders themselves, the point is to keep asking, "What are we doing? Why are we doing it? How might we do it better?" As Shaich says, "Figuring out what you want to accomplish is a continual search—and questions are the means to the search."[7] Try asking yourself some mission questions. There are five below that will help create the vision statement for your upgraded life. Answering these questions is a key step toward executing that goal. Try to be specific. Incorporate something from all five of the following categories.

1. **WHO?** This is the most important question to ask yourself. Whom do you envision your future with? Whom do you want to spend time with? Whom do you want to collaborate with, live with, have fun with, work with? Are you currently in a bad relationship that needs revaluating? Are you seeking a new business partner? Put as much detail as you can into your descriptions of the people you envision working with and spending your life with. If you think you'd rather be alone or don't see yourself ever settling down with just one person, write that down. If having children—or not having children—is important to you, put that down too.

2. **WHAT?** What is it that you want to be doing with your life and your career? We work for many reasons: to support a family, to support ourselves, to give back, or to fulfill a sense of purpose. We want to find happiness and a sense of meaning in our careers. You'll also need to evaluate the type of lifestyle your career will allow you to lead. Will it give you free time for interests and hobbies, for family and friends? What type of balance are you seeking between work and life? Will it allow you to be creative and be yourself? Will it tap and harness your expertise and skills? What kind of life do you want to live? An adventurous life filled with travel and exploration? A fulfilled life at a slower pace? Do you want to help others? Don't think only about what you can get paid for doing; think about what you might do as a volunteer or as a hobby.

3. **WHERE?** Where we live and work has a major impact on our happiness and overall well-being. Many aspects of our lives are tied to our communities, from friends, family, religion, extracurricular activities, and cultural offerings to schools, healthcare, and more. You need to ask yourself which community is the right fit for you.

Does it reflect your personality? Does it make you feel welcome and valued? Is it a place you want to commit to and invest in? Is it a place where you can put down roots and raise a family?

- Climate is important too. Does the weather help or hinder the types of activities you're interested in? Not only do your city and your neighborhood matter, so does the type of home you want to live in. Try to picture it. Is it a town home in a walkable neighborhood, a loft in a bustling city? Does it have a yard, a garden, a view?

- The outside is a part of the where, but so is the interior. The type of home environment you live in greatly affects your outlook, mood, and behavior. Is it a place of calm and a retreat that allows you to recharge and reflect, or is it a cluttered, noisy, dark mess that causes anxiety and stress? Envisioning where you live, inside and out, will help you get there.

4. **WHEN?** Every life stage matters. People live longer than they once did, and many of us are not content to accept retirement at the conventional age of 65. Setting realistic timelines for where you want to be and what you want to be doing at different stages of your life is important. Envision your life in college, after college, in your career, with a family, as an empty nester, as a retiree (or perhaps starting out in another career).

5. **WHY?** Do you want this vision for your life? Does it give you a sense of purpose and meaning? Is it motivating and inspiring to you? Are you helping others? Are you being productive? Does it connect deeply with your spiritual, religious, and moral beliefs? Digging deep into your own sense of why will help you understand what's wrong and what's right with your life today—how much you need to change and how.

These five points make up a vision statement for your life that will be a touchstone and guide as the next chapters unfold. If you can answer only a few of them at this stage, that's okay; just get down whatever it is you're certain of. Going back to check in, reevaluate, and add to or change your statement is part of the constant upgrading process.

Here are some sample vision statements that vary wildly but incorporate all five questions:

I am a 55-year-old health freak, so I want to be an active cyclist living in a bungalow in Colorado with my same-sex partner and a big network of friends. I want to have a job at an environmental agency within the next two years. My passion is the planet.

I want to fully realize my skills as a defense attorney and my passion to help the wrongly convicted and be on track to a partnership by the age of 40. I want to live in a high-rise apartment in a global city and end up with a woman who shares my interest in education and culture. This career makes me feel good about helping others while enabling me to maintain the lifestyle I desire.

I want to be a happily married stay-at-home mother to the boyfriend I'm dating now. I want to take care of two kids by the age of 33, living in a house with a yard in a small friendly community on the East Coast because family means everything to me.

By the age of 25, I want to launch a tech start-up that will help feed the hungry. I want to live in an apartment in Silicon Valley. I will get married later after I have some fun and hope to have some kids. I will create a work-life balance that will allow me to enjoy the outdoor recreational opportunities that the West Coast so richly affords.

Here are some examples of partial or vague vision statements that will need to be filled in and reevaluated at a later stage:

I want to ride a scooter through Europe.
I want to lose 40 pounds and start my own retail business.

I want to be a professional scuba diving instructor at the Great Barrier Reef.

I want to open my own organic restaurant and bakery.

I want to adopt two children and go back into healthcare management.

I want to be a violinist performing in an orchestra.

I want to take cooking classes in Tuscany.

I want to launch an online magazine.

Sure, these are all great things, but adding more parameters, such as the age you'd like to be when you achieve a goal and the reasons it is important to you, will make them come to life. Avoid grand statements such as, "I want to foster world peace," and, "I want to feed the hungry." As admirable as such sentiments may be, they're not very helpful unless they're incorporated into a fully realized vision statement. "I want to foster world peace and harmony," for example, can be translated to, "I want to move to New York by the time I'm 30, where I can work for the United Nations to help change the world for the better." Or, "I want to move to Washington, D.C., within the next six months and work for the World Bank, focusing my efforts on poverty reduction in African nations."

"I want to feed the hungry" can be translated to, "I want to get a postgraduate degree in agronomy at Michigan State University so I can help Third World farmers increase their crop yields using the tools and resources that are at their disposal. After traveling for five years, I would like to teach so others can continue this important work."

If you can't communicate your vision through words, draw a picture. Really. Ten years ago a friend asked me to draw the house I would like to live in. "Add as much detail as possible," he urged. I had no idea what he was getting at or why, but I followed his instructions.

I drew a big house surrounded by green space: tall trees, a garden, wildlife, with a backdrop of interesting buildings. Inside, there was a fireplace, a big open kitchen for friends and family to gather in, and lots of bookshelves. I added a couple of stick figures with smiles on their faces and a big bright sun shining down. When I was content with my drawing, I showed it to him. He studied it for a long time without saying a word, holding his hand on his chin. Finally he said, "I give this exercise to all my friends to see how they picture their future."

"Did I do it right?" I asked.

He said, "Out of the last 20 tests I've given, you drew the biggest house and the biggest sun shining down. It's also interesting to see the tall trees and wildlife and lines and lines of bookshelves."

He filed the drawing, and I never gave it another thought until years later, when I realized the house I'd moved to in Washington, D.C., was surrounded by magnificent trees, a beautiful garden, and lots of wildlife, situated as it was close to Rock Creek Parkway near the National Zoo. The home I live in now is in the city but on a ravine that is also filled with wildlife and great big trees. Both neighborhoods have strict ordinances against chopping down trees; the walls of both houses are lined with books as my husband is a professor and also an author and when we moved in together, we combined our big libraries.

Draw your house, draw your office, draw who you'd like to be working with or living with. Draw what your desk looks like or what you're wearing; feel free to draw even the expression on your face, as I did. Every little detail can give you clues to the future you want to have. Get that pad of paper out and start sketching.

Why Aren't You Doing It?

Now that you have begun to think in a serious, systematic way about what you want to do with your life, there comes a second and much harder question: Why aren't you doing it?

Why is it that most people don't get to live the life they want to live? As dissatisfied as they may be with their lives and current situations, many are literally paralyzed when it comes to making the changes they need to make, whether it is an awful job or a toxic relationship or obesity they are struggling with. Many of us stay frozen in time in a state of managed dissatisfaction. What holds us back from moving toward a better life? Sure, change is difficult for all of us. It carries uncertainty and risk, and it is often stressful and tumultuous. Even if we have an idea of the direction in which we want to go, many of us feel helpless to set our own course, much less change it. We feel that our lives are beyond our control.

The cure, believe it or not, is optimism. Brody continues, "Many worriers think the solution is positive thinking. Dr. Chansky recommends something else: think 'possible.'"

Merely opening your mind up to the possibility of change brings change. Rather than following a path that goes around in circles out of a conviction that life's circumstances are unmanageable, optimists set themselves toward an end result that they believe is achievable.

This may sound like fluffy BS, but this isn't just touting the power of positive thinking; there's a considerable amount of science to back it up. In his well-regarded books *The Optimistic Child, Child's Play, Learned Optimism, Authentic Happiness,* and *Flourish,* the American psychologist Martin Seligman makes his important theory of *learned helplessness* accessible to laypersons and applies it to everyday life. He began to formulate the theory while conditioning dogs for laboratory experiments. He realized that some animals behaved as though they were helpless in certain situations to avoid an adverse circumstance even though they had the power to change it or escape.

When some people feel that they have no control over their lives, they too behave in a helpless manner, which, ironically, can close the door to opportunity and the possibility of change. For example, a child who performs poorly on math tests may come to feel that *nothing* he or she may do can ever make any difference when it comes to math. When these children are faced with number-related tasks later in life, a paralyzing sense of helplessness may overcome them.

Depression, anxiety, phobias, shyness, and loneliness can all be exacerbated by learned helplessness. A woman who feels shy in social situations may eventually withdraw from other people altogether, turning her bashfulness into a crippling disability.

And here's the thing: the idea that you *can* change is almost as potent as the idea that you can't.

A childhood friend who went on to a thrilling life filled with ups and downs in the fashion and movie industries told me she'd "always felt the pressure to follow the rules, and if you don't follow the rules, you'll be a loser." She rebelled against it early on. "I just felt like I didn't fit into that environment and their definition of success," she said. "I had to find my own way. I was always a driven and passionate person, just not in that traditional way. I didn't fit in. If you're a passionate person who is driven, that gives you the fuel to prove them wrong."

The solution to learned helplessness is learned optimism. Sometimes it takes a deliberate act of will to break the cycle of self-fulfilling negativity. Why do people stay in ruts? If they're so unhappy, why not do something about it? What is there to lose? If you can't take a chance on yourself, whom can you take a chance on? Whether it is trying to prove someone wrong or envisioning a more fulfilling future, find the inner fuel to start your engine.

The Importance of Environment

What's going on outside our heads matters too. Your physical space and surroundings have a profound impact on your mood and your overall sense of well-being and happiness. Simple things such as tidying up, removing clutter, organizing, and letting in sunlight could easily serve as a catalyst for change and make you more productive and ready to tackle change. Gretchen Rubin, the *New York Times* bestselling author of *The Happiness Project*, decided to spend a year of her life documenting how she could squeeze more happiness out of her life. When she took a look around at her own environment, she found that, "Household disorder was a constant drain on my energy; the minute I walked through the apartment door, I felt as if I needed to start putting clothes in the hamper and gathering loose toys." She spent the next few weeks cleaning out closets, shelves, and "dump zones, the places where everyone dumps their stuff."

"Having fewer clothing choices made me feel happier," she said. "Although people believe they like to have lots of choice, in fact, having too many choices can be discouraging. Instead of making people feel more satisfied, a wide range of options can paralyze them." It's called clutter for a reason. "Who knew," she added, "that doing something so mundane could give me such a kick?"[8]

Appealing to four of the five senses is important when you're thinking about your environment. Sight, sound, smell, and touch. You can save taste for the dinner table. Hotels and department stores use your senses to manipulate your mood. Loud thumping music is supposed to make you more impulsive so that you'll buy more. A space that's packed with merchandise puts you in a frenzy to buy multiple items. A quiet, uncluttered space induces calm. Just look at how children behave when they enter a space that is clear, uncluttered, and open. One of the first things you'll see them do in that space is dance, jump, and skip.

Every time guests visit our condo they say, "Your lobby is so nice, it smells so good and fresh. It is so relaxing here." I decided to do some research and asked the building management about the scent. "We hired Dr. Aromas to consult on the fragrance for the building," said David, the young man at the front desk. "Dr. Aromas is actually a company?" I inquired. "Yes," he explained. "It's pumped through the ventilation system. The building owners worked with the consulting company for months to find the right scent that would appeal to residents and prospective buyers." I guess it worked, as in just two years, all 60 units have sold. Dr. Aromas' sales pitch says, "Our clients—both commercial and residential—have come to learn that the way their business or home smells influences moods, experiences, and decisions. Our commercial clients have discovered that our fragrances positively affect their sales. Hotels discovered that guests love the sweet smell that wafts through their lobbies, prompting visitors to relax and stay longer." Your space is the foundation on which everything else will build. Why not curate it, clean it up, and make it appealing?

My friend and former boss Ron Kagan, the director of the Detroit Zoological Society and one of the world's leading experts on animal welfare, made international headlines when he decided to relocate the Detroit Zoo's elephants to a better home, a sanctuary in California. The way exotic animals experience life in captivity is determined by the homes zoos give them. Animals need the right amount of indoor and outdoor space and the right terrain, lighting, temperature, food, healthcare, enrichment, activities, and social environment to thrive. For example, male tigers are solitary creatures, whereas gazelles and zebras travel in packs. When zoos place these creatures in spaces that do not meet their needs, the results are evident in the animals' neurotic behaviors, such as the pacing that giant cats are prone to or the swaying seen in elephants. When all their physical, mental, and social needs are attended to, they thrive and even reproduce.

We have a social responsibility to ensure a proper environment where animals can thrive, but how often do we assess our own physical spaces at home or at the office?

Zoo animals can die or suffer psychological and physical damage if their environment doesn't meet their needs, and the same thing is true of the place where you spend more than 40 hours a week. Take a look at your office environment.

Most of us spend the majority of our office time sitting: sitting in front of our computers, sitting in meetings, sitting for lunch, sitting in the boss's office. But there's no reason to neglect our health or put aside our need for a healthy physical space just because we are at work.

Stand Up for Your Health

"The health studies that conclude that people should sit less, and get up and move around more, have always struck me as fitting into the 'well, duh' category," Steve Lohr writes in his *New York Times* article, "Taking a Stand for Office Ergonomics." "Still, scientists have determined that after an hour or more of sitting, the production of enzymes that burn fat in the body declines by as much as 90 percent. Extended sitting, they add, slows the body's metabolism of glucose and lowers the levels of good (HDL) cholesterol in the blood. Those are risk factors toward developing heart disease and Type 2 diabetes."[9] It turns out that being stuck behind a desk isn't just soul-deadening but can be deadly for your body too.

Some call it a sitting crisis, others call it the problem behind us, but it's no joke; the offices we've imprisoned ourselves in are increasing our healthcare costs and taking a toll on our productivity and mental health. Diligent workers, the ones who are rewarded with raises and promotions, are the ones seen putting in long hours slaving away at their desks. It hasn't always been this way. "In the 19th and early 20th centuries," Lohr notes, "office workers, like clerks, accountants and managers, mostly stood. Sitting was slacking."

In the *Wired* magazine article, "Get a Standing Desk," Shoshana Berger writes, "Your job is killing you. If you sit at a desk for more than four hours a day, you increase your risk of death from any cause by nearly 50 percent and boost your risk of heart problems by 125 percent."[10] It doesn't have to be this way. In a *Harvard Business Review* article titled, "To Stand or to Sit at Work: An Auto-Analytics Experiment," Susy Jackson writes, "I eventually began sitting on an exercise ball to combat Spam Butt." Soon afterward the rest of the office started to follow suit. "While I was sitting on the yoga ball, a curious thing was happening all around me. Heads started popping up and staying up. Standing desks were all the rage."[11]

I've seen it myself at *The Atlantic*'s Washington, D.C., offices in the Watergate building. There are beautiful views of the Potomac outside the windows, but when I work from there now, there is something interesting to look at inside as well. Writers and editors are working standing up, with music stands or podiums configured to hold their laptops, or they are sitting, rolling, or shifting around on exercise balls to strengthen their core and keep their muscles working. There is a growing movement among workers to take matters in their own hands and create makeshift solutions to get out of their chairs.

We all need to change our mindset and get up off our behinds. Whether we are spread out in isolated campuses and industrial office parks or packed into suburban strip malls or towering skyscrapers, our offices are unnatural and uncomfortable places for most of us to be.

Get 'Em While They're Young

Why do we accept these environments? Because we have been programmed to accept them since we were too little to know any better. At the age of two, three, four, five, or six, we are shipped off to a foreign environment, away from mom and dad and our siblings, and are told to sit still at a desk to listen and learn. As I child, I remember being too shy and nervous in such a rigid environment to even raise my hand to ask for permission to use the washroom.

When I watched the way my nieces and nephews do their homework, I reached some interesting conclusions. My nieces lie stomach down on their pink beds with their feet kicking back and forth, surrounded by dolls and stuffed animals. Two of my nephews slouch down in their beanbags doing their homework on their iPads. My other nephew sits at the kitchen table munching on a grape or carrot between math problems, tapping his pencil on the table while he thinks. Every now and then, he'll walk over to Larry, his pet lizard, and play with him, and then come back to finish his work. When I asked my sister-in-law

Anastasia how two-year-old Zaiden was liking his three-hour-a-week class, she said, "I think he's getting used to it. But he insists on sitting on Mary Jane's lap, his teacher, for the entire session, until I pick him up." My mom told me that when she asked him how he liked school, he confessed to her, "Jideh [Arabic for grandmother], I like it, but I cwy a li'l bit." Jideh responded, "You cry Zaiden, why?" Zaiden chimes in again, "Yeah! I cwy a li'l bit, but then I stop!" After watching my nieces' and nephews' working styles, something occurred to me: Why don't most classrooms have beanbags, sofas, and floor space to roll around in? What's to stop kids from learning while they're standing, wiggling, jumping, or lounging? Children are literally bursting with energy, but early on, our schools slowly damp the enthusiasm out of them. Is it healthy for them to repress all that boundless energy for hours a day, five days a week, with only minor breaks during recess to run outside and play? I understand that education is struggling across the country and that schools are broke. They don't have the resources for a major redesign that is programmed to make our children perform better.

But does that mean we should accept 30 desks lined up theater style, with the instructor at the helm, just as we did in the 1800s? Minor changes in our schools, offices, and home environments can greatly enhance our overall health and mood, make learning more fun and less intimidating, and work more productive.

Think about the type of environment *you* need to thrive, whether it is at home or at the office. What kind of physical space do you need to get the most out of you? What kinds of people, leaders, and networks do you need to surround yourself with to be engaged and motivated? What kinds of tools and resources do you need to most fully optimize your potential? What learning and professional development do you need to grow? These may seem like simple questions, but the implications of your answers may well be profound.

Just as the solution to learned helplessness is learned optimism, the cure for a toxic environment is often a revamped or new environment: a different place with different people. Sometimes it takes an act of deliberate will to break the cycle of self-fulfilling negativity.

Think about these questions and devise solutions that will make you a happier, more engaged, and more productive person. Create a list of actions and steps you can take tomorrow. Whether it is time for spring cleaning to eliminate the clutter so that you can clear your head, better lighting, more green, music to enhance your mood, or ergonomically correct furniture for better health, there are several little things you can do today for a better tomorrow.

Surround Yourself with People Who Create Their Own Opportunities

My friend felt stultified in her environment in the suburbs; it was as if she were living by the wrong set of rules, trying to please the wrong kinds of people. "I decided early on that I couldn't do it their way," she said. "When I looked around, however, I became frustrated as I didn't see any other examples of success veering from this path. So my first step was to put myself in an environment to see the change so I could be the change. I knew I had to surround myself with other people who were creating their own opportunities instead of waiting around for opportunity to magically fall into my lap." She did just that, leaving her suburban home for the Big Apple.

Whether it is setting your own vision or getting on board with someone else's, you need a guiding vision. Think about life as a game with an end goal of winning a home, a mate, children, a leadership position, fame, recognition, accomplishment, or success. In every game, whether it is Monopoly or Angry Birds, there are twists and turns and levels to ascend, obstacles and challenges to overcome, and setbacks to deal with, whether it's picking up a "Go to Jail" card or being slung through the air to crash into a stack of sturdy crates.

The point is that no matter how many times we have to pay taxes, endure penalties, fall down, lose our winnings, give up our homes, or go back to square one, we keep playing in the hope of a better endgame. No one expects to master the game from the get-go. We accept that failure is built into the system, and we move on. But when we experience a few setbacks in life, too many of us are too quick to throw up our hands in surrender, content to waste the rest of our lives not trying to achieve anything.

Knowing Your Goals Can Transform Your Life— and a Whole City

While I was growing up in Michigan, my friends and family and I went on many road trips to Chicago. I was always excited at the end of the four-hour drive when we approached Lake Shore Drive and saw the big-city lights.

Chicago's longest-serving mayor, Richard M. Daley, helped lift his city from a place that was beset by scandal and racial divisiveness to one of the nation's best-run cities. He improved the mass transit system and ignited the cultural scene with public art and green initiatives. His focus on aesthetics and quality of life permanently transformed the city.

Not too long ago, my husband served on a panel with him at the Aspen Ideas Festival; the topic was cities and place making. Afterward, we went out to dinner with him at a cozy restaurant at the foot of the ski slope.

I asked Daley about the importance of staying focused on a core agenda. "In any work that you do there will be obstacles and setbacks," he told me. "But you cannot allow yourself to become so consumed with those issues that you forget about your main goal."[12]

One of his goals was to beautify Chicago even though many rallied against him and considered it to be a waste of money; he vastly increased the city's investments in museums and public spaces.

Millennium Park—a once-disused railroad yard that is now a green space filled with art, music, and people—is perhaps the greatest public work he undertook. But he also is well known for his simpler but no less effective efforts, for example, the foliage-filled planters that can be seen throughout many neighborhoods and the public art displays that draw tourists and residents alike to the Navy Pier. He is now well regarded as a pioneer in city livability issues.

When you look at your goals, accept the fact that there will be obstacles along the way, but consider how those goals will affect others. What effect will they have on your friends and your family? Perhaps knowing that they might also greatly enhance the lives of several others may motivate you to start moving toward them.

All the Other Kids with the Pumped-Up Kicks

Until we know what our life goal is, we can't identify the obstacles that stand in our way, let alone formulate an effective strategy for overcoming them. When we play Monopoly, we know that our goal is to amass homes, hotels, and money while keeping ourselves out of jail. In life, sometimes the toughest impediments stem from a lack of resources such as time. Sometimes people hold us back; sometimes we hold ourselves back with our own bad choices.

Sometimes the path that society pressures us to take traps us. We go to school, then college, then have a career and family, and end up feeling like a hamster, spinning a wheel that goes nowhere. We make just enough money at each stage of life to make it harder to risk losing what we have already aquired. We fill our houses with things; we become addicts. We look around and see "all the other kids with the pumped-up kicks." We want the bigger house, the faster car, the flat screen TV, the newest devices, or the flashiest handbag.

Just take a look at our homes during the holidays. The decorations indoors and out make them look more like department stores than houses. The numbers of gifts we shower on our toddlers at Christmas and their birthdays is obscene. Easter is now a cross between Halloween and Christmas, kids get baskets of candy *and* gifts. Little girls demand bigger and bigger Barbie houses every year, teaching them at a young vulnerable age that bigger and more are better. Our garages are jam-packed with stuff, and our basements and closets are filled with unnecessary things that we continue to clutter our lives with. Open your closet or walk down to your basement if you have one and take a look at all the things you've acquired. DVD players, air hockey machines, wires, electronics, crates, and crates of toys, old new clothes, which you purchased months ago but the tags are still on. Things we think we'll need on a rainy day, when we throw a party or some "what if?" happens. We enslave ourselves to consumerism; we can't help it. We are surrounded by television, ads, and media that force-feed this glossy lifestyle to us 24/7: *Pimp My Ride*; MTV *Cribs*; HGTV's *Top 10 Kitchens, Pools, TV Rooms, Outdoor Rooms, Great Rooms*; *My Super Sweet 16*; home makeover shows; fashion makeover shows. We become dope fiends, wanting more and more. Sure, the new bike, the new high-def flat screen, and the new Fendi bag feed into our happiness for a little while, but it's a hedonic treadmill and no one can win that game. No one can keep up. There's an old adage among the wealthy residents living across from Central Park in New York. The Upper West siders will brag that their yacht is better, while Upper East siders will boast that their plane is bigger. The reality is that consumption is just a way to make you work harder. These things may give us an instant rush of excitement but do little to upgrade our lives.

It took me a long time to figure this out. But I wised up one year after exhausting myself at the malls during the holidays dealing with traffic, lines, and congestion, the mobs of people like me running around frantically trying to purchase dozens of perfect gifts for family and friends. When I finally returned home with my 10 bags of stuff and sat down to wrap everything individually, I thought, how are these purchases going to enhance my loved ones' lives? They were not going to do that, I realized. After they rip off the wrappings, they're going to put them away in their full closets and basements, where they will sit unused with the pile of other stuff. So, I concluded, from here on out, I am never purchasing another thing: no Abercrombie & Fitch sweaters, no J Crew moccasins, no pajama sets from Target, or fancy ties from Saks, no trendy Skull Candy headphones, lotion kits from Sephora, and the like. Just no more stuff!

I am buying them experiences: tickets to the basketball game, the baseball game, the opera, the ballet, a concert, an event, the science center, a performance, an airline ticket, or even a dinner gift card. I am going to spend that money on fun things that friends and family and I can enjoy together. We need to place more value on experiences than on things. At the end of our lives, we treasure our memories more than our things.

Gram Hill, a successful entrepreneur who sold his Internet company in 1998 for more money than he thought he would earn in a lifetime, wrote in *The New York Times*. "We live in a world of surfeit stuff, of big-box stores and 24-hour online shopping opportunities," Hill said. "Members of every socioeconomic bracket can and do deluge themselves with products."

He advised, "There isn't any indication that any of these things makes anyone any happier; in fact it seems the reverse may be true."

It took him 15 years of traveling to get rid of all "the inessential things I had collected and live a bigger, better, richer life with less."

Intuitively, we know that the best stuff in life isn't stuff at all, and that relationships, experiences and meaningful work are the staples of a happy life."[13]

Knockout Knickknacks

I am not the only one thinking about the clutter we fill our homes with. Kara MacNeill, a World Vision Canada volunteer, wrote in the *Huffing-*

ton Post, "My husband is a very neat and organized kind of man, and one of his pet peeves is clutter. He was determined to avoid covering every surface in ornaments and trinkets. He would very patiently tell me, 'Kara, just say NO to knickknacks.'"

She took his advice to heart and really did start saying no to stuff and clutter, not only getting them but giving them as well. Instead of buying her family and friends yet more clutter to fill their homes, she made a donation on their behalf to families abroad in need of medical supplies, clothes, and other essential items.[14]

Don't get me wrong; I realize that we all like and desire nice things. But the intangible always outweighs the tangible in the end. I learned this the hard way when I saved up $2,500 to go backpacking through Europe with my cousin Deanna and my sister Leena when I was in college. We had a great time in Athens and the Greek Islands hanging with family who, unknown to us, heavily subsidized our living expenses. After we parted ways and started our own journey, I decided to allocate $2,000 to clothes and souvenirs and just $500 to hotels and travel. We had no idea what was in store for us.

Our first stop was Barcelona. We had booked a cheap room with two double beds online; we didn't spend much time checking it out when we arrived. We ran in, dropped off our bags and took off, eager to check out the city. When we returned from dinner, clubbing, and a walk down Las Ramblas, we started getting ready for bed. As we were preparing to tuck ourselves in, a small rodent or a very large insect scurried across the floor. The three of us jumped on the bed, clutching one another and screaming for dear life. "Oh my God, Oh my Cuss, that was disgusting!" We called down to the front desk, still balancing on the bed. The attendant pretty much said that there was nothing they could do this late and we should just go to bed. The three of us took turns staying up all night, on guard so to speak. The next day still groggy from our night shift duties, we checked out and took the train to Paris. When we checked into another dark, grim, and cheap hotel, the person at the front desk told us that only two were allowed to stay in a room. We assured her that "our friend" was just visiting from another hotel. After we "got away with it," we unpacked and were getting ready for our first night on the town. We were excited to check out the nightlife of Paris. Two of us were blow-drying our hair at the same time with our portable CVS handhelds, which were rigged with a U.S. to Euro converter. "Hey, Rana, check out my hair dryer, the rods are bright red. Is this going to burn my hair?" Deanna asked. I looked at my hair dryer. "Mine is the same way. I guess it just must be the power conversion." Though we started to smell something burning, we pushed forward, anxious to get our night started. All of a sudden we heard a pop, and the room went pitch black. "Uh-oh, what happened?" Leena said. "I think we blew the fuse," I said. Apparently our minor infraction caused the electrical system to blow, making the entire hotel dark. The front desk woman followed the scent of burned electricals and came running upstairs, yelling at us in French, *"Merde! Merde!"* When she realized that we had lied to her, she kicked us out on the street, wet hair and all, while shouting *"Sortie, sortie!"* At that point, I told my sister and my cousin that saving the extra money to go shopping was just not worth it. "This sucks! Let's upgrade our experience," I suggested. "If we put our dollars there, we'll get a lot more fun out of our trip than any new Parisian fashions and souvenirs we'd show off back home."

We quickly agreed and, with the help of Deanna's mom, we secured a beautiful four-star luxury hotel. We hid our backpacks as we knew what most Parisians thought of American college backpackers and tried hard to look as put-together as possible when we checked in. When we opened the door to our room, we started going crazy, jumping up and down on the bed and screaming with delight. The room was gorgeous: light-filled, spacious, with amazing views of the Eiffel Tower. We felt like we were on top of the world. We knew we were making sacrifices. No shopping sprees, no fancy clothes and purchases. But we were content to explore the city through our new upgraded experience.

We all have these choices to make in our everyday lives. We need to think about trade-offs. My cousin and my sister and I upgraded our experience by sacrificing our shopping. Hill goes on to say, "Our fondness for stuff affects almost every aspect of our lives. Housing size, for example, has ballooned in the last 60 years. The average size of a new American home in 1950 was 983 square feet; by 2011, the average new home was 2,480 square feet. And those figures don't provide a full picture. In 1950 an average of 3.37 people lived in each American home; in 2011 that number had shrunk to 2.6 people. This means that we take up more than three times the amount of space per capita than we did 60 years ago."[15] Can we really afford that big mortgage payment or, should we downsize to something smaller and invest all that freed up capital in the experiences that make us happier?

To pursue our vision, some of us might have to live in a smaller house than our spouses might like; some of us must trade job security for risk. We gain flexibility and ownership of our own schedules, but the price we pay is volatility and ups and downs. When a close friend of mine came face to face with the potential loss of her business, she was philosophical. She said, "Following your passion means the possibility of having everything and nothing, making it and losing it. It ebbs and flows; you must have flexibility and an adaptable personality." You need to trust your instincts and be ready at all times for new challenges.

The world-renowned education authority Sir Ken Robinson told me, "Some people can make a living from being in their element, others can't or don't want to. They just do it for the love of it. Whatever your circumstances, you need to find time to be in your element—to do what gives you energy rather than what takes it from you."[16]

Most people want a safe job with no risks and a steady path. Others look deep inside and find a different sense of purpose. "For me it felt like I had a sense of responsibility," my friend continued, "a strong determination to explore part of myself. I see that a lot of people don't even tap into it, afraid of the risk or content with the status quo. I don't know why."

You only live once, so why not go for your vision? Let's get practical, though. Some of the ties that bind us are real; we have families, we have student loans and mortgages, insurance payments and car payments, and mounting credit card and cell phone bills. We have a million things we have to do every day. How much more can we add to the list? For those of us with steady jobs, feeding into our vision seems like a frivolity. There are only so many hours in a day.

The good news is that you don't have to have more before you can pursue your own vision. You have to first identify what you want your life to look like, learn how to leverage the resources you already have, prioritize your needs, and knock out time wasters. You'd be surprised at how many of your goals are within reach.

Marshall the Resources Around You

I was recently one of a handful of women business leaders attending the major European annual gathering, the Ambrosetti Forum in Lake Como, Italy. The night before my husband was to give a speech, our friend and collaborator Riccardo Illy invited us to the famous Harry's Bar on the lake for dinner, along with his daughter, who also works for Illy Caffé.

Before he became CEO and president of the global coffee empire Illy Caffé, Illy had been a member of the Italian parliament, the mayor of Trieste, and the president of the Friuli–Venezia Giulia region.

We joined him at a gala dinner with fireworks on the lake the next evening too, but this time we were part of a larger party. Israel's then prime minister Shimon Peres, along with Senator John McCain, Texas governor Rick Perry, and Senator Joe Lieberman were in attendance, and more security guards than guests scoured the room. Not content to enjoy the amazing view of the lake and delight in the great food and wine, I asked Illy if he was ever tempted to enter the field of politics again, and he gave me a politician's judicious answer: "Maybe." His daughter chimed in and said that she'd prefer for him to give his attention to the business and that politics takes too much energy and time.

It seems to me that politicians—like most of us, come to think of it—have a pretty long list of to-dos awaiting them every day, not to mention all the emergencies and unexpected situations that arise, the fires that have to be put out, the disasters that sometimes literally fall out of the sky and upend entire agendas. "How do you juggle the day-to-day and at the same time set a vision for the future?" I asked him. Vision was at the very heart of his answer. "To be an effective politician, you need to be able to envision the future, to understand the needs of your constituents, and to plan and act using human, financial, and intellectual resources," he said. "Not least, you must communicate to persuade."

It was so refreshing to hear a successful political and business leader admit that he needed to marshal the resources around him, that he couldn't do it alone. Drawing on Illy's advice, once you have your vision on paper, the next step is to plan and act using every resource at your disposal. Friends, family, and colleagues can all help move your vision forward if you clearly communicate it to them and engage them along the way. If you have a goal and communicate it clearly and display your passion about achieving it, it is amazing how many people will support you and help you get there. Most of us are inspired by others' passions and want to jump on board to help the cause.

If You Can't Find Your Own Way, Join Someone Else's

If after you've thought about it, your piece of paper is still blank, think about all the people or organizations whose missions pique your interest and consider getting on board with one of them.

"Benjamin Franklin once said that 'there are three classes of people in the world: those who are immoveable, those who are moveable, and those who move,'" Ken Robinson observes. "Some people just don't get the need for change or don't want to. They're fixed in their position, and no amount of argument or evidence is likely to shift them. My advice is to leave them alone and put your energy somewhere else. There are others who may not be convinced yet but they're willing to listen. Work with them. Then there are those who are already moving. Align with them and support each other."[17]

A few years ago, my husband and I, along with a dozen or so others, were invited to a Toronto hotel suite to meet the rock star Bono. He was there to talk about ONE, the global charity he cofounded to reduce global poverty and combat climate change, AIDS and other infectious diseases, and hunger. Bono had been an idol of mine since I was a teenager. I went to all the U2 concerts in Detroit, bought all their albums, and plastered my bedroom walls with their posters. I was so nervous, it was all that I could do to say hello. A year later, we were invited to a larger but still intimate session that the *Globe and Mail* had organized with him and the rapper K'naan. The two were looking to bring attention to the poverty and famine in K'naan's native country, Somalia, and open a dialogue about what the West could do to help.

Since I was too starstruck to talk to Bono, I interviewed ONE's executive director and cofounder, Jamie Drummond. "There's already a lot of vision out there, with lots of people invested in their various visions," he told me. "The key is to find the best of it and help it build toward things which are both visionary and prophetic, but which notch up serious, incremental, measurable wins along the way."[18]

As Ken Robinson puts it, "When enough people move, that's a movement: when a movement gathers enough momentum, that's a revolution."[19]

If you can't find your own way, join someone else who has found his or hers. Some of us are meant to lead and others to follow, but we can all decide for ourselves which vision we want to be a part of. Amanda Burden, the director of the New York City Department of

City Planning and the woman who reshaped New York City for the better, introducing such game-changing projects as the New York City High Line, says, "It starts with being able to articulate a great vision. People respond to ambitious, transformational ideas."[20] Find a vision that inspires you and think about how you want to incorporate it into your own life.

Your Homework

1. Ask yourself what you want to do when you grow up. Meaning *now*!
2. Write down your vision statement. Be sure to incorporate all five pillars of the statement: who, what, why, when, and where.
3. Try to understand why you're not living the life you want to live.
4. Then knock out those obstacles.
5. Upgrade your environment for productivity and change.
6. Wake up and realize that life is filled with trade-offs.
7. Assess and figure out what's important to you and what trade-offs you're willing to accept.
8. If you can't find your own vision, join someone else's.

CHAPTER 2

WHAT'S YOUR PASSION?

*The saddest people I've ever met in life are the ones who don't
care deeply about anything at all. Passion and satisfaction go hand in hand,
and without them, any happiness is only temporary,
because there's nothing to make it last.*
—Nicholas Sparks, *Dear John*

If you are familiar with Washington, D.C., you know how brutal its summer weather can be: hot, sticky, muggy, with temperatures in the range of 90–100 degrees for days on end. When the sun sets, there is no relief from the heat, and to exacerbate the situation, the rivers, swamplands, and parkways provide breeding grounds for mosquitoes that go on the attack at dusk. That is why most Washingtonians escape to the beaches of Rehoboth, Dewey Beach, or the Outer Banks. I had a demanding job with little time off, and so we were trapped in the summer heat. Since there were not very many, if any, pool clubs to join, I called around to find a gym membership that included the use of an outdoor pool. We finally found one, the Embassy Marriott, just across the street on Connecticut Avenue.

After a long and exhausting week and several delayed flights, my husband and I decided to decompress by the pool one Saturday afternoon. I brought along a stack of pop magazines—the kind you're embarrassed to show the covers of in public—and purposely left all my devices at home. While I was scooping up all the latest news about Cameron, Kim, Jay-Z, and JT, Richard was lying there in the sun as if he didn't have a thought in his head. Then, all of a sudden, he turned to me and started talking about economic inequality and the "spiky world."[1] Before either of us knew what was happening, he began to articulate his now-famous theory of mega-regions, the 40 or so clusters of cities that dominate the global economy.

Intellectual breakthrough or not, I looked at him like he was crazy. While I was content to casually flip through some magazines and unwind, his wheels had been grinding about the distribution of prosperity across the world's cities. Some people are born with a passion for something that's so strong that it determines everything they do even when they are supposed to be relaxing by the pool on a hot summer day. I soon discovered this was not an isolated incident. Richard thinks about his work constantly; it gives him great joy and a sense of accomplishment.

Peter Diamandis, the CEO of the X Prize Foundation, a humanitarian nonprofit that launches innovative global initiatives, and the founder of Singularity University, told me that he has been obsessed with the idea of space exploration since his earliest childhood. Though his path diverged for a time in school (he earned an MS in aeronautics and astronautics from MIT but also took time out to earn an MD at Harvard Medical School), he has always remained true to his first love. "I consider my passion for opening up the cosmos one of the most important things I have in my life," he said. "Whenever I'm down, whenever I'm confused, whenever I'm not sure what I want to do, that passion serves as a guiding star to help me reenergize and focus."[2]

There are so many other people who are truly passionate about what they do, from fashion to food to architecture and design, from finance to music. A lot of people don't have to ask what it is they are interested in.

Let Your Passion Take Care of Itself

When I was in my twenties, I asked myself what pursuits I was truly passionate about. I cast my net wide and tried several different things. I liked music, and so I worked for a radio station and a record label and was on the board of a symphony orchestra. I liked fashion, and so I worked for major retailers from the Gap to Saks. I liked food, and so I tried my hand in restaurants and took cooking classes. I liked art, and so I served on the board of a museum and took several art classes. I enjoyed media, and so I dabbled in writing for newspapers and worked as a contributor for the local news channel. I liked travel, and so I worked for an airport developer studying airports across North America and served on the board of Airports Council International in Washington, D.C. You see, unlike my husband, who is passionate about one thing—cities—or Diamandis, who is passionate about space exploration, I tend to dabble in a lot of different things.

But when I tried to name the one thing I knew best, the one pursuit that I was truly passionate about, I was disappointed. No matter how hard I tried, I came up empty. Then I got smarter and asked myself a slightly different question: What makes me happy? Here again, my list was quite long: I like to cook, travel, and learn; to stay active, play tennis, follow arts and culture, fashion and film, work with nonprofits; I like all forms of media; and I enjoy traveling, reading, and spending time with friends, family, and creative people. I had worried that my passions weren't passionate enough, and then all of a sudden I realized that doing things that gave me moments of happiness and joy was enough.

Daniel Pink is the *New York Times* bestselling author of a book that launched a revolution, *Free Agent Nation: The Future of Working for Yourself*. A former chief speechwriter for Vice President Al Gore, he is a terrific speaker himself. His book, *Drive: The Surprising Truth About What Motivates Us*, gives us a path to achieve high performance.

He told me, "You know, I'm not a huge fan of the concept of passion when it comes to careers. Instead of trying to answer the daunting question 'What's your passion?' it's better simply to watch what you do when you've got time of your own and nobody's looking. *That* will give you the deepest insights into what you should be doing. . . . If people tap their strengths and use them in the service of something larger than themselves, passion will take care of itself."[3]

I'm a huge fan of the popular chef Ina Garten and her show *Barefoot Contessa*; I record it on my PVR and watch it when I can. She's been on the Food Network for 10 years. Some might imagine that she had been cooking barefoot from her earliest childhood, but the fact of the matter is that she didn't start off as a chef. She didn't discover her passion for food until she visited an open-air market in Paris when she was on vacation, and she began to experiment with cooking only when her husband, Jeffrey, was serving in the military in Vietnam. He later went on to become dean of the Yale School of Management and before that served as undersecretary of commerce for international trade in the first Clinton administration.

Garten herself had a job in the bureaucracy of the White House. After climbing the ranks, she eventually attained the position of budget analyst, which entailed writing the budget for nuclear energy and policy papers on nuclear centrifuge plants. Who could be passionate about that? Cooking and entertaining relieved some of the stress of her high-pressure job. After she left the White House at age 30, she purchased a specialty food store in East Hampton, New York, and that was when her passion became her livelihood. Garten's cookbooks have been nominated for James Beard Awards and have sold hundreds of thousands of copies, and her cooking shows have been nominated for and received Daytime Emmy Awards. As she told *The New York Times* some 30 years ago, when she was just at the start of her second career, "My job in Washington was intellectually exciting and stimulating but it wasn't me at all."[4]

Like Garten, most of us were not born with an innate talent for cooking, music, art, or math that we were driven to develop from a young age. Many of us in fact are working in jobs just because we followed a linear path after our studies or, worse, just to bring home a paycheck. I love Pink's advice to gauge what you enjoy doing in your free time and the way Garten stumbled upon that.

But you don't have to "follow" a single grand passion to give your life meaning. Dan Gilbert, an investor in more than 60 companies; the founder and chairman of Quicken Loans, the largest online mortgage company in the world; a major leader helping to revitalize downtown Detroit, and the owner of the Cleveland Cavaliers, recently shared the 27 most important lessons he'd learned in business, "If you believe tomorrow will be even more exciting than today, then you have discovered what passion really means."[5]

Find a way to fit the activities you find most satisfying into your daily life or, better yet, find a way to use them toward a larger purpose. Wayne Pacelle, the CEO and president of the Humane Society, the nation's largest animal protection organization, is seriously passionate about animals. Whether he is working out in the field, raiding a cockfighting operation, lobbying lawmakers on Capitol Hill on behalf of animal protection legislation, or saving seal pups in Atlantic Canada, he is a nearly superhuman force.

I worked with Pacelle many years ago on a major pet adoption event in Detroit. When I interviewed him recently, I learned that his passion for activism started during his years as an undergraduate at Yale University, where he majored in history and environmental studies. Though his career provides a great example of the role that a singular passion can play in effective leadership, he offered a realistic perspective on passion's pitfalls. "There's no guarantee that your passion will be rewarded with continued employment or career advancement," he told me. "But putting your passion on display is a powerful thing."[6]

If your passion is animals and you always wanted to be a veterinarian but you somehow ended up in media, why not volunteer to work at an animal rescue shelter or a conservation organization in your free time? If your passion is art but you're a cardiologist, why not collect art or volunteer in a gallery? Teach a children's art class? Immerse yourself in art expeditions? Tour art fairs? Start a blog, a Twitter account, an Instagram or Pinterest your passion. If your passion is dance but you ended up being the principal of a high school, why not take dance classes in your free time, teach dance class in the school, and go to dance performances? You will find that any connection to your passion, be it small or large, can greatly enhance and optimize your life.

If you are like me and the millions of others who don't have a singular passion, make a list of the things you enjoy doing in your free time and find a way to routinely incorporate them into your daily life. Sure, you might say, "I'd love to golf every day, but that's just not realistic." Yes, most of us have long commutes to work and spend hours in the office, leaving little or no time for the things we enjoy. But Chapter 4 will show that it's not about getting more time; it's about managing the time you have to knock out the time suckers and trade them for the things that bring simple buckets of happiness to your life.

At this point, don't worry about finding the time. The important thing now is to get your list on paper.

What If You're Great at Something You Hate?

I spent many a weekend in my past glued to the television, marveling at Andre Agassi's will and determination. His achievements on the tennis court are easy to count: eight Grand Slam titles, an Olympic gold medal, and 60 titles overall. He is one of only five male singles players to achieve a career Grand Slam: a victory in all four Grand Slam championships (Wimbledon and the Australian, French, and U.S. Opens). He was inducted into the Tennis Hall of Fame in 2011 and into the U.S. Open Court of Champions in 2012.

I was surprised to learn that the tennis legend has no great love for the game. Sometimes even people who are great at something can't summon up much passion for it. When I interviewed Agassi, he told me how he compensated: "By making it part of a larger project for which you do feel passion. When I realized that I wasn't born to play tennis, that I was made to play tennis, I searched for other things to which I felt more deeply and emotionally connected. Like education. I then made tennis part of that work. Anyone can do this with any job. If you don't love the task at hand per se, make it about your family, make it about serving others, make it about simply being conscientious. Make it about something other than your own fleeting wants and needs, work at it with everything you've got, and then stand back—the results will be magic."[7]

Since he retired from the game in 2006, Agassi has shifted his legendary focus and determination to his true passion: education reform. His Andre Agassi Foundation for Education opened a charter school, Andre Agassi Prep, in West Las Vegas, Agassi's hometown. Devoted to transforming U.S. public education for underserved youth, the foundation has raised almost $177 million for its mission. That's a passion that has made a difference in the lives of many children.

Now it's time to take out that piece of paper again. Underneath your personal vision statement, write down 10 things that make you happy: anything from cooking to cycling to spending time with your kids; from gardening, reading, playing the guitar, fishing, painting, jet skiing, and volunteering to helping the elderly. Make the list. Once you have all 10 things down, prioritize them from great to good.

Keep that list handy and review it constantly to ensure that you are always focusing on ways to incorporate these things into your life. Try to find a way to incorporate the top 2 into your daily life, the top 4 into your weekly life, the top 6 monthly, the top 8 quarterly, and all 10 annually. You'll be surprised how much happier you can be when you spend your time doing what you like. Yes, it really is that simple.

CHAPTER 3

GET CREATIVE

Creativity is the single most important thing that I have.
—Peter Diamandis, founder of the X Prize

I read a staggering statistic the other day. On average, kids smile 400 times a day.[1] Adults? Twenty times a day. What makes adults so damned miserable, I wondered. I started to explore this topic and stumbled upon the importance of creativity to our overall happiness, well-being, and success, in both our personal and our work lives. From studying the subject matter and listening to the experts, I reached the following conclusions:

- As we get older, creativity is squelched out of us.
- Creativity grows in a yes environment.
- Creativity needs a playground as an outlet.
- Creativity is all around us; learn to harness it.
- Creativity is a prerequisite for success.
- Creativity requires a diversity of people and convergence of view-points.
- Creativity comes though exploration and discovery.

Society Squelches Our Creativity

Within the course of just a few generations, the age of agriculture has given way to the age of industry; we've passed through the knowledge epoch and are now living in the Creative Age. But despite all that, our schools, our governments, and most of our businesses and organizations are still ossified and bureaucratic. From a young age, our creativity is squelched. As Sir Ken Robinson, the internationally recognized leader in creativity in education, has said, "We are educating people out of their creative capacities."[2] I felt that instinctively as a schoolgirl. Even though I got good grades, I hated school with an unholy passion.

You already may know that my husband is a professor; several of my family members are elementary and high school teachers. Teaching is a profession I greatly admire; our educators' endless dedication, passion, and motivation are amazing and inspiring. To report every day and educate 30-odd kids must be mentally and physically exhausting. However, although our teachers give their all, our schools are a different story.

I can remember sitting at my desk in the fourth grade, staring at the big clock on the wall and thinking, How can I do this for another eight years? I felt trapped and faced every weekday with the same dread every ungodly early morning. I remember thinking how uncomfortable my chair was and how boring it was to be lectured to when I had already raced through my homework for the day. I wanted to get up and move around, to be engaged. I wanted to be active, flip through books, and talk to people but was forced to sit quietly at my desk. I remember thinking that it was sheer torture; I'd look around and wonder if the other kids had the same thoughts racing through their heads. Most of them looked content, so I imagined something was definitely wrong with me and kept my feelings to myself. I felt helpless and even remember going to the washroom and crying on a few occasions during breaks. The only way I got through it was by consoling myself with the thought that one day I would be free.

It's odd to hear my husband the professor saying the same thing.

He obviously loves to learn, do research, and write, but he hated school as well. "Every single minute," he professed. He cut most of his high school and college classes to play in his rock band.

Robinson's TED Talk was called "How Schools Kill Creativity." The video went viral and is the most viewed Ted Talk ever, seen by millions of people all over the world. "Creativity," he said, "now is as important in education as literacy, and we should treat it with the same status." Instead, our schools systematically stigmatize it and stamp it out. "All kids have tremendous talents—and we squander them pretty ruthlessly,"[3] he adds.

To be creative, to try something new, you have to take a chance on being wrong. Children are natural risk takers, but by the time they finish school, that propensity has been educated out of most of them. At a conference of the Scottish Book Trust, Robinson noted that when a group of 1,600 children between the ages of three and five were tested for their ability to think in divergent, out-of-the-box ways, 98 percent of them achieved positive scores. By the time they were 8 to 10, the percentage had fallen to just 32. When the same test was administered to youths between the ages of 13 and 15, only 10 percent passed. And when 200,000 adults age 25 years took the test, only 2 percent could think creatively.[4]

When I asked Robinson what schools and businesses can do to encourage creativity, he answered, "Everything. Creativity is a practical process, and we can learn how to be more creative. I said that creativity is putting your imagination to work. A more formal definition is that creativity is the process of having original ideas that have value. Creativity is a process. Often the ideas we start from are not the ones we end up with. They evolve as we work on them, and the dynamics of this process can be learnt and practiced. Creativity involves generating new ideas. They don't have to be new in the history of humanity, but they do have to be new to you. There are techniques to question old ideas and generate new ones. Creativity also involves judgment in deciding what works and what does not. These techniques can be taught in schools and businesses. The first step is to recognize how important it is to do that and to treat them as seriously as we do literacy and numeracy."[5] Fortunately, Robinson's advice is now being taken up as a national policy issue. Richard spoke recently at the Creativity Conference in Washington, D.C. He served on a panel opening the session and former President Bill Clinton gave the closing remarks,[6] "We need to have a more explicit framework to nurture and support creativity."

Don't Be a Hater

"No, no, no, no, no!" We live in a "no" society. A friend of mine who is a mother of three says she loves her children but feels terrible at the end of every day. "Why?" I ask. "Are you exhausted from chasing after them and running around?"

"It's not that at all," she answers. "I don't actually mind that part; it keeps me active and young. I hate having to say no to them all day long: 'No, don't do that!' 'No, you can't have three chocolate cupcakes and a Coke for dinner!' 'No, you can't bring our dog with you to school today,' 'No, you cannot color on the dining room walls.' I'm mentally exhausted, upset, and deflated at the end of every day from having to say no to the three people I love so much. Their passion and energy are so great, but all day I'm saying no to protect them or to stop them from fighting, and I hate the way I sound. Like a nagging witch!"

At least parents mean well. But saying no is draining and exhausting in your personal life and for businesses too. Have you tried calling a customer service line recently? "Uh-oh, it looks like we got charged twice for the same movie on our cable bill," I'll remark to my husband. "For the film *This Is 40*, they charged us $6.00 twice, there it is," I say. "I didn't want to watch that silly movie anyhow, you should call," he answers, which irks me. And then, when I go to pick up the phone, I remember that the $6.00 savings is not worth the agony, frustration, and time lost. Sitting southside at a cafe on Lincoln Road in Miami Beach on a beautiful 75-degree morning, having coffee with my mom, who was visiting from Michigan, I was reminded why I try so hard to avoid all such matters.

Since I had a few minutes to spare, I decided I would call AT&T to see why anytime I tried to use the FaceTime app without Wi-Fi, it would give me an error message to call to upgrade my service. I was already annoyed that I couldn't have the option to do this by just clicking on a link. I dialed the number and after pressing several number keys to get to the right department, punching in my phone number twice, and holding for eight minutes, I finally had a live voice on the other end. "Great," I told my mom. "I have someone now. This shouldn't be long."

"Hello, this is Ann Marie. This call may be recorded for training purposes. Who am I speaking to?"

"Rana Florida," I answered.

"I'm sorry, who?" Ann Marie asked.

Aren't they trained to listen to the answers of the questions they just asked? I thought.

"Rana. R, A, N as in Nancy, A. Last name Florida, just like the state."

"Florida? Can you spell that for me?"

"Florida, just like the state, F, L, O, R, I, D, A," I responded.

"Okay, Ms. Florida, can you tell me your phone number?"

"Sure, but I already entered it in twice on the keypad before being connected to you, so don't you already have it?"

"No, that information does not come to us. Can you please tell me your phone number starting with the area code," Ann Marie instructed.

I rattle off the number and am eager to get to the matter at hand, but before I can tell her the reason I called, Ann Marie is back at it again, "Can you tell me your account number?"

"I don't have my account number, but can't you just look it up with my name and the number I just gave you?" I roll my eyes, and am now feeling guilty that I left my mother sitting there with no one to chat with on our coffee date. I hold up my finger and promise her just one more minute. She waves a hand at me and says she's fine, carry on.

"Okay, Ms. Florida, this is for your own security, please understand. If you don't have your account number, can you give me the last four digits of your social security number." I give her my ss. "Ms. Florida, just a few more questions for you. Can you tell me the last amount of your bill?" "No, sorry, I have no idea," I said. "How about the street you grew up on or the name of your first pet." I dig back into my memory and tell her Beach Road. I start to tell her the name of my first dog Lucky, who was run over by the school bus, but then I say, "No, no I think maybe Hugo, my cat, who was mauled by a dog while I was standing up at my best friend's wedding." After I finally get the answers right, she gives me the green light to proceed with my question. "I get an error message every time I try to use FaceTime without Wi-Fi, even though I signed up for an unlimited data plan and pay an arm and a leg for it."

"I understand your concern, Ms. Florida. Let me look at your data plan. Please hold." The fear of God is in me that she will never come back or I will accidentally but really on purpose be cut off. After two full minutes of boring hold music, she comes back on the line, "Yes, you're right, you do have an unlimited data plan." Really, you needed two minutes to figure that out? "I believe I'm going to have to transfer you to sales, as this is a new feature you'd like to add," she says. "No, no, no, please don't transf . . ." Click, hold music, and there I was sitting across from my nice mother, who was visiting from Michigan and anxious to catch up over our morning coffee. I rolled my eyes again, and said, "So sorry, Mom, just one more minute, I promise." The fact that my mother doesn't use a smart phone, so she had no text messages or e-mails to respond to, or Twitter or FaceBook or Instagram accounts to browse on, no reading material, and no one else to talk to, put the pressure on me to hurry up and try to get off the phone as quickly as possible. "Hello, this is John, can I please have your phone number starting with area code?" "I just gave her all of that info, don't you have it all?" I pleaded. "No, sorry, this is a new department, phone number starting with area code, please?" He drilled me with the same series of questions. Ten minutes later, he concluded that even though I had an unlimited data plan, FaceTime was not a feature that could access the data plan and I would have to either pay extra for the feature or switch data plans, which he advised would be more expensive. "How do I have an unlimited data plan if I can't use FaceTime because it takes up too much data?" I questioned. "I know, ma'am, I had this same call yesterday and was wondering the same thing myself," he admitted. Now I was furious. Not only was my precious Saturday morning being wasted, but there is obviously a glitch in their system, and I wondered why it wasn't being taken care of. So I asked John if he had kicked the problem upstairs to management. "No, ma'am, I haven't, but it's a good idea," he said. "Look, if multiple people are having this problem, then it's really an issue that needs addressing. Can you please talk to management about it?" "Sure, ma'am, I will do that." I shook my head, hung up the phone, and looked at the duration of the call: 28 minutes. And instead of spending a nice morning with my mom, I was now furious. My mother could sense my agitation, which made her a little uneasy, and she asked if I wanted anything else to drink.

I wondered why employees are never empowered to say yes, let's make that happen. Instead the odds are overwhelming that the answer we'll get will be no: "No, we can't do that," "No, we don't do that," and flat out, "Sorry, we can't help you." Some of us will demand to speak to a supervisor, who will validate our concerns but still go on to say no. Wouldn't it be a groundbreaking idea to have a customer service group that found a way to say yes to the customer at least once in a while? Too often, I feel that way in life as well.

Be it in work or in life, nothing stifles creativity like rejection. As frenetic and frustrating as so many of our lives are, it's a miracle that we manage to get dressed and come to the office every day, let alone think up the occasional new idea.

Creativity Needs a House of *Hell*, Yes

For creativity to rise and shine, it needs a yes environment. In business as in life, you need to surround yourself with a team that is ready to say, "Yes, let's give it a try," "Yes, let's do it—the worst-case scenario is we'll learn something," and "Yes, I'm in!"

Squelchers are people who instinctively throw water on new ideas: "No, that won't work," "No, we can't do it that way," "That idea is crazy. It will never fly." In fact, the seatbelt in cars was dismissed as a stupid idea until it was finally accepted a decade later.

A colleague at *The Atlantic* put it this way: "I call it a soufflé. You have this big amazing idea, and when other people dig into it, they just cause it to deflate." People who say no dampen down ideas and spread anxiety. I know I don't enjoy being around them. Their energy is negative; they are what I call Debbie Downers. Not only do they say no in their professional environments, but I see them carry the mantra through their personal lives as well: "No, I don't want to try that new restaurant." "No, I don't want to try snowboarding for the first time at the age of 35." "No, I don't want to go to that event or that new exhibit. Why would I want to do that?" In science a positive and a negative equal a zero. So to overcome the effects of a negative person, you need two positive people. Negative people are a huge drain on businesses too. Their constant stream of rejection is toxic to new discoveries and ideas in the work environment, and, frankly, they are a drag to be around.

"Can we just find a way to say yes?" I am constantly asking.

Many of us will just stop working on a crazy idea or a new project due to outside discouragement. But Dan Gilbert advises that it's not us, it's them. One of his 27 lessons is: "People who are constantly negative, pessimistic and cynical are not spewing their venom toward you or your ideas. They are talking about themselves. Never forget that."[6]

At Toronto International Airport recently, I walked up to a gate agent with boarding passes and passports in hand for a flight to Dallas. My husband and I each have a gazillion points that we seemingly can never use; I wanted to ask if we could get upgrade to first class before those points got wiped out when the airline merged or filed for bankruptcy, which it was always on the verge of doing. But before the words could leave my mouth, she was shaking her head no. "Why are you shaking your head no?" I asked. "I haven't even had a chance to ask you the question!"

"Whatever it is, I can't help you," she responded with her head down, frantically typing on her keyboard.

Too many people try hard to keep us from an upgraded life. So many of us are used to this treatment. Call your cable company, your phone company, your energy company, or an airline and all you'll hear is no, no, no. We hang up the phone and are fuming and angry, but it's not their fault. They are merely the ones on the front lines. All of their decision-making capability has been squelched out of them.

"The vision is really about empowering workers, giving them all the information about what's going on so they can do a lot more than they've done in the past," Bill Gates, cofounder of Microsoft, famously declared of the computer age.

We've all spent countless hours on the phone trying to argue with these poor robots. "Let's try to find a way to say yes," I plead. "I've been a customer for five years, always paid on time; can we move forward in a productive manner?" Inevitably I become so frustrated that I hang up before things devolve into a shouting match that I would regret.

How can companies continue to operate this way? Thanks to some freakish coaching, customer service reps now all repeat a mantra: "I understand you are frustrated," or, "I can understand you are upset." I'm frustrated that they haven't been empowered to solve problems. I'm frustrated that they don't encourage a better way. I'm frustrated that these monopolies are still in business with such antiquated ways of treating their employees and customer base.

Gilbert has a lesson about this too: "Thinking (going deep) about problems, challenges, new ways of doing things and creativity is one of THE hardest things you will ever do. It also will bring you the finest results."[7] I can't control the gas company or the airlines or the credit card company, so I've made a point of surrounding myself with people who say yes at work and in life. I seek out collaborators and colleagues who think, believe, and act in a "yes we can" way: "Yes, let's do it! Yes, that's a great idea!"

During the aftermath of Hurricane Sandy, President Obama "ordered his staff to follow a '15 minute rule,'" Julie Pace reported in *The Huffington Post;* his staff had to respond to any state or local official who called within that time frame. "'If they need something, we figure out a way to say yes,' he said."[8] This simple yet powerful statement, finding a way to say yes even during a crisis when resources were limited and staff was already overworked did wonders to solidify his position as the leading presidential candidate of 2012 just one week before the election.

When You Can't Say Yes All the Time

I encourage my team to find a way to say yes. The client doesn't need to know the hundred things you had to do to get to a yes answer, but let's do our best to set that course.

Although the reality is that it can't always be yes, there is a better way than just saying no. I learned early in my advertising career that if you want to change something, you have to do it in a constructive manner. I saw creative teams put in countless hours on campaigns for clients that would get turned down and rejected within minutes. "No, that's not what we want," the client would respond. "No, that doesn't represent our brand." The creative teams would go back to their offices deflated and uninspired.

One day when I was managing my own advertising teams and we were presenting campaigns to senior leadership, I witnessed a powerful thing. The creative teams had stayed up late the night before to lay out all the story boards on the conference room table in the big board room. This board room was mainly used to win new business and impress clients. They came in early, had coffee and bagels on the side table, adjusted the lighting perfectly, and set up mood boards on easels behind each campaign. One manager walked quickly around the conference table, with a coffee in one hand and an everything bagel in the other. As he took bites from the bagel, the poppyseeds and seaseme seeds dropped onto the creative work. He didn't seem to care. He just shook his head no to everything he saw with a grimace on his face. The other leader walked slowly around the table. He took the time to gaze at each creative, stopping and pausing along the way with his arms behind his back. He asked the creative team questions, inspected the mood boards, and took a few notes. It took him much longer to offer his feedback. When he finally spoke, he did an interesting thing. He first listed all the positive things about each one. He said, "I really like how you did this here," or, "It's really smart that you incorporated these concepts in this one." "I really like the fonts and the colors used in this campaign." When he was finally ready to communicate his thoughts on taking the campaign in an entirely different direction, the team not only was inspired but was open and receptive to feedback and changes.

Unfortunately, too many of us too often communicate only the negative, not realizing the huge consequences this can have on colleagues, clients, friends, and family as feelings of rejection, ill will, anger, and being taken for granted rise to the surface. Contrarily, when you communicate the positive, it inspires people and encourages them to work harder and more productively. When you are happy with something or like something, it's important to take the time to communicate it. It's a much more effective way to motivate teams and encourage creativity.

Creativity Needs a Playground

The playground of X Prize founder Peter Diamandis is outer space. "I envision what doesn't yet exist and use my passion and drive to get others to help support that vision and make it reality," he says. "It's what I do." Whether he's free-floating in a zero-gravity cabin or tinkering in a rocket, he says, "I love the creative process and I love the entrepreneurial process and the two go hand in hand for me."[9]

We need to feed the inner child in us that yearns to be creative, the one that was squelched into conformity years ago. What better way to do this than to give yourself a recess. We all loved this playtime as children, but so few of us will give it to ourselves. We try to get a lot done in a day and feel that goofing off on the playground is a waste of time. But it's important to find a playground for our bodies so that we can unleash our minds.

Tennis has been my recess. Even though I didn't start playing the game until my early twenties, being on the tennis court brings me back to my childhood. I can yell at the ball, jump around, run, fall, scream, wail, laugh, and have fun. Most of the time I play outdoors on clay courts under the sun. I get sweaty and hot, and the clay dust coats my legs; I feel like I did when I was a kid, spending a long day at the park.

Best of all, I'm not checking e-mail, tweets, texts, and phone messages. When I get off the court and back to my normal workday, I feel recharged, reenergized, and ready to take on more work and tackle challenges in a more optimistic way. It also helps spark new ideas. "Sweat is like WD-40 for your mind," Chris Bergland wrote in *Psychology Today*, "It lubricates the rusty hinges of your brain and makes your thinking more fluid. Exercise allows your conscious mind to access fresh ideas that are buried in the subconscious."

Bergland also notes that Albert Einstein claimed to have thought up the theory of relativity while he was riding his bicycle, adding, "Anyone who exercises regularly knows that your thinking process changes when you are walking, jogging, biking, swimming, riding the elliptical trainer, and so on. New ideas tend to bubble up and crystallize when you are inside the aerobic zone. You are able to connect the dots and problem solve with a cognitive flexibility that you don't have when you are sitting at your desk. This is a universal phenomenon, but one that neuroscientists are just beginning to understand."[10]

We all need to find a playground. "A new and growing body of multidisciplinary research shows that strategic renewal—including daytime workouts, short afternoon naps, longer sleep hours, more time away from the office and longer, more frequent vacations—boosts productivity, job performance and, of course, health," Tony Schwartz, the CEO of The Energy Project, noted in a *New York Times* op-ed.[11] Whether it is cycling, yoga, rock climbing, walking, pilates, paddle boarding, skiing, snowboarding, mountain biking, or something else, find an interest that engages your body so that you can release your mind. "Regular exercise and sleeping well go hand-in-hand," Bergland notes. "Regular exercise allows you to sleep deeper and dream better. The more regularly you exercise, the better you will sleep and the more of a creative powerhouse you will become."[12]

Many of us feel too overwhelmed to think creatively. Our work and home lives are filled with a gazillion things to do. The reality is that it's not just the one hour work out that we have to commit to, but getting ready, putting the gear on, packing the gym bag, getting to the gym, and cleaning up takes additional time and constant self urges of willpower to make sure you don't let yourself back out of the committment. But another recent study from Scotland suggests a simple walk in the park can ease brain fatigue and refresh your brain for new thinking.

"The idea that visiting green spaces like parks or tree-filled plazas lessens stress and improves concentration is not new," Gretchen Reynolds wrote in a *New York Times* blog. "Researchers have long theorized that green spaces are calming." But using portable electroencephalograms, a team of researchers from the University of Edinburgh proved it. When people wearing the devices walked through urban settings, their brain waves patterns showed signs of arousal; when they walked through a park, they became more meditative.[13]

"The study suggests that, right about now, you should consider taking a break from work," Dr. Roe said, and, "It's likely to have a restorative effect and help with attention fatigue and stress recovery."[14]

Your health and well-being are essential to everything you do, how creative and productive you are, how you lead and manage, how you approach every day. If you are stressed out, mentally exhausted, physically out of shape, it's time to upgrade it now as it will effect everything else you do. If your home and office are your temples, your body is your vehicle for getting around. Take care of it; keep moving.

Our fast-paced society bombards us with work. Actually carving out the time to treat yourself to a romp seems impossible, but remember that it not only is fun and healthy but can lead to more productivity, creativity, and innovation.

Googleplex Your World

If you are a manager of a major organization or an entrepreneur with your own staff, it's time to put these principals into practice. The payoff will be immense. Consider following the lead of innovative organizations such as Google, which promotes activity and fitness on its campus in Mountain View, California. The Googleplex has four core buildings on a campus that is spread over a 26-acre site that includes green space and a large public park connecting it to the Bay Trail.

When my husband and I visited the vast green campus a few years ago, we were blown away. We saw staff on roller blades, on bikes, jogging, walking with family members, friends, and dogs—and not just at lunch but in the middle of the workday. There were water features, ponds, fountains, pathways, plazas, and big art structures.

Inside, it was just as exciting: 18 food stations, cafeterias, and buffets with diverse menus featuring free food for all and free laundry rooms, swimming pools, and multiple sand volleyball courts. Googlers are encouraged to take breaks and release some physical energy so that they are equipped and ready to take on new mental challenges and make new discoveries.

When *New York Times* columnist James Stewart went on a tour through the Google office in Chelsea, New York, he described the experience as a "dizzying excursion through a labyrinth of play areas; cafes, coffee bars and open kitchens; sunny outdoor terraces with chaises; gourmet cafeterias that serve free breakfast, lunch and dinner; Broadway-theme conference rooms with velvet drapes; and conversation areas designed to look like vintage subway cars."[15]

He saw libraries, secret rooms, and bookcases hiding private reading areas. He saw play stations and hooks and ladders, and even interrupted a scavenger hunt in progress. Googlers had their dogs at work. While some strolled the halls, others napped anywhere they felt like.

"Google's various offices and campuses around the globe reflect the company's overarching philosophy, which is nothing less than "to create the happiest, most productive workplace in the world," according to a Google spokesman, Jordan Newman. "Google lets many of its hundreds of software engineers, the core of its intellectual capital, design their own desks or work stations out of what resemble oversize Tinker Toys. Some have standing desks, a few even have attached treadmills so they can walk while working. Employees express themselves by scribbling on walls. The result looks a little chaotic, like some kind of high-tech refugee camp, but Google says that's how the engineers like it." "We're trying to push the boundaries of the workplace," Mr. Newman said, in what seemed an understatement."[16]

Don't Think Impossible

When I was a very little girl, I remember my father saying to me and my siblings, "You can do anything if you put your mind to it." Such a simple yet powerful statement.

His own life proved that adage. He grew up in the old village of Madaba, a short drive away from Amman, Jordan. He was ranked at the top of his class and even taught classes in math when he was still a student. At the age of 18, he decided that he was going to leave his parents and six brothers and sisters to make a better life for himself in the United States. There was no Internet to help him learn about the region, the cost of living, the jobs available. With just $120 in his pocket, he kissed his family goodbye and left to start a new life in a foreign land. Without ever having visited it before and not knowing a soul, he made the move, first to Greenville, Illinois, then to Toledo, and then to Detroit, where he worked as an usher in the Fox Theater and as a wall washer in Henry Ford Hospital to pay for engineering school. He chose Detroit because he had heard that there were opportunities for engineering jobs with the Big Three automakers.

He attended university at Wayne State, where he became great friends with my uncle, who is a retired professor from the University of Michigan. My uncle introduced him to his sister. My father said he took one look at her and decided that she was the girl for him. Amazingly, my parents grew up 20 minutes away from each other in Jordan but met only after they'd both moved to the United States. They were married for 42 years, raised six children, and had nine grandchildren before my father passed away.

I took my father's advice to heart and truly believed it. Now, when people say no to me, it gives me the fuel to try that much harder. When an editor of a prominent media outlet told me that I couldn't be a contributor, it gave me the drive to prove her wrong. I landed a blogger position at the *Huffington Post*, which had 35 times the unique viewers! Many of my posts were featured on the home and business page next to posts from Arianna Huffington, Mayor Michael Bloomberg and other thought leaders, authors, business CEOs, and celebrities. Some of my posts were picked up by other news outlets, including *The Washington Times, Top News Today, World News Today*, local business, finance, and legal pages, style and fashion blogs and websites, and even *The Hollywood Reporter.* One of my posts, "How to Get a Raise," caught the attention of the *Today Show* producers and landed me a guest expert spot on the *Today Show*. Before I knew it, I was being interviewed by Meredith Vieira and Hoda Kotb. NPR's *Talk of the Nation* also invited me on air as a guest contributor. I didn't take this position lightly and used the platform to interview all the amazing minds in this book. This caught the attention of my now literary agent, which led to this deal for this book with McGraw-Hill, one of the largest publishers in the world. As painful and annoying as it is, rejection is part of the game; you can't let it stop you. Use it as fuel to start your engine.

"I've never been to design or business school, but in some ways that has helped me because I didn't think about impossibility," the fashion designer Tory Burch, whose distinct logo can be found at more than 70 Tory Burch stores around the world, told me in a recent interview.[17]

I love Burch's outlook. She became super successful in fashion design because she didn't box herself into believing she wasn't an expert in fashion and therefore shouldn't even try. Instead, she dived right in and went for it.

In a recent blog post at *The New Yorker*'s website, the neuroscientist Gary Marcus posed the question, "Should we keep doing what we are doing, or should we tackle new challenges? If you're seven, or twelve, or twenty, it's easy to think about new ambitions: learn Spanish, learn to paint, do a flip off your skateboard. But what if you're older?" Is there hope for us to reinvent ourselves—to learn a new language or play an instrument—if we didn't start early in life?

Marcus charted his own experiences trying to learn the guitar in his book *Guitar Zero*. "I imagined that I was alone in my quest," he wrote. "The conceit was that I was going to practice for ten thousand hours, because nobody else my age would ever be willing to invest that kind of time. But in the past year, I've been deluged with e-mails from other adult learners. A journalist wrote to say that her seventy-six-year-old father had learned the guitar late in life, and had just told her that he was starting a band with his friends called 'The Three Grandfathers.' In Portland I met (and jammed with) Rick King, an engineer who was keeping an Excel spreadsheet tracking every hour of his practice, having returned to the guitar in his sixties after surviving a heart attack."

Don't think you're alone or ridiculous in wanting to try something new, something that you're not an expert in. Everyone started as a novice.

"Whether or not picking up a new skill makes you smarter, it can certainly make you happier," Marcus concludes. "We can't all be rock stars. But, as the cliché goes, the journey can be every bit as rewarding as the destination." Think about the things you've wanted to do but put off your entire life. "Whether your dream is to play piano, cook steak *sous-vide*, or finally learn to speak French, the lesson from all this new research is clear: there is no better time than now to take on something new."[18]

Gretchen Rubin writes about happiness in *The Happiness Project*. "We are happy when we are growing. Contemporary researchers make the same argument: that it isn't goal attainment but the process of striving after goals—that is, growth—that brings happiness."[19]

Juic'n

Every creative person has his or her own unique process. "I want to design things that combine intellect, emotion, craft, and functionality, and in order to do that, I've had to devise a process for myself that is both disciplined and open-ended. So I start with color—not general shades but very specific, precise hues—then I consider materials, which naturally lead to shape and construction," Tomas Maier, the creative director of the luxury brand Bottega Veneta, told me. "Always, from beginning to end, there's a particular question or idea that animates the process for me."[20]

For Maier, the creative process is precise; however, most of us no longer have a creative bone left in our bodies. We have been programmed to engage in a routine and to think about creativity as a frivolity, something perhaps to dabble in only in our free time. How do we encourage creativity, and where do we go for inspiration when so many of the mundane tasks of life conspire to stifle it? What is our juice to get going?

Tim Brown, the CEO of IDEO, the design firm that created the first mouse for Apple and the second mouse for Microsoft, had this to say: "For me, changing context is often the best way to encourage new ideas. Travel helps."[21] Changing your environment and seeing new places truly does open up your thinking and offers new ways of looking at the world. Not only seeing new places and experiencing new cultures but the very act of getting you moving and out of your routine helps. It opens your eyes and mind to fresh new ideas in ways that watching a movie or reading a book about a new place often can't do.

For thousands of years, people believed the earth was flat. The Renaissance astronomer Nicolaus Copernicus proved otherwise in the 1500s, but his theory was debated for another century. A mind that is open to new ideas is the key to moving forward.

Not only is creativity important for growing and learning, but it is essential for success in business. Whether you are creating a new line of clothes or coming up with the newest Twitter meme, "Creativity is vital, particularly today, given the acceleration in technological progress and global competition," the coffee magnate Ricardo Illy told me. "You need to continually innovate, and creativity is at the core of innovation."[22] Change may be the only constant we have in our fast-paced world. Either we learn to embrace it, or we fall behind.

What made the Big Three U.S. auto manufacturers fall behind, bringing the great city of Detroit to its knees? Failure to innovate.

When I asked her about the importance of creativity, the architect Zaha Hadid said, "I'm always curious about the next step, the next big thing. The rapid developments that computing has brought to architecture are incredible. . . . There is a strong reciprocal relationship whereby our more avant-garde designs encourage the development of new digital technologies and construction techniques—and those new developments in turn inspire us to push the design envelope ever further."[23]

Turning a Drug Den into an Art Museum

Constant innovation and change take energy and time. "We are all creatures of habit," says my friend Mera Rubell. But slight tweaks to our routine can help. "Even a mundane alteration to our lens can affect the way we see the world. For me this change of lens gives me a certain freedom and complexity to see the world in color and not just in black and white."

Rubell was born in Russia to a family of Polish war refugees. Though she arrived in New York without a word of English as a girl of 12, she went on to attend Brooklyn College and Long Island University, where she received an MA in education. She was a teacher for Head Start when she met her future husband, Don, a medical student. The two quickly discovered that they shared a passion not just for each other but for art and business, she told me. With hardly any money, they made a plan to explore New York galleries, meet promising artists, and purchase some of their paintings. The pieces they bought, by the likes of Jean-Michel Basquiat, Keith Haring, Damien Hirst, Jeff Koons, Cindy Sherman, and Andy Warhol, now make up what is arguably the most important privately held collection of contemporary art in the world.

In the early 1990s, they bought a former federal Drug Enforcement Agency facility in the crime-filled Miami neighborhood of Wynwood and turned the 45,000-square-foot space into both a museum and their private residence which includes a library and a tennis court, spearheading the movement of galleries, cafés, and artists into the once desolate district. Rubell was a powerful force in the redevelopment of South Beach as well and played a pivotal role in bringing Art Basel to Miami Beach.

"What spice is to cooking, creativity is to my life," she told me. "I see it as a daily mind set: How can I challenge myself to inject a surprise into the way I normally do or see things? Creativity leads to innovation, and I do believe that creativity and an open mind allow the world to move forward."[24]

Find your creative juice and incorporate it into your personal and professional lives. If you are stuck in a rut, push yourself outside your comfort zone. Whether it is travel or a new environment or context, find what motivates you to look at things differently. If you are a leader mentoring others, find ways to encourage and reward creativity in the workplace. Don't squelch new ideas and discourage others by telling them their ideas are nuts. Pushing the boundaries of the status quo will lead to learning, new discoveries, and personal growth.

Multi-platinum-selling singer, songwriter, producer, dancer, and actress Nelly Furtado saw her career take off in 2001, shortly after she released her debut album *Whoa Nelly!* which went on to sell 6 million copies worldwide. For all her awards (a Grammy, a Latin Grammy, and 10 Juno Awards) and gold and platinum records, I found her to be very down-to-earth, warm, and engaged when I had the pleasure of dining with her. "Creativity is the juice that keeps me alive," she said. "My main goal in life is to stay passionate—whether that means honoring the muse, surrendering to the moment, leaving yourself open to spontaneity—whatever it takes—you need to live and feel in order to be creative, and relish your high moments and your low moments."[25]

19,000 Ways to Serve a Cup of Coffee

Creativity is all around us. Just look at what's on offer in any shopping mall. What was once exceptional is now the norm. Colors, sizes, shapes, scents, and packaging are more vibrant than ever before. Consumers expect products to constantly reinvent themselves. Customization is key.

What ultimately makes or breaks a brand is not marketing budgets and advertising campaigns but something much more fundamental: the business leader's ability to make the most of his or her creativity and attract and leverage the creativity of the people on his or her team. When we spoke about how he had built his empire, the billionaire founder of HDNet and owner of the Dallas Mavericks Mark Cuban put it this way: "You have to re-earn your customers' business every day and creativity is a big part of that."[26]

Starbucks has more than 19,000 ways to serve a coffee. Venti half caf soy no foam latte, grande skinny mocha, tall chai tea extra hot, triple shot sugar-free vanilla cappuccino: whatever it is, Starbucks doesn't say no. Could this be why there are Starbucks cafés in 61 countries and counting?

Nike lets you design your own shoes. Their online slogan is, "You Design It. We Build It." Customers can choose from a spectrum of colors to apply to all areas of the shoe and from a variety of specially engineered mesh uppers. They have a choice not just of sizes but of widths and can choose how much cushion they need and the appropriate tread for surfaces such as streets and sidewalks or outdoor trails and how much flexibility they need to support their gait.

I recently customized my own Nike Frees. In 10 easy steps, I was able to design my dream shoe, starting with a specific shoe for inspiration, then selecting one of 16 cool colors for the Upper, the Overlay, the Swoosh, the Lining, the Lace, the Midsole, the Midsole Topline and the Tongue ID. The default Tongue ID is Nike on both the left and the right shoe. But I picked R for the right shoe and Flo. for the left, so when you looked at them straight on, it read, R.Flo, a moniker I thought sounded like a professional runner's. And Nike's business savvy doesn't stop there. After you design your perfect shoe and place the order, Nike prompts you to share your design through social media. "I designed this @NIKEiD What do you think?" is the default Twitter, Pinterest, e-mail, Instagram, and Facebook message, with a photo of your show. Everyone is a creative artist.

Consumers want to have it their own way. Hard Candy nail polish was created by two Iranian sisters, Pooneh and Dineh Mohajer, and Dineh's ex-boyfriend Ben Einstein. Their first product was a startling shade of blue they called Sky, created by serendipity in 1995 when Dineh tried to match her nails to her sandals. After receiving several compliments, she decided to sell her polish at the popular Santa Monica retailer Fred Segal. Before she knew it, celebrities started wearing it and talking about it in interviews, and the brand exploded. Within two years, it was generating $10 million a year. In 1999, it was acquired by the luxury brand Louis Vuitton Moët Hennessy (LVMH).

When Hard Candy launched, it made a huge impact because the names it gave its colors were fun and wacky but, more important, because the colors were so vibrant and daring that its rivals' traditional reds and beiges paled in comparison.

Now celebrities such as Katy Perry and Lady Gaga are pushing the boundaries of fashion off the grid. Not only are nail polishes available in thousands of new colors, their textures have changed. Katy Perry's collaboration with the nail polish maker OPI resulted in a new line called Cracked, which takes on a shattered appearance when applied to a nail. Glitter, shimmering coatings, and shellacs, which promise long-lasting colors, are all new additions to the creative mix. The coverage for the Golden Globes' and Oscars' red carpet awards now includes a "mani cam" to capture the wild and eclectic manicures of celebrities.

Keep Creating or Die

Thinking creatively leads to new ways of doing things, which lead to business success. Not so long ago, Blockbuster was the dominant player in the video rental business, with stores all over the United States. Going to the video store with your girlfriend, boyfriend, spouse, or kids was a fun thing to do to kick off the weekend. But it wasn't fun having to return the movie. Blockbuster had the choice of losing money while videos it could have been renting sat in someone's player or charging high late fees and turning its customers' laziness into a profit center.

In the 1990s a little start-up based in Scotts Valley, California, called Netflix entered the market, offering customers the ease and flexibility of dropping a video in the mail whenever they felt like it, with no late fees and no hassle. Netflix now has over 27 million subscribers and is responsible for 33 percent of all streaming video traffic. It has partnership deals with every major studio and network and has rights to the content of over 250 suppliers. Blockbuster declared bankruptcy in 2010. Netflix took the store model to a mail-based model, then quickly shifted to an Internet and streaming model, and now it is even producing its own original content. If you are not constantly rethinking and readapting, even a multi-million-dollar business with millions of customers, 60,000 employees, and thousands of stores can close down very quickly when a smaller, nimbler, outside-the-box-thinking company comes to market.

Fast Company's Linda Tischler interviewed Ken Carbone and Leslie Smolan of the design firm CarboneSmolan, who have been business partners for 35 years. As in any business, they've had their fair share of ups and downs, great years and tough ones, but their relationship has stood the test of even the most difficult times. Tischler writes, "Framed above a doorway in their office is a sign that Carbone found in a fortune cookie: 'The road to success is always under construction.' It is, they say, their firm's mantra. 'If you stay the same, you'll die,' Carbone says. 'Granted it's exhausting, but staying off balance builds different muscles.'"[27]

Constant change, creativity, and innovation are the key to success. If you sit back and think you have the perfect product or service and don't constantly upgrade, tweak, and change it, business will pass you by. In business as in life, we need to constantly upgrade ourselves—our mental awareness through discovery and learning and our physical bodies by exercise and a healthy diet.

"Amplifying our creativity is the single most important task ahead of us today," Bruce Nussbaum, professor of innovation and design at the Parsons School of Design, told me. "We face the challenges of a VUCA world—Volatile, Uncertain, Chaotic and Ambiguous—that can only be met with a creative mindset. The culture of efficiency that we grew up with can't cope with this magnitude of cascading change. We need to acknowledge that creativity is at the core of economic value and we need to build a new Economics of Creativity."[28]

Diversity Is Key

Diversity is both a driver of creativity—you need different kinds of people if you want to generate new and different ideas—and a selling point in and of itself, a fact to which many ad campaigns bear eloquent witness. Old, young, straight, gay, black, white—all races, genders, and ethnicities are potential consumers and expect to see themselves reflected in a company's marketing. MAC Cosmetics was among the first brands to use an openly gay spokesperson back in the 1980s; Apple painted Microsoft uncool in its PC Guy campaigns by associating it with the stuffy middle-aged white businessman John Hodgman played in the commercials.

Creativity requires diversity; organizations and entrepreneurs must move away from the one-size-fits-all model. Embracing diversity in the workforce means welcoming young and old, straight and gay, men and women. A rainbow of different races and ethnicities equals a wide spectrum of different inputs and viewpoints: the recipe for innovation and discovery. Not only must employers embrace nontraditional workers, but they need to adapt to nontraditional working styles. There's no reason for the 9-to-5 chained-to-your-desk work style of the 1950s in today's business climate.

Girls, *Lean In!*

Facebook COO Sheryl Sandberg's book, *Lean In*, and Anne-Marie Slaughter's blockbuster *Atlantic* cover story, "Why Women Still Can't Have It All," both provoked a tsunami of chatter about women juggling high-profile careers and families. While Sandberg hit the media circuit, Slaughter led a sold-out lecture tour and landed a seven-figure book contract, pretty much proving that they can.

But most working moms still struggle with the challenge of having a fulfilling career with colleagues and bosses who value their skills and knowledge and grant them the flexibility to pick up the kids at school, stay home with a sick child, and maybe carve a little time out of the middle of the occasional day to coach a sports team or accompany a child on a field trip. Some employers do this, but too many are unnecessarily rigid, forcing moms into the 40-hour-plus workweek, making them beg and plead for the privilege of being late once in a while. Working mothers are made to feel that they are not doing enough at work rather than being rewarded for trying to balance work and family.

Then there are all the stay-at-home moms, who are the most underutilized resource in our society. So many highly skilled mothers in the 30- to 50-year-old age bracket could easily be incorporated into the workforce if they were granted flexible hours, had the option to telecommute, and, most important, were trusted to manage their own workloads and lives.

My sister Reham is the divorced mother of my two amazing nephews, ages 9 and 11. She graduated with top honors from the University of Michigan, but instead of going to a corporate job where she'd have to clock long hours and put her kids in daycare, she accepted a position with the Creative Class Group as director of events and operations in which she has the freedom to work whenever and wherever she pleases, often taking calls at home from such important clients as the office of the prime minister of the United Kingdom while her kids are enjoying a play date in the next room. Sometimes she'll have to use the mute option and shush them: "Boys, quiet! I am on an important call!"

She will meet with clients such as Philips in Amsterdam via Go-ToMeeting, pick up the boys from soccer, make them dinner, and then sit down and help them with their homework before returning to her own work late at night, long after conventional office hours are over. If the boys are on a school break, she may take them to London or Greece or Abu Dhabi or to New York or DC without having to turn in a vacation request. She manages her own workload and her own schedule. This arrangement is mutually beneficial—she gets a work-life balance, we get the benefit of her skills, and we get them at a discount too, since she traded a higher salary for flexibility. It's unfortunate that more companies don't take advantage of this untapped resource.

It's no surprise that more women are leaving hostile and rigid work environments, preferring to take their chances with businesses they can launch from their homes.

In November 2011, my husband and I attended the Asia-Pacific Economic Cooperation (APEC) Summit in Honolulu, where Richard gave a speech on the past and future of cities. In the previous two weeks we had been to meetings and events in Toronto, Amsterdam, Utrecht, Maastricht, Seoul, DC, and Miami. We were so maxed out with travel that we almost considered turning down the invitation. But it was a huge honor to play a role in this dialogue between North America and the Asia-Pacific nations, and we knew we would be in good company.

A few days before the event the roster of speakers was finalized. The rundown was as follows:

United States Secretary of State Hillary Clinton
People's Republic of China President Hu Jintao

Richard Florida, senior editor, *The Atlantic*
United States President Barack Obama
Indonesia President Susilo Bambang Yudoyono
Dr. Eric Schmidt, executive chairman, Google, Inc.

We were blown away. "Oh my gosh, Richard is speaking before President Barack Obama!" I forwarded the e-mail to Richard and our team. The entire team was thrilled and thought it was the coolest thing ever, except for Richard, who was very nervous. He has been speaking at events around the world for over 20 years to audiences large and small. Using his photographic memory, he typically reviews the talking points and background material and finalizes what he is going to say 10 minutes before hitting the stage. But opening for the president of the United States was a new experience even for him.

The Secret Service was everywhere when we arrived at the hotel; white vans labeled "Field Operations" were parked at every corner. We were instructed to take a long back route down service elevators and through the kitchen on the way to our green room, which we shared with the president of Indonesia and Google Executive Chairman Eric Schmidt. As Richard was preparing his notes, I couldn't help thinking about the inspiring speech Secretary Clinton had just delivered, in which she focused on women as a vital source of economic growth.

Among the statistics she cited, a few stood out. Women own nearly *8 million* businesses in the United States, accounting for $1.2 trillion of gross domestic product. Over the last 40 years, women have gone from 37 percent of the workforce to 48 percent. The productivity gains that can be attributed to women's increased participation in the labor force amount to $3.5 trillion in GDP, almost a quarter of the this nation's total GDP and more than the GDP of all of Germany.

But despite all of women's economic contributions, most countries and even most U.S. corporations don't recognize them. When women decide to have children, many will not return to work, as antiquated policies don't leave them enough room to juggle their careers and families. Sure, the Family Medical Leave Act entitles new parents to 12 weeks' leave, but when those three months are over, women are expected to resume their jobs in exactly the same way they did before—if those jobs were not eliminated while they were away.

A friend of mine who is an editor at *The Wall Street Journal* recently fretted that her youngest daughter's school had burned down, and so she had to work from home for three days in a row.

"Can't you work from home whenever you want?" I asked. "Most of your work is done electronically anyhow."

"Are you kidding?" she responded. "They make you feel guilty for not being there."

I asked her if anyone had said anything to her.

She said, "No, but you can just tell. Even though I can do twice as much editing as them in half the time, my colleagues look at me like I'm slacking."

"But you have three small children!" I said to my friend. "Why can't you just get your work done from wherever you want whenever you want?"

"I can work from home better; there are fewer distractions. But the assumption is if you're not at your desk, you're not working. I'm also working on Thanksgiving Day, Christmas Eve, and Christmas this year," she added.

"This is how they treat a loyal senior editor who has been with the company for 20 years? I don't understand why you have to be at your desk. Can't you just ask your boss for more flexibility while managing the same workload?"

"I can't," she said. "They really think it's important to pick up on the chatter in the newsroom."

"What about using instant messaging or chat?"

"The online group does that, and it works well, but we have yet to transition."

No wonder the newspaper industry is dying, I thought.

Writing in *The New York Times,* Robert Pozen a senior lecturer at Harvard Business School and a senior fellow at the Brookings Institution, and author of *Extreme Productivity: Boost Your Results, Reduce Your Hours.* bears her out:

> *It's 5 p.m. at the office. Working fast, you've finished your tasks for the day and want to go home. But none of your colleagues have left yet, so you stay another hour or two, surfing the Web and reading your e-mails again, so you don't come off as a slacker. It's an unfortunate reality that efficiency often goes unrewarded in the workplace. I had that feeling a lot when I was a partner in a Washington law firm. Because of my expertise, I could often answer a client's questions quickly, saving both of us time. But because my firm billed by the hour, as most law firms do, my efficiency worked against me.*

Pozen mentions a study published in 2010 by University of California, Davis, Professor Kimberly D. Elsbach and others. The study "interviewed 39 corporate managers about their perceptions of their employees. The managers viewed employees who were seen at the office during business hours as highly 'dependable' and 'reliable.' Employees who came in over the weekend or stayed late in the evening were seen as 'committed' and 'dedicated to their work.'"[29]

Mad Men

This point is driven home in the TV show *Mad Men.* "A Little Kiss," the first episode of the fifth season, begins as the head secretary, Joan, is out on maternity leave, exhausted and stuck at home with the new baby while her doctor husband is stationed in Vietnam. When she gets dressed up and visits the office with her baby, the staff ooh and ahh and uncomfortably pass the baby around while hustling to get back to work.

Joan is desperate to return to work, a startling change from the first season, in which she had seen her job as a way to get a husband and kids. The dramatic change in domestic politics that the 1960s wrought is captured in this powerful exchange with her mother:

Joan's mother: "[Greg's] not going allow you to work."
Joan: "*Allow* me?"
Joan's mother: "'Where thou goest, I will go.'"
Joan: "And how'd that work out for you?"[30]

The contrasts and consequences of women's choices are starkly illustrated throughout the episode. Peggy, Joan, and Megan choose to work, whereas Trudy and Betty's suburban dream has left them bored, frustrated, and increasingly obsolescent.

What's disheartening is how little has changed since the 1960s. It's amazing that some offices have done as much as they have to enliven workspaces, even allowing employees to bring their pets to work, but have done so little to support working mothers.

Having children, one of the most wonderful and precious experiences of people's lives, is welcomed socially by families and friends but shunned professionally. Our corporations and organizations mostly look at it as a hindrance. Most women are forced to choose to give up their professional careers to care for their children or be stressed out messes and juggle demanding hours at work with neglected or subpar child care.

Society needs a serious wake-up call. Working women are here to stay, and they are always going to be having children. Current maternity leave practices need a total overhaul. Sure, give new mothers time off to adjust to their new situation, but don't shock them back into the workforce a few months later. Allow them the freedom and flexibility to juggle their workload and new family members on their own schedule. An infant doesn't march to the drumbeat of the 9-to-5 time clock. Recognize the need to come in later, pop out during the day, and work later or work odd hours.

Not all jobs can be performed remotely, of course, such as manufacturing and service jobs. If you are a nurse or a retail worker, keeping certain hours in the shift makes sense. But why are so many organizations reluctant to adjust to the needs of mothers who work in knowledge jobs? Give them the flexibility to manage their own workload. If their work suffers, then reevaluate. But the time, money, and resources needed to find and train a new employee far exceed what it costs to put a little freedom, trust, and flexibility into their schedules.

At the APEC summit, Secretary Clinton spoke eloquently about the barriers that women face around the world and the incredible obstacles and inequities they must still overcome in the workplace. The removal of those barriers would increase the size of U.S. gross domestic product by 9 percent, the Euro Zone's by 13 percent, and Japan's by 16 percent. What an incredible untapped opportunity!

Even in the twenty-first century, even at the richest, most forward-looking companies, the glass ceiling has not gone away. Women are notably few and far between at the very top of the pyramid. Chrystia Freeland's book *Plutocrats: The Rise of the New Global Super Rich and The Fall of Everyone Else* talks about this. In an interview with *Elle* magazine, Freeland says, "My book editor asked me, 'Are we going to do a chapter on women?' There *are* no women. Oprah, the Walton heiresses, Sheryl Sandberg, the wives, the widows, the woman who invented Spanx—it's a very, very small group. Most plutocrats will accept that there are women with enough brain cells to get there. What they will tell you privately is that women don't have a willingness to take risks, and they don't have the killer instinct. It's another way in which the world of the plutocrats is different. In Middle America, more and more women are breadwinners. Then you get to the plutocracy, and it's the 1950's. None of the women work. None of the plutocrats have female colleagues of comparable power—none."[31]

Creativity requires diversity in ages and genders. But there is still a big gender gap; just take a look around. The majority of our governments and businesses are still run by middle-aged white men. Take a look at the U.S. Senate. Out of 100 members, the 113th Congress has only 20 female senators. While this is the most ever in the United States, it is still a minority. We need to empower women to integrate their work lives with their personal lives.

If you're a woman who's looking for a job, look for a company that gives you the freedom and flexibility to get your work done on your own schedule. If you're an employer looking for top talent, recognize the needs of the changing workforce and understand that many people would accept less pay for more flexibility and control over their schedules. Tap into the mothers who want to raise children in a well-balanced environment but want to work from home. The children we raise today will be the leaders of our society tomorrow.

Getting Creative Spoils the Corporate Mold

Not only is creativity important to our new ways of living and working, but our work environments could stand some shaking up too. The space you work in is very important to the output of your product or service. Companies such as Steelcase, Herman Miller, and IDEO study and research the science of optimal work environments. Creative environments, whether at work or at home, can more than pay for themselves with increased productivity.

These days there are two broad categories of workspaces. The first are the traditional old-line models, with corner offices for executives, smaller offices along the perimeter for less senior management, and look-alike meeting rooms and featureless warrens of cubicles in the interior. The second is the free-form urban tech/creative campus, such as Google's digs and Red Bull's London headquarters, as well as Pixar's headquarters in Emeryville and Vodafone's in Portugal. Filled with amenities such as Ping-Pong tables, cafés, and big comfortable common areas where people can come together for informal exchanges and dialogues, these edgier spaces are designed to stimulate a talent pool, to energize and inspire it at every turn.

But for every business that has caught on to the importance of a properly designed workspace to productivity, many more are still in the dark. I talked to Bruce Kuwabara, a partner at Kuwabara Payne McKenna Blumberg Architects, about the challenges of office design. "Think about how the redesign of the building can support concentrated individual and team work, mixing and interaction," he said. "We all need quiet time to think, write and work but there is also a time when we need the input and exchange among our colleagues and other experts."

"The second part," he continued, "is the interior fit up. You need to develop a vision of how you want to work and play."[32] There's no harm in experimenting. Think of your workspace as a flexible loft in which you can shift spaces around to encourage innovation and improve productivity. Why not get your teammates on board by setting up working groups to discuss functionality and the element of design?

That experimental spirit was nowhere in evidence when I toiled in corporate America. I still crack up when I remember what happened at one of my jobs. I had been spending hundreds of hours in the air and in hotels and had exceeded all of my performance goals. When I was back in my office, I wanted it to be a place that reflected my personality and felt like home. I didn't think it was a big deal when I outfitted it with some modern egg-shaped chairs I had purchased from Design Within Reach. Little did I know.

The trouble began as soon as I took them out of their boxes. A pair of senior executives stopped and gawked, their heads tilted to the side, clearly trying to understand what they were seeing. "Wow, those are some way funky chairs," one of them said after a while. A few minutes later someone from the finance team walked by and joked, "Where are those chairs from? Outer space?" I rolled my eyes and got back to work. More and more people stopped outside my door and stared. I said to myself, "Okay, what is the big deal here? Why is everyone making such a fuss about these two cool new modern chairs?" Another manager chimed in, "I'm not so sure, I'd refer to them as 'cool.' Perhaps weird is the word you're looking for."

I stepped out of my office, took a long look around, and began to understand. Before me was a sea of gray drab cubicles, endless rows of beige metal filing cabinets, and thickets of chairs with aqua blue and green floral cushions. I was much younger than most of the senior staff, and I was also new. I had been shaking things up with my new PR and communications tactics, but it seemed my taste in furniture was not welcome.

The next day, I was paid a visit from a human resources executive. Standing at my door with a clipboard in her hand, she looked at the chairs and then looked at me. "I'm sorry to inform you that they cannot stay here," she said. "They are not part of our standard office furniture package."

"But that's ridiculous," I protested. "These chairs are just here, tucked away in my office." Then I tried to rationalize with her, "I bought them personally; I'm saving the company money!"

"If they are not removed by the end of the week, we will have them removed for you," she replied. Then she walked over to my desk, dropped a catalogue on it, and said, "Senior-level staff are permitted to choose from one of the two guest chair options offered here on page 192. You can fill in your requisition and leave it with Mary." Before I could say another word, she turned on her heels like a drill sergeant and quick-stepped away. I looked at the page she had tabbed with a yellow 3M sticky and saw the same ugly floral cushions. Two choices: one with arms and the other without.

Poof. Just like that, all the goodwill I had for the company, the excitement I had to take my work to the next level, just vanished, dissipated instantly thanks to a rigid, antiquated policy that seemed to have been devised to make even senior staff feel depersonalized and interchangeable.

Sir Ken Robinson says, "Creativity is the fruit of imagination and imagination is what makes us human. Imagination is the ability to bring to mind things that aren't present to our senses. Through imagination you can visit the past; you can empathize with other people's points of view and you can anticipate the future. Creativity is putting your imagination to work and it manifests in every field of human achievement. Creativity is the fountainhead of human culture and it couldn't be more important. It's all the more tragic that it's so often stifled in our schools, businesses and institutions. We pay a heavy price for that."[33]

Delivering Happiness

A few years ago, our company received an e-mail from Tony Hsieh, the young CEO of the Internet shoe seller Zappos. It started off direct and to the point: "You probably receive a lot of emails like i do, so i'm going to use bullet points instead:

- i am ceo of zappos.com, doing over $1 billion/year in gross sales
- i am author of "delivering happiness," on the ny times bestseller list for 26 weeks in a row
- we are going to transform the culture of downtown las vegas by building our future campus at the current las vegas city hall
- video 1 to watch which describes the vision, based on some of your ideas:
  http://blogs.zappos.com/blogs/ceo-and-coo-blog/2010/11/29/secret-downtown-project
- video 2 to watch shows highlights from the las vegas city council meeting:
  http://blogs.zappos.com/blogs/zappos-family/2010/12/02/zappos-family-goes-city-council-hearing
  this is probably the only opportunity in your lifetime to put your

theories to the test in a major city and watch everything unfold in less than 7 years.

let me know if you'd like to be involved!

————Tony Hsieh

Follow me on Twitter: http://twitter.com/zappos

My book: http://www.deliveringhappinessbook.com

Bus tour: http://www.deliveringhappinessbus.com

The e-mail was clearly passionate, but its author didn't bother with small stuff like capital letters or punctuation and got right to the point.

Hsieh is a figure to be reckoned with. He sold his first company, LinkExchange, to Microsoft for $265 million when he was just 24; a decade later he sold Zappos to Amazon for $1.2 billion. Even so, he puts on no airs or pretensions. He communicated with us the way I communicate with my team, my friends, and my family. With a single stroke, he broke down the old walls of formality and invited us into his world.

Could you imagine getting a letter like that from a law firm, a government organization, or a university? Not really. I still have to beg my legal and accounting team to fire off e-mails rather than draft lengthy letters on thick letterhead with date stamps. I explain to them that as I am constantly traveling, I check for snail mail about as often as I check for voice mail—never. They don't understand the subtly yet importance of the statement, *the missed call is the new voice mail.* They have a hard time understanding the changes in our society and still attach a lengthy boilerplate about confidentiality to every communication they send.

Recently I sent my younger brother, Ramiz, an e-mail and recieved the funniest auto-response I have ever read; I nearly fell out of my chair laughing. "Out of Office. Dear Sirs and Madams," it began. "I will be out of the office on business May 15–May 20th. In my absence, please contact my Deputy, NAME, EMAIL and Number."

I quickly dialed my sister. "Oh, my God! Oh, my God! I am send-ing you the funniest e-mail ever," I said. "I am forwarding it to you and right now." I sent it to her and cc'd my other siblings. She replied, "Okay, I got it. What is this?" And then she said, "That is crazy!" We couldn't stop laughing. Both of us kept saying, "Sirs and Madams" and "My Deputy." What the hell was this, the 1950s?

My brother was just 29 years old at the time! He works in manage-ment for a global auto parts manufacturing company. When we all teased him about it at our next family gathering, he confessed that it was stan-dard company boilerplate that he had been instructed to use. He told us that this European company has a rich and formal 100-year-old culture. It is among the largest, most profitable privately held automotive com-panies in the world. He explains, "One of every three vehicles on the road has our parts in it. 'Sirs and madams' are here to stay!" That may well be. But whether they mean to or not, his organization's Old World standards make its employees come across like a bunch of stuffed shirts.

A few months later, we flew out to Las Vegas to consult with Hsieh and his team. We were dressed in business casual, blazers and dress shoes. Hsieh and his team were dressed in jeans, T-shirts, sneakers, and backpacks. We extended our hands to shake, and a member of his team said, "We don't shake hands; we give hugs." And they did. When we offered him our business cards, he said, "We don't have business cards either."

His first order of business was to give us a tour of the company. Hsieh explained that the tour we were getting was also available to the public. Zappos doesn't hoard proprietary information behind closed doors, away from the prying eyes of competitors; it encourages anyone who is interested to come see how it works. Every Zappos employee is allowed to talk to the press: no media training, no clearing it through the public relations department, no talking points. Any reporter from the *New York Times, Vanity Fair,* or the *Wall Street Journal* is encour-aged to speak to any associate, and the associates are not afraid to be quoted. "We believe in total transparency," Hsieh said. And the truth is, it's their mantra.

The hourlong tour began at the registration desk. The wall behind it was festooned with cut ties, establishing the antiestablishment culture. Everyone was encouraged to be himself or herself. Employees (who are not called employees, by the way; they are associates) sported purple hair, blue hair, shaved heads, piercings, and tattoos and wore ripped jeans, shorts, or whatever else they wished. Nearby was the Zappos corporate library, a wall of books on creativity, innovation, and personal development such as Timothy Ferris's *4-Hour Work Week,* Steven D. Levitt's *Super Freakonomics,* and Jim Collins's *Good to Great.* I noticed *Drive* by Daniel Pink, *The Tipping Point* by Malcolm Gladwell, and Robert Sutton's *No Asshole Rule.* Associates are encouraged to check out reading such as *Stumbling on Happiness* by Daniel Gilbert, *Marketing Made to Stick* by Chip and Dan Heath, and Spencer Johnson's *Who Moved my Cheese?*—as many books as they want.

The tour included a photo opportunity at the throne where Zappos's Queen (or King) for a Day is crowned. I took a look around and shook my head, remembering that long-ago debacle with my two white chairs. Zappos associates are encouraged to decorate and design their spaces however they wish. Not only was the office filled with mismatched furniture of every description, but there were bikes, toys, surfboards, streamers, posters of shirtless men, beanbags, and stuffed animals hanging from the walls and ceilings and crowding the aisles. There wasn't a "standard office furniture package." In fact nothing was the same. Even the restrooms were decorated with fun games, sayings, and trinkets.

But this was a real business, not just fun and games. I walked by a sign that posted the day's sales. It read:

Inventory for 3/31/11
We're a Service Company that just happens to sell . . . Shoes, Handbags, Clothing, Eyewear, Watches, Accessories, and so much more!

Yesterday Sales $5,620,815.58
Today, Zappos.com has 5,604,681 Units in Stock
218,566 Styles on the Site
Record-Breaking Day: $12,814,142 on 12–13–10

When the tour was over, I walked away with a smile on my face, still thinking about my office chair experience and those blue-green floral cushions.

The Mayor's Bullpen

When I toured the mayor of New York City's office in 2011, I learned another lesson in office design. Of course, nothing about Mayor Mike Bloomberg is ordinary. His estimated wealth, according to a profile in the March 2012 issue of *Forbes* magazine, is $22 billion, making him the twentieth wealthiest person in the world, the eleventh richest in the United States, and the second richest in New York City.[34] His Bloomberg Philanthropies have donated hundreds of millions of dollars to causes that benefit public health, the arts, the environment, and education and that promote innovation in government. As mayor of New York he declines to receive a city salary and collects annual pay of $1.

Bloomberg has taken a number of tough stands, some of which have earned him a considerable share of notoriety. He has been courageously outspoken on gun control and didn't hesitate to condemn the anti-Islamic hysteria that surrounded the so-called Ground Zero Mosque. Thanks to Bloomberg, the Smoke Free Air Act of 2002 made New York the first major city to ban smoking from bars and restaurants. He has championed the fight against obesity by introducing a measure (so far unsuccessfully) to bar the sale of sweetened drinks in containers larger than 16 ounces and called for a ban on the use of trans fats in restaurants. Another measure he pushed through requires restaurants to post calorie counts for standard food items.

Bloomberg has supported Transportation Commissioner Janette Sadik-Khan's groundbreaking efforts to take the city back from cars to make it more friendly to pedestrians. Though their attempt to introduce congestion pricing failed, they have undertaken a number of innovative traffic calming measures, closing several thoroughfares, including the busy intersection at Herald Square, where they set up chairs, tables, and potted plants, providing an unusual place for residents and tourists to sit and read the paper, have a snack, take a break, and people watch.

Bloomberg's innovations don't stop on the city streets. He even rethinks the traditional office environment where the boss has a big window office and his staff is squashed into cubicles nearby. Instead, the mayor of one of the top global cities chooses to sit in a small cubicle, right in the middle of the bullpen, where the action is. The original large mayor's office is now a conference room.

"Bloomberg imported the cubicle concept from his Wall Street days, and he sits at a desk the same size as the 51 others," wrote Chris Smith in *New York Magazine*. "His closest confidante, First Deputy Mayor Patti Harris, is within arm's reach. He donated the computers and pays for the snacks (bagels in the morning, salad in the afternoon). 'As a workspace, it is something that you do not think that you can ever get used to,' says a former bullpen resident. 'But when you see the mayor hosting high-level meetings in clear sight of everyone else, you start to understand that this open-communication model is not bullshit. And that it works.'"[35] It makes a powerful statement, both to the people he works with and to outsiders, about the importance of his team.

Let's shake things up and try new ways of doing things in our personal and professional lives. Too often we look to the past for confirmation of the right way of doing things when in fact the future holds better alternatives. True pioneers are the ones who step up and challenge the status quo. Whether it is Google's management of office environments, Zappos's "delivering happiness," or Bloomberg's out-of-the-box initiatives to make our cities more livable, these small changes can greatly enhance our lives. Managers and bosses, leaders and public figures, have an important obligation to lead in a way that affects future generations. Think about which old policies should be buried and which new ones can be introduced in workspaces and even home environments.

Creativity Is the Right Way

It's time to break the old molds, to lose the old structures, the old rigid ways of thinking and acting. We need to forget the lesson we learned in school that there are only right and wrong ways of doing things. New companies have lost the formality of the 1950s and cut the ties. There are all kinds of imaginative, innovative, and bold ways of doing things. We need to transform the old system that has so long imprisoned and squelched our inner children and start finding ways to say yes. Whenever you find yourself saying no, train yourself to find the route to yes.

I learned this in my media training courses. There is *always* a way to turn a no into a yes. For example, "We don't serve processed food with trans fats" is clearly a no statement. Change it to "We serve delicious and fresh lunch and dinner, using locally grown and organic herbs and produce." Same statement but now clearly a yes statement.

We need to acknowledge that everyone—not just children—needs a playground. We gave ourselves recess in school, but as adults we've taken away our time that was devoted to having fun. Get it back. Find a way to incorporate it into your life and into the lives of your associates. It will make you and those who work for you more productive.

Creativity is all around us and growing bigger as a business model. It's everywhere: in our companies and in our brands, products, and services. If you don't constantly innovate, you will die.

Creativity requires diversity of people and convergence of viewpoints. Young or old, straight or gay, black or white, male or female, every perspective is essential—and not just at the bottom of the ladder but at the top too. Too many of our CEOs and political leaders are middle-aged white men. We need to find a way to tap the resources sitting idly in our society by giving educated women the freedom and flexibility to manage their time and workloads rather than being forced to choose between family and work.

Creativity comes through exploration and discovery. Encourage your team and yourself to embrace new ideas. If we stop learning, we stop growing.

Think about your physical environments, about ways you can change them to increase productivity. Push yourself out of your comfort zones. I've achieved my greatest personal growth when I was thrust into uncomfortable, new, and foreign situations. Being able to observe, learn, and discover is the key to professional and personal advancement.

CHAPTER 4
DESIGN YOUR TIME

People chase money and forget that time is
our most precious resource.
—Andre Agassi

Time. It's the one thing we can't buy, trade, or get back. The *Boston Globe* calls it, "A problem so common it may qualify as a new American epidemic: We've got no time. Too busy. Overwhelmed by work, family obligations, and the fast-paced nature of a run-ragged world, many Americans—especially working adults, parents of young children, and those with college degrees, according to polls—feel strapped for time and are leading less happy lives as a result.

"Researchers in the 1990s gave this familiar, if dreadful, feeling a name: time famine. More recently, they coined a term to describe the opposite: time affluence, that elusive feeling of being rich in time. Time affluence, it appears, has real benefits in our lives. If time famine can create a state of rolling personal crisis, studies have shown that feeling 'time affluent' can be powerfully uplifting, more so than material wealth, improving not only personal happiness, but even physical health and civic involvement."[1]

Let me try to make this as simple as possible: there are only three things to do with your time:

- Have fun
- Be productive
- Give back

That's it; there's nothing else. Having fun is pretty straightforward. Take vacations, spend time with your friends, indulge and pamper yourself at blissful spas in Arizona, get crazy drunk, fall in love, dance and gamble all night long in Vegas, visit museums in Paris, drive a convertible up the Pacific coast, go sailing in Amalfi, sip rosé in Cap D'Antibes or Prosecco in Sardinia. Lie on the sofa and watch football, go bowling, or play your Xbox or Wii. Maybe jump out of an airplane. Whatever your definition of fun is, please indulge it.

Being productive can mean going to school, getting a job, starting a business, taking a class to learn a new skill, continuing your education, engaging in professional development, and working on your health and well-being—pretty much anything that moves you forward personally or professionally.

Giving back occurs when we channel our resources toward others: healing the sick, educating others, investing in the community, taking care of children and family, organizing our efforts for a charity or common good, and volunteering our time.

Those three things—having a blast, feeling a sense of accomplishment, and cultivating a sense of a larger purpose—are all that really matters in life. Anything that falls outside those three categories is clutter or filler and a waste of your time, and you need to eliminate it from your life immediately. Not only is it a waste of time, but it interferes with getting to the three buckets that do matter.

Balance is the key. If you are having fun living like a rock star, the constant flow of stimuli will be hard to maintain, and when it does slacken, your overall happiness will be reduced. Adding productivity to the mix will give you a sense of accomplishment. Giving back will give you a sense of higher purpose and with it the type of happiness that is achieved only when you are contributing to something that is bigger than yourself, something that has meaning to you. The goal in life is to maximize these three key things while striking the right balance in your life to achieve maximum happiness.

I constantly review how well I am doing on keeping my buckets filled; I keep running notes on all three of them, and that allows me to see how I'm spending my time and when I should shift my focus and efforts to filling the other buckets. As for having fun, I have maxed this category out. I've gone skydiving, camel riding in the desert, dune bashing, paddleboarding with family at sunset on New Year's Eve, parasailing in the Bahamas, and snorkeling at the Great Barrier Reef. I've discovered great events and met fascinating people in every corner of the world. I've attended parties of every sort from backyard BBQs to red carpets and black-tie affairs. I've been to exotic spas, on African safaris, and on adventures throughout Asia. I've checked out the Burj Khalifa, the world's tallest building, and been to the top of the Eiffel Tower. I've heard concertos performed by world-renowned violinists, rocked out with Nirvana, and road-tripped across country with friends to see Graceland. I've petted a penguin, fed a giraffe, and enjoyed a champagne brunch among warthogs. I've enjoyed fun times with my husband, friends, and family. If I died tomorrow, I could surely say I had the time of my life.

Being productive covers everything from going to school and graduate school to working hard; running a business, reading, writing, and learning; taking classes and lessons in everything from cooking to painting, photography, and sculpting; eating healthy, and exercising. I try to pack in as much productivity as possible in my job and in my professional and personal development. I am constantly pushing myself to grow, explore, and discover.

Giving back means everything from serving on the boards of nonprofits and cultural institutions, to helping families in need, to volunteering in a hospital. In my current job, I am helping through important initiatives such as the Philips Livable Cities Award and partnering with organizations such as the United Nations and the Institute for Human Activities. In my personal life I try hard to be there for my family, for my 12 nieces and nephews, and for my aging relatives.

These are my examples of the three buckets; your own may be completely different. Think about yours. Take out a notepad or your go-to device of choice and start to fill them. Take a long look at these buckets and evaluate which one needs more filling. Remember that the goal is to maximize all three.

This may be a hard concept to grasp because we are all taught that a bucket list is something on which you check everything off before you die, in other words, that your goal is to empty your bucket. This principle guides you to fill up your buckets and even hope that they overflow.

Try to think about them routinely. I know I do. When making tough life decisions or just contemplating everyday minutiae, think about how your choices affect each of the three buckets. If something falls outside of them, it's time to eliminate it from your life.

One thing is for certain: we are all going to die. Therefore, why not try to make the most of the time you have while you are still young and healthy?

Manage Your Time

Effective time management is one of the most important keys to success. It is so easy to let others fill up your days. A good friend who is a successful attorney, real estate developer, and family man has three words on the subject of time management: "Let's do lunch." Want to grab dinner with him? You're out of luck. That time slot is reserved for his family. Casual friends and prospective business partners have to content themselves with an hour or two in the middle of the day.

It's a line in the sand and a necessary one to preserve both his sanity and the life he wants to lead.

Many of us say yes to too many things and too many people. In his book *How Will You Measure Your Life?* Harvard Business School professor Clayton Christensen makes a salient point about how great influence always comes with a catch: the more people there are who recognize and appreciate your contributions, the more people there are who are clamoring for your insights, your energy, or 30 minutes of your time. Even when you know what's most important to you, how do you choose from among all those competing demands?

Those decisions need to be made daily. "In fact," Christensen concludes, "How you allocate your own resources can make your life turn out to be exactly as you hoped, or very different from what you intend."[2]

It took a while before I learned to place a value on time; others have caught on much faster. When I interviewed Andre Agassi, he said, "I feel time running through my fingers every day. I've always been hyper-aware of time, ever since I was a kid. People chase money and forget that time is our most precious resource. So for me it's a daily struggle to find a balance between work and friends and family. The first step is accepting that there's no foolproof system, no perfect formula for time management. All balance requires constant tweaking."[3]

Lose the Time Wasters

So many of us have people in our lives who take up our time without adding any value. I've come up with a rating system for the people in my life. This may sound harsh or cynical, but it is a critical first step in managing your time. We complain that we don't have enough time to get to the things on our happiness list or to execute on our vision for the future and that life is already too busy. This exercise allows us to free up our time to put ourselves first.

Make a list of the people you spend time with. Now make one of these three marks next to their names: a negative (–), a zero (0), or a positive (+).

A negative person is someone who drains you of energy and adds no value to your life socially, professionally, or otherwise. You know exactly who and what I'm talking about. We all have them in our lives: they just take, take, take.

A zero neither adds nor takes away value. These people always seem to be hanging around or texting: "Hey whatcha up to? I'm bored." They are always bored. They target you and make you spend your most precious resource—*time*—to entertain them. These are people I consider filler.

A positive, in contrast, is someone who adds real value to your life. You are learning from this person, who is helping you move forward.

Take a long, hard look at your list. Put a plus, negative, or zero next to each name. Really think about that person. Don't get caught up in emotions. Try to think about it systematically. What contributions, what value are these people really adding to or taking away from your life? When you've given everyone a score, it's time to cross off all the names you've marked with negatives and zeros. If you're serious about improving and upgrading your life, it's time to banish these people from your life or minimize your interactions with them. With your newfound time, you can go back to your passion list and devote more time to the activities that make you happy. It sounds simple, and it is once we get past the emotional side of the connections. (Maybe it's not so simple if some of your zeros and negatives are close relatives. But even in those cases, it's important to set up and enforce boundaries.)

Seinfeld on Events

Years ago, I saw Jerry Seinfeld perform live in a theater. In one of his monologues he made fun of married life as a series of events you have to attend as a couple. He said his wife is always nagging, "Come on, honey, get ready for the event. We have to go to the event. We can't miss the event!" The audience burst into laughter as we could all relate, whether it's wasting a precious Sunday afternoon at a baby shower, attending a Friday night function, or going to a birthday party for a child you hardly know only because you feel a sense of obligation. "What are all these events I did not sign up to go to?" Seinfeld screams to the audience.

I know what makes us RSVP "yes" to events we have no interest in. Most of the time the invitations arrive in our in-boxes when we are sitting bored at our desks. They promise excitement, entertainment, great food, VIP treatment, live performances, and an all-around good time. After looking at all those photos on Facebook and Instagram of smiling people having fun, you start to get excited about what this evening might hold in store for you. But the reality is that most events don't come close to meeting your expectations.

How do they disappoint you? Let me count the ways. First, you have to rush home from work to get ready; already you're starting to feel regret as you wish you could just flop down on the sofa. Even so, you push through and put together a suitable outfit. When you arrive, you have to pay for expensive valet parking or search for a space. You're starving when you finally get inside; you search frantically for the food you were promised, but there's nothing in sight except a mountain of cheese and crackers. You look around for a few of your friends and don't see any, but someone you don't want to see grabs you on the way to the bar and pulls you into a long, boring chat. You finally make it through the long line at the bar only to find out that you have to line up somewhere else to purchase a roll of tickets to exchange for drinks. You slam your first drink down on an empty stomach and get another. Now you are buzzed, your friends have arrived, and you are starting to worry that you're drastically overdressed or terribly underdressed, and you feel like a loser either way. You drink some more. Finally you see a waiter with a tray of hot food and nearly trample four people to snag a mini-crab cake. More drinks; some drunk dancing; photo uploading to Facebook, Twitpic, and Instagram; some shouted conversation over loud blaring music; long lines at the washroom; and then a 45-minute wait for your car.

You go home, pass out, and wake up the next morning with a hangover from the fruity drinks. Later on, you try to convince yourself the event was a blast. Hey, you have the Facebook photos to prove it. But the reality is that you wasted a precious Friday night on a lame event. Not only are the events themselves time suckers, but consider the time you wasted preparing for them, the hours at the mall buying the perfect gift or outfit.

And it's not just social events that disappoint. We were taught to network, network, network, the buzzword of the 1990s, which created a flurry of useless events held in Marriott or Hilton hotel conference rooms. Every event was exactly the same, from the registration table at the door, where you picked up your lanyard, to the mixing and mingling over drinks at 6:00 p.m., the sit-down dinner of rubber chicken and soggy carrots and broccoli, and all those boring speeches and long video messages synched to their agenda.

Businesses too get caught in the cycle to put on events without fully understanding the drain on time and resources that they cause. Ask yourself what the goal of the event is. Is there a financial benefit? Are you cultivating new clients or partners? Is it media attention and buzz you're after? Are you conveying information to a board of directors? Are there more efficient ways to reach this goal? Learn to think systematically about the costs in time and resources versus the expected payoffs and end results.

It took me a while, but I finally wised up and learned to asses the impact of such events. I see friends and family wasting precious time running around, willingly sacrificing their weekends to mundane errands, traffic, and lines. I am not saying you should miss Nonna or

Papu's seventy-fifth birthday celebration and little Levi's bar mitzvah, but we do need to train ourselves to stop and evaluate. Will this experience add value to my life, or is it just taking time away from my vision statement and happiness list? Earlier you thought it wasn't realistic to spend 10 hours a week on the things you added to your happiness list. Now I want you to reevaluate the possibility.

If the answer to the next question isn't "heck, yes," I won't go. The next question is: Will it be more fun than staying at home in my pajamas, lounging around by the pool reading books, playing tennis, going for a walk, or anything else I added to my happiness list?

Just Say No

So many of us wear ourselves out racing to nowhere by saying yes to everything. We need to learn to say no too so that we can protect our time. It took years of boring events, cheap wine, and rubber chicken dinners before I figured this out.

Here's an easy way to learn to say no: place a dollar value on your time. Say you make $75 per hour. Now figure out how much time you spend each week dropping off dry cleaning, going to the bank, and grocery shopping. Let's say it's 10 hours. Then add up all the other obligations you've said yes to: the dinner party on Friday, the birthday lunch on Sunday—and don't forget about the time you spent preparing for them, picking the right outfit, the hostess gift, and the birthday present. Let's say that's another 10 hours: 20 hours × $75 = $1,500. You just spent $1,500 on stuff you don't want to do! Would you pay someone $1,500 to run these errands for you? Probably not, so why do you sell yourself short? Learning to say no to things that feel like a chore or an obligation is the key. Outsource errands by hiring a high school or college student for a lot less and find a better use for your time. Wouldn't you rather spend those 20 hours having fun, being productive, or giving back? Companies need to address the same valuation. Too often they will just consider the direct costs of holding an event, rather than the impact of indirect costs, such as employee time and opportunity costs.

Although we can take control of much of our personal time, many of us still can't control the amount of time we spend at work. The good news is that some employers are starting to respect work-life balance.

"Rather than work-life balance or work-life separation, we focus more on work-life integration," Zappos' Tony Hsieh told me. "That's why we encourage employees to be their true selves when they come to the office. This way, they end up forming real friendships, not just co-worker relationships."[4]

I have been stuck in my share of unsatisfying jobs. But it's only in retrospect that I've been able to appreciate how much time they stole from me. I had bosses who watched the clock to make sure we didn't take a minute more than our allotted hour for lunch and bosses who expected me to spend my weekends with them road tripping to corporate retreats.

The value of being able to control your own time, work at your own speed, and manage your own schedule is a form of freedom that few of us get to enjoy. Those who do, ironically, are much more efficient than those who have to punch a clock.

As the bestselling author of *Drive*, Dan Pink, told me, "It's actually easier to stay motivated working for yourself than it is working for others. First, if you don't get stuff done, you don't earn anything—and therefore can't pay the mortgage or feed the children. Second, most people working for themselves are doing things they enjoy. They've got autonomy in day-to-day efforts and a deeper connection to the work itself."[5]

The old order is dying. Whereas most of our parents held stable jobs for years, our unstable economy has taught us how chimerical the notion of job security now is. My cousin told me, "From an early age, I knew that I would be an entrepreneur and manage my own schedule."

When I asked him how he knew, he recounted a traumatic experience in his childhood. "My father came home with a pink slip from the automotive company where he had been an accountant for the majority of his life. I remember my mom crying and the two of them being very worried." This, he told me, taught him an invaluable lesson: he should rely on no one but himself to be in charge of his livelihood. Today he has his own thriving law practice.

The Gift of Time

Luke Johnson, a business writer for the *Financial Times,* recently wrote about a survey he conducted. What was their most important driver, he asked a group of business leaders: wealth, power, or fame? Uniformly, he reported, the answer was something else entirely: the desire for autonomy.[6] Not only can no one fire you when you're your own boss, but the ability to manage your own time is truly a gift.

"Death is the destination we all share, no one has ever escaped it. And that is as it should be because death is very likely the single best invention of life," Steve Jobs wisely said.[7] It's amazing how much money men and women will spend on cosmetic treatments such as Botox and Restylane to turn back the hands of time. But so many of them will not do what they can to optimize the time in their schedules, allowing others to cram them full of unnecessary meetings and events.

My friend Ryan Prince, an entrepreneur and partner in a business whose portfolio includes healthcare, real estate, and hospitality, tells me he manages his time with an iron fist. A husband and a father of young twin daughters, he understands the need to protect it. "I have systems set in place for both my professional and personal needs," he says. "If I let my staff come to me whenever they want to deal with administrative duties, such as signatures, banking, forms, etc., it would interrupt the flow of my work. So I designated a two-hour window every Monday morning to attend to their needs. I have other weekly slots for internal operating meetings with various teams (healthcare, hotels, residential)."

Ryan Prince on Time Management

I read an article in *Vanity Fair* in which Michael Lewis interviewed President Obama. Obama told him that his whole life is about making important decisions, so he's tried to remove all unnecessary decisions in his life. I take this advice to heart. For example, I don't like to waste time every morning trying to figure out what to wear, so I purposely own only two blue suits and two grey suits, one black suit, and one white tux. All my shirts are white and blue, so that every tie goes with every one of them. I will never purchase a patterned shirt, as cool as it may look. My next time management trick will be to create a lunch menu for myself, so I never have to hmm and hah about what to eat every day. Chicken salad, sandwich, whatever it is, I don't want to waste the time agonizing because I don't really care.

I use a BlackBerry for the Note app. It allows me to keep lists that sync constantly. These are my AAA lists:

- Daily list—I don't put more than three things on this list because I have to be realistic about how much I can accomplish in a day
- Weekly list—I have about 5 to 10 important things on it
- Monthly list—These are things I need to get to but not urgently

I keep an annual list, too: What are those 12 things over the next 12 months I want to accomplish professionally and personally? Sort of like someone's New Year's resolutions.

I look at these lists about 20 times a day. If someone says don't forget this, I just add it to one of them; it goes in and goes out. The big mistake people make in life is to focus on what's urgent, not on what's important (my dad taught me that).

I am constantly checking my annual list and trying to integrate it into tasks for my AAA lists. It has a mix of professional and personal goals to achieve, e.g., get involved in a charity, renegotiate certain work contracts, wake up earlier in the morning, pay off the home mortgage, take one of my daughters for breakfast once a week.

I'll take a look back and map where I spend my time. Look at last week, last month, and evaluate how much is useful versus not useful. I'm less good at managing meetings, but want to get better. I feel that they go on too long. I need to balance effective time management with the time investment that I need to keep the team motivated. I doubt I'd ever try it, but I like the concept of stand-up meetings, which I think would be more efficient and keep people on pace. I generally think meetings should just present options and recommendations. If someone wants to meet just to canvass my views before coming to their own, then I'd love to see that on the agenda.

As for e-mails, I have a system where I use auto rules and folders. If my name is on the cc line, it doesn't go into my in-box. Same with newsletters and listservs. They go into specific folders that I give low priority to; I get to them when I can. I used to have 500 e-mails in my inbox, and it was a complete nightmare. This makes a big difference.

I used to write very shorthand e-mails; now I take the extra five seconds and write the extra few words to say what exactly it is I need, to avoid a follow-up e-mail asking for clarification. I think the back-and-forth communication is too time-costly. Take the extra step to do this.

I used to just block junk mail, but now I take the extra three seconds to unsubscribe.

On average I send and receive 400 e-mails in a day, and half are not necessary. I never use an Out of Office. If you do, you shouldn't be in the job.

More lists: A couple of times a year, I sit down and write, "I enjoy XX (fill in the blank), I'm good at XX (fill in the blank), I'm not good at XX (fill in the blank)." What's my overall view of the world? What are the opportunities that exist within my world, stuff I like, stuff I'm good at? Financial analysis: I try periodically to assess the best bang for my buck, biggest asset to my time. I always try to find the inflection point of maximizing fun while making the most money. Sure, I could find work that maximizes money but makes my life miserable, so I try to strike a balance. I want to work with people who I like and respect.

While I manage my professional time closely, my personal time is run by my wife. If it weren't for her, I would have no social life. I'd be sitting home every night eating pizza. In order to never have that fight, "you said you'd be at the lunch" or "you said we'd go to the dinner party," my wife and I organize our social schedule through Outlook invites. She sends me an invite, I accept or reject, and that's how we run our social lives. That way if it's not on the calendar, then it wasn't my fault for missing it!

How Do You Measure Up?

My husband is a big believer in the same principles Prince espouses. He always buys Brooks Brothers black midcalf wool socks so that he won't have to match them, something he believes is an utter waste of time. He does the same with the rest of his wardrobe. It might look like he wears the same uniform every day, but he has 20 of the same shirts in different shades of black and gray and several pairs of the same jeans and one pair of boots. This may sound borderline OCD, but any little tricks you can do with your daily routine to optimize time can save you days over the course of your life. Tim Ferris writes in his *New York Times* bestselling book, *The 4-Hour Workweek*, "Considering options costs attention that then can't be spent on action or present-state awareness. Attention is necessary for not only productivity but appreciation." He concludes:

> "*Too many choices = less or no productivity*
> *Too many choices = less or no appreciation*
> *Too many choices = sense of overwhelm.*"[8]

Managing all those lists and analyzing how you spend your time might sound like a lot of work, but they make it possible for Prince to have space for his personal and professional goals, spend time with his family, think, and enjoy life.

His practices are based largely on the new phenomenon of self-tracking. One hundred years ago, when consultants did this with factory workers, it was called Taylorization, after the efficiency expert Frederick Winslow Taylor. In a *Harvard Business Review* article, "You, by the Numbers," H. James Wilson writes about "auto-analytics," the practice of collecting data about oneself with an eye to self-improvement. "Athletes have long used visual and advanced statistical analysis to ratchet up their performance," Wilson writes. "Now auto-analytics is flourishing in the workplace, too. With wearable devices, mobile and computer apps, and sophisticated data visualization, it has become fairly easy to monitor our office activity—and any factors that might affect it—and to use that information to make better choices about where to focus our time and energy."

Wilson's analysis concludes, "What exactly can you measure? Using successful cases and research, I have developed a framework that includes three arenas where auto-analytics can be useful: the physical self, the thinking self, and the emotional self (body, mind, and spirit)."[9]

Self-tracking and "the quantified self" are not new notions; Kevin Kelly and Gary Wolf coined the term five years ago in *Wired* magazine,[10] but the concept has been around for hundreds of years. Benjamin Franklin did some of it in his *Autobiography*.

Now technology has supercharged it. A plethora of apps for smartphones and computers and countless new mobile devices, such as the Nike FuelBand, a digital accelerometer that you wear on your ankle, make it possible to keep track of everything you do. Digifit monitors your heart rate, pace, speed, cadence, power, and more. Your data can then be uploaded to a number of pro sites for analysis, including TrainingPeaks and New Leaf.

MyFitnessPal is a smartphone app that logs food consumption and eating habits. A listener I heard on an NPR program called it her "personal lie detection device." A listener from Buffalo, New York, said she uses Fitbit to count her every step. While using it, she went from a mere 5,000 steps a day to 13,000 steps and lost more than 15 pounds.[11]

There's so much more. Are you in a rotten mood most of the time? MoodPanda.com can help. You rate your happiness on a scale of 0 to 10 and optionally add comments on what's influencing your mood. Foursquare gives you a history of places you visit as well as tracking where your friends are. Following the premise that 80 bites of food is all our bodies need to feel full, an app called 80Bites monitors the number of bites you take every day. Need to destress? Equanimity is a meditation app that gives you reminders of when to start and end your sessions. Sleep Cycle links to the accelerometer in your iPhone to track your motion during sleep, graphing the patterns as you shift between deep sleep, shallow sleep, and dreaming. Asthmapolis helps asthma sufferers by tracking when and where they have attacks. The device, which attaches to inhalers, includes a GPS and a clock; the data it collects give patients insights into both their own bodies and the air quality in different places, allowing them to better manage the disease.

Whatever app or device you use—and thousands of them are unveiled at the Consumer Electronics Show in Las Vegas every January—the goal of self-tracking is to eliminate subjective qualitative assessments and replace them with the kind of hard quantitative information that allows you to tweak your behaviors for optimal performance.

If you go to the app store and search "time management," hundreds of results will pop up. Find the app that works best for you, your business, and your associates. Technology helps, but it's not strictly necessary. Just being more attentive can make a big difference. I started analyzing my own time and implemented a lot of these rules in my life.

Technology Can Help, but You Control the Commands

I hadn't realized how much time people and tasks can take away from you until I started traveling. With your workweek shortened by the 10 to 40 hours taken up by transit, every hour on the ground is that much more important. I have started unsubscribing from e-mails, junk mail, and newsletters, as well as snail mail. Outlook is the key to my scheduling. I will not take a meeting unless there is an agenda with goals and deliverables, and it cannot be replaced by a conference call.

I don't accept invitations to events out of a sense of obligation anymore unless I know they are going to add value or be a lot of fun. I go back to that rule of mine and force myself to ponder whether the event is going to be more fun than lounging around at home, making dinner, and watching a movie.

I have to admit that I loved hosting dinner parties until it became such a production. The *New York Times* wrote a piece titled, "Guess Who Isn't Coming to Dinner" declaring the dinner party dead: "The seated dinner, with its minuet of invitation and acceptance, its formalities and protocols, its culinary and dietary challenges, its inherent requirements of guest and host alike is under threat, many say." In addition to all that, my guests started to linger well after dessert was served, until 1 or 2 in the morning, sometimes cutting into my valuable sleep time.

The *Times* continues: "Increasingly, such gatherings seem outmoded, squeezed out by overcrowded schedules."[12] Now when I want to see friends, it's at a restaurant, where I know I don't have to invest the extra production hours and can leave without having to kick them off my sofa. This may sound terrible, but I assure you I love my friends and family. Still, when you have only so many hours in the day, each one that is hogged up becomes a reason to stress.

Making Work Work for You

I love the coffee king Ricardo Illy's take on time: "Many people combine business and pleasure easily, blurring the lines without one dominating the other," he says. "I'm not one of them—work is pleasurable for me, but business comes first." The secret, he added, "is to follow Aaron Burr's advice, who said, 'The rule of my life is to make business a pleasure and pleasure my business.' Then you're really managing every aspect of your time."[13] Most of us can only dream of such a luxury.

I was finally able to do this myself when I took the big leap and left my corporate job to join my husband in our business. I used to spend hours commuting from DC to Virginia and Maryland, stuck on the Beltway in traffic. As if the daily traffic jams didn't cause enough stress, there were the constant detours and stoppages caused by the president's and other dignitaries' motorcades. That wasn't the worst part. Halfway through my eight-mile journey, I drove past CIA headquarters in Langley, Virginia, where the massive antenna array caused my cell phone to cut out. Too many meetings and conference calls, too much travel and traffic all took their toll, but it wasn't until later that I realized it was more than just the overload. It was the loss of control. Too many people besides me—my bosses and my peers alike—had a say in my schedule.

Psycho Bosses

I had one boss who was more like a prison warden than an inspirational leader from whom I could learn. After being on the job for five years and exceeding performance review measurements and goals, I accepted the fact that we were not getting raises for the third straight year because of cuts in city and state funding. I enjoyed my work and pushed forward despite the disappointment. I had just come off a six-month branding campaign that had received international attention, putting in time in the mornings at home before I showed up at work, checking for news stories at 5 a.m., working weekends, and talking to media well into the evening. I remember once even stepping out of a relative's funeral service to take a call from a reporter on deadline. I felt like I was overdelivering on everything.

One workday, I went to lunch with some colleagues and potential partners. The lunch ran a bit long, but it was more of a meeting than a personal lunch, and so I didn't think anything of it. When I returned to my desk, my phone rang; my boss was on the other end.

"Um, Rana, do you know what time you left for lunch today?" he asked.

"No, I'm not sure. Why?" I responded.

"Because I watched what time you left, and you have been gone for an hour and twenty minutes," he said.

I was fuming; it took all I had not to call him a cussing fat cussing idiot cussing cuss and slam down the phone. But I needed the job and the paycheck and did not have a backup plan, nor did I have the three-month emergency fund saved up just yet. Instead, I informed him as calmly as I could that my lunch was with colleagues and potential partners.

"Well, it doesn't set a good example for the rest of the staff," he chided me. "Next time you go off-site for a meeting, please report into me with a list of names of who you're going with, where, and the purpose of the meeting."

Next time I go off-site!!?? I wanted to pull my hair out. Did he think that he was our warden and that we could leave the prison yard only with his approval? Why was this person given a position as a leader? How was he motivating, mentoring, inspiring? Why did he get to control my time? I was doing my job—in fact, I was doing a damn good job—but he wanted control over every minute I was there.

The idea that someone can pay you for the privilege of controlling your time is a strange concept. I can understand paying people to deliver expertise, tasks, and services, but to want ownership and control over their schedule is demoralizing, and demeaning. Why not just monitor the quality of their work? Of course, as I noted earlier, there are jobs such as retail, nursing, and education for which strict shifts are required. But for most creative white-collar jobs, schedules can be flexible and work can be delivered from almost anywhere.

Overthrow the Dictators

Early on, I realized the value of changing my vocabulary. *Subordinate, employee,* and *staff* became *colleague* and *team* because ultimately that's what we all are in the workplace. When I began as CEO at the Creative Class, I told my team members that I was not their boss. "Please don't call me boss, don't send me approvals like I'm your boss, don't ask for approval to go on vacation. There is no vacation request form," I said. "We are all *colleagues.* You are getting paid for your expertise. I am not going to do performance reviews or expect status reports. It is up to you to manage your own workload, to manage the clients, and to deliver a quality service."

"I don't care when you work, how you work, or where you work," I told them. A few of them did not understand and still wanted to report in to me. I had to constantly remind them not to fill up my in-box with such trifles. "Great, you're going on vacation with your kids and won't be checking e-mail," I'd respond. "Have fun. Find a colleague to manage your clients and make sure your clients know how to reach them."

I thought about those conversations when I was interviewing Mayor Richard Daley. "I can't recall many instances when I was mayor where an issue was so crucial that my staff had to awaken me in the middle of the night," he told me. "I hired very competent managers who knew I expected them to work hard. They knew they couldn't be afraid to make a decision. Sometimes the decisions were right, and sometimes there should have been a different approach. The important thing is that the decision was made."[14]

Josh Patrick, the founder and principal at a financial advisory services firm, told *The New York Times,* "One of the things we constantly told employees was the following statement: *'You are the expert at your job.'* It took several years for some of our people to actually believe it. But I've used this mantra in my business life ever since. The key is that when you make this change, you stop telling people what to do and you start asking them their opinion about the best way to get something done. This can produce all sorts of benefits."[15]

I've had bosses who didn't just want to control my professional time but wanted to be included in my personal life and hang out with my friends and me outside the office. I've had bosses who wanted me to give them home and fashion makeovers and who wanted me to host parties with them. I always gave in a bit, thinking this surely was my way to the top. It wasn't. The more time I gave, the more time they took.

Jason Fried wrote an op-ed piece for the *New York Times* on managing time at his software company, 37signals:

We take inspiration from the seasons and build change into our work schedule. For example, from May through October, we switch to a four-day workweek. And not 40 hours crammed into four days, but 32 hours comfortably fit into four days. We don't work the same amount of time, we work less.

Most staff workers take Fridays off, but some choose a different day. Nearly all of us enjoy three-day weekends. Work ends Thursday, the weekend starts Friday, and work starts back up on Monday.

The benefits of a six-month schedule with three-day weekends are obvious. But there's one surprising effect of the changed schedule: better work gets done in four days than in five.

When there's less time to work, you waste less time. When you have a compressed workweek, you tend to focus on what's important. Constraining time encourages quality time.[16]

I've never had an employer who believed in this system. All of them assumed that if you're not sitting at your desk for long hours, you're not really working. Sometimes exactly the opposite is the case. Rather than sneak out early and risk the piercing looks of colleagues and bosses, many an efficient worker will ride out the last hour or so of the day at his or her desk, playing around with Facebook or instant chatting with friends. Being productive does not translate to being busy.

As the productivity expert Tony Schwartz wrote in a *New York Times* op-ed, the best way to improve employees' productivity is to encourage them to relax. "The importance of restoration is rooted in our physiology," he wrote. "Human beings aren't designed to expend energy continuously. Rather, we're meant to pulse between spending and recovering energy."

In a study of nearly 400 employees, published in 2011, researchers found that sleeping too little—defined as less than six hours a night—was one of the best predictors of on-the-job burnout. A recent Harvard study estimated that sleep deprivation costs American companies $63.2 billion a year in lost productivity.

Having more vacation time is beneficial. In 2006, the accounting firm Ernst & Young did an internal study of its employees and found that for each additional 10 hours of vacation employees took, their year-end performance ratings from supervisors (on a scale of 1 to 5) improved by 8 percent. Frequent vacationers were also significantly less likely to leave the firm.[17]

Another one of Dan Gilbert's 27 lessons is very much to the point. He says, "Working longer hours does not automatically make you more successful. Working smarter does."[18] Consider the case of Sheryl Sandberg, Facebook's COO, who leaves the office at 5:30 every day. "I walk out of this office every day at 5:30 so I'm home for dinner with my kids at 6, and interestingly, I've been doing that since I had kids," she declared in a recent interview. "I did that when I was at Google,

I did that here, and I would say it's not until the last year, two years, that I'm brave enough to talk about it publicly."[19]

James Vaupel of the Max Planck Research Center in Denmark believes that everybody should work shorter hours but continue to work well past the traditional age of retirement. "A 25-hour work week will allow younger people to spend more time with their children, take better care of their health (which will help raise average life expectancy), and improve their over-all quality of life," he says, "while for the older population—many of whom have more time on their hands than they know what to do with—work can serve as both a psychological and physical outlet."[20]

Beg, Borrow, and Steal Back Your Time

Even if you don't have your own business, there are several things you can do to protect your time. You don't have to be at the mercy of your crazy boss.

One of my friends called me from her car not too long ago to get my advice on whether she should apply for a full-time job as a political analyst, earning $22,000 a year more than she does now. Still, she was torn about whether she should be looking to leave the job she's been in for 13 years, which allowed her the flexibility to spend time with her three young children. "I'm just leaving Kyla's class," she said. "I spent the morning volunteering in her classroom and getting ready for the upcoming Halloween party. If I take this job, I won't be able to do that. But this new job is so close to my house." I asked her how much time she currently spends commuting to her job. "Thirty minutes each way," she said. I calculated that though the new job may or may not allow flexibility in her schedule—that was still to be determined—it would give her the gift of an additional five hours a week. "That's five extra hours to volunteer in your kids' classroom, take the kids to the park, or however you want to spend it," I told her. When calculating time costs, too many of us fail to count our commutes, the way I haphazardly did when I took my job in DC.

I was recently in Los Angeles on business; its freeways brought back bad memories of all the time I used to spend commuting. Not only is commuting a waste of time, a study released by the Centers for Disease Control, the National Institutes of Health, and the American Cancer Society has confirmed what many have long suspected: lengthy car commutes are terrible for your health.

In a blog post titled, "The World's Worst Commutes," my husband noted, "Commuting is among life's least enjoyable activities, according to research by Nobel Prize winner Daniel Kahneman and others." He went on to point out that commuting is expensive too. The annual Urban Mobility Report calculates that commuting costs Americans an estimated $90 billion per year in lost productivity and wasted energy: "Kevin Stolarick, the research director of the Martin Prosperity Institute (MPI), has found that every minute shaved off America's commuting time is worth an estimated $19.5 billion dollars. That translates into $97.7 billion for five minutes, $195 billion for 10 minutes, and $292 billion for every 15 minutes saved nationally."[21]

When 37-year-old Yahoo! CEO Marissa Mayer banned working from home in a memo to employees in 2013, the reaction was immediate. A *Forbes* headline read, "Back to the Stone Age."[22] The *LA Times* wrote, "Now working moms are in an uproar because they believe that Mayer is setting them back by taking away their flexible working arrangements. Many view telecommuting as the only way time-crunched women can care for young children and advance their careers without the pay, privilege or perks that come with being the chief executive of a Fortune 500 company."[23] As the head of a corporation that is supposed to embody an ethos of creativity and innovation, Mayer did take a step back in time. Employers should be required to tier their employees' schedules, giving them the freedom to come in at 7, 8, 9, 10, or 11 a.m. This system would not only allow employees to pick the right schedule for their lives, but it would alleviate the congestion on our highways, which look more like parking lots.

Here are some tips to help you negotiate your time:

1. If you're wasting time in traffic every day, ask your boss to shift your schedule so that you can commute during hours when the traffic is lighter.
2. Ask to shift your schedule from Monday to Friday to three days in the office and two days at home.
3. Offer to work four 10-hour days instead of five 8-hour days.
4. Suggest working from home at the beginning and end of the day, coming in for meetings and other needs in the middle of the day.
5. If more than a few of your colleagues share your commute, make the case for a satellite office. Communicate the productivity gains of the collective team to your boss.

When we are interviewing, many of us are afraid to ask too many questions because we just want to land the job. But it is your life, your career, your health, and your mental well-being. Devoting your time, skills, and energy to an employer is a major commitment. You are going to be spending more waking hours with your boss and colleagues than you are with your family. I'm not exaggerating. Here is a letter I received at the *Huffington Post* from a reader who wanted my advice on corporate retreats. Read it and weep.

The Difference Between Needy Behavior and Team Building

Dear Rana:

My team works very hard, sometimes up to 70 hours a week. Most of them are young and energetic and like to have a lot of fun. I want to reward them with an all-expense-paid team-building trip somewhere great. I'm not sure which experience would be best: A dude ranch in Texas? A group hike in California? A biking trip in Portland? Are there any work retreat packages or companies you can recommend that provide both the experience and the take-aways for team building?

Kate

Tampa, Florida

I responded as follows:

Dear Kate:

You sound like everyone's nightmare boss. If your team is working 70 hours a week, the last thing they want is to spend yet another weekend away from their families. A work-related trip might be fun if you're unattached, but the married folks and parents among your employees won't see it the same way. You must be single and have no life. In this case, you're blurring the line between needy behavior and true leadership—does your team want a "team-building" trip, or do you?

Let me be clear: no one wants to go to a dude ranch with their boss. I couldn't think of a worse torture. I've been on bowling outings, road trips through Virginia, and team trips to Orlando, and I can tell you that all of them were a waste of time when it came to building team morale. You can't make associates like each other and work better together by forcing them to go on a trip.

But the question remains: Whether it is setting up an obstacle course or silly trust exercises where you let yourself fall backwards and hope your team will catch you, do team-building exercises really work? Of course the companies that specialize in them say that they can. According to Meeting Facilitators International, a successful retreat contains seven key ingredients:

1. The right people
2. The right agenda
3. The right process
4. The right prework
5. Action planning
6. Follow-up
7. A comprehensive meeting report

If you don't choose the right people to be involved, they warn, the whole thing can backfire. The last thing you want to do is invest all that time and money and have it turn into a disaster.

Adventure Associates is another company that specializes in such retreats, while Backroads is a great one-stop shop for organizing full-service bike trips almost anywhere in the world.

But I've been in the corporate world for a long time, and experience is in this case valuable. Not only do I think that these retreats are useless—I can vouch for the fact that forcing me to engage in nonsensical games and exercises with coworkers—not my friends—in what would have (and should have!) been my free time only made me despise my workplace more.

Creative and knowledge workers value intrinsic rewards, freedom, and flexibility. They won't find any of those on a group retreat. Try asking your team what they'd prefer as a reward and put it up to a vote. We'd all be interested in hearing back from you.[24]

Make sure the job, the culture, and your colleagues are the right fit for you.

Turn the Interview Around

With that in mind, here are some questions every job seeker should make sure to ask:

1. **HOW WOULD YOU DESCRIBE THE CULTURE OF THE ORGANI-ZATION?** Is it a high-intensity, fast-paced, independent-working culture such as a stock trading floor, or is it a lively, fun, teamwork-inspired environment such as a trendy communications agency?

2. **HOW WOULD YOU DESCRIBE A TYPICAL WORKDAY?** Find out if you'll be in meetings from morning until late evening, or if you'll be on planes all the time. Ask if the work is routine and predictable or if there are often surprises and emergencies to tackle.

3. **WHAT TEAMS WILL I BE WORKING WITH? WILL I HAVE THE OPPORTUNITY TO MEET THEM?** Some of you will be spending more time with your colleagues than with members of your family. It's important to make sure you'll get along with them; otherwise, your work environment can be a source of great stress in your life.

4. **DESCRIBE YOUR WORKSTYLE.** Don't be afraid to ask your potential boss to describe the way he or she works. You might have to read between the lines, but it's important to find out whether he works by micromanaging employees, overseeing every detail, or if he is hands off. Does she plan several staff meetings a week and expect constant status reports? Will he give you freedom and flexibility to manage your own work load? Is she prepared to be a mentor?

5. **HOW WILL MY PERFORMANCE BE MEASURED?** Most companies have long drawn-out annual performance reviews. Find out who comes up with the goals and objectives to measure your performance. Are they dictated in a top-down approach, or do you and your manager come up with these goals together in a reasonable fashion?

6. **WHAT CHALLENGES DOES THIS POSITION ENTAIL?** Each position has its fair share of challenges. Whether it is operating on a shoestring budget, getting controversial legislation passed, or dealing with a difficult board of directors, there's always an obstacle or several that will make your job more difficult. Getting

the inside scoop early on will help you decide whether you are equipped to deal with it and whether it's the right job for you.

7. **WHAT SUPPORT AND RESOURCES WILL I HAVE TO DO MY JOB?** Again, you might have to read between the lines, but if you can find out how big your budget will be, whether administrative support is provided, and how big or how small your team will be, you'll be way ahead. Understanding the full scope of resources available to you is paramount.

8. **WHAT IS YOUR DEFINITION OF SUCCESS?** Success can be measured in a number of different ways. Understanding what criteria you're going to be judged by and promoted on is key to your success. Is it sales numbers, media impressions, research published, client satisfaction, new business development? Ask the questions to ensure that you're simpatico from the get-go. If the interviewer is cagey, that will tell you something too.

9. **SPECIFICALLY WHAT MILESTONES AND ACCOMPLISHMENTS WILL YOU EXPECT ME TO REACH?** In addition to your normal workload, often there will be special projects and milestones to contribute to: 75th anniversary communication plans, 10,000 patients evaluation plan, and the like. Understanding what the long-term goals and plans are for the organization and how you will be expected to pitch in is important.

10. **HOW DO YOU VALUE WORK-LIFE BALANCE?** Most people are afraid to ask this very important question, thinking it will negatively affect the interview. But it must be asked, especially if you have young children. Does the organization expect you to pitch in around the clock or work late into the evenings to get the job done?

11. **WHAT ARE YOUR BENEFIT PACKAGES AND VACATION DAY OFFERINGS?** Do you get 10 paid holidays and one week of vacation per year? Or is it five weeks a year? Do you need permission to use your vacation days? Is it frowned upon to use all your vacation days? Does the company encourage productive breaks? The

last thing you want is to find yourself working overtime on New Year's Eve. Get the lay of the land.

12. **WHY OUT OF ALL THE JOBS YOU MIGHT HAVE HAD DID YOU PICK THIS ONE**? Your prospective boss has key insights into the company. Try to glean them.

13. **WHAT'S GREAT ABOUT THIS COMPANY?** Follow up the question by asking why it's great to work there. Sure, you've done your homework and read all about the organization, but an insider's perspective is more valuable than anything you might read in the media.

If your interview has been like most others, you've been made to jump through hoops for a mere chance to get the job. Your prospective employer probably has dragged you through a series of interviews; asked you to show credentials, perhaps even transcripts and examples or your work; and brandish references. It's now your turn to do the asking, so don't be afraid to get the answers.

Show Time Suckers the Door

Apply these time-saving techniques to everything you do. Every time you establish a "contract'" with a person, formal or not, your goals and expectations should be clearly laid out in advance.

A friend who built a very successful real estate investment firm does this with his personal bike trainer. He explains that he would like to get in three one-hour rides a week, and within five weeks he'd like to excel at climbing big hills. "If you are not the person to help me do that," he says, "let's be clear now so we don't end up wasting each other's time." He will add incentives to reach his goals. "If I am climbing those hills within five weeks, then I will sign on for an additional six months." At the six-month renewal, he will add additional goals and more incentives. He also negotiates points for canceled appointments and lateness. "Look, my time is very valuable to me," he says, "so I'd like to lock in these days at this time. For any change, cancellation, or delay, you have to give me one free session."

I thought of this story, when a trainer friend of mine who was looking for new business asked my advice on what potential clients look for when hiring trainers.

"You have to be able to communicate quickly and effectively via e-mail or text," I said. "It's hard enough to juggle everything you have in one day and when you want to squeeze in a work out, you want to know right away if it's possible."

I also advised, "Don't be late! It's not just the hour workout that people schedule, it's the half an hour before, getting ready, changing, hydrating, etc. and the half hour after to shower and change. If you're 15 minutes late, it could send people into a tail spin for the remainder of the day."

He replied, "Yes, I learned this the hard way. I was running late for my first session with a new client, a successful and very busy entrepreneur with four children. When I called to let him know I was going to be 15 minutes late he replied, "Don't bother coming. Just turn around." I think he was setting a precedent so I'd know how valuable his time was. This taught me a valuable lesson, and I was never late again. I'm still training him five years later."

Any relationship can suck up your time if you don't set clear boundaries and parameters from the beginning.

There's nothing that makes me crazier than rushing the entire day so that I can get to an appointment on time only to be made to wait. Fifteen minutes, twenty minutes, five minutes; whatever it is, I could have used that time better doing what I needed to do rather than waiting for someone else. Hairdressers', dentists', and doctors' offices are typically the biggest culprits of the make-me-wait game as they have no way of predicting how long each patient or client will take. I always ask their offices to send me an e-mail or quick text if they are running more than 10 minutes late. And I usually call and ask if they are running on time before I leave. I do the same thing at work. The morning of every meeting, I e-mail to confirm the time and place. I do it in my personal life. If I invite someone to dinner and she is more than 20 minutes late, she will not be invited again unless she has a really convincing excuse. My time is too valuable to wait for others, and so is yours!

Whether it is your landscaper, assistant, new partner, trainer, dentist, dog walker, or baby-sitter, use these five tips to lay out the parameters of the engagement. Make your expectations clear early in the first meeting and constantly remind this person of them if he starts to slip.

1. Clearly state the value proposition (I am exchanging X for Y.).
2. Set time boundaries (Monday, Wednesday, and Friday 10 to 11 a.m. sharp for five weeks).
3. Set goals and expectations (If I don't see XX results in XX time frame . . .).
4. Use incentives (if you are successful in getting me to my goal in number 3, I will sign on for additional sessions, pay a bonus, and so on).
5. Establish a failure clause (if you are late or do not meet our goals, you owe me a free lesson or our contract will end).

Big, Bad, and Slow

Here are some big time suckers we can reduce or eliminate:

1. **E-MAIL.** Hours every day can be sucked up by e-mail (more about this below).
2. **SNAIL MAIL.** Every time we make a purchase, retailers ask for our mailing address. Do not give it to them. Nothing wastes time

like weeding through a pile of junk mail to find the one important letter. Most snail mail consists of direct mail solicitations and advertising junk. It fills up our trash bins that much faster, and then we have to spend time taking it out. Unsubscribe to the repeat offenders and be cautious about who you give your mailing address to. My husband likes to watch me go berserk when the huge Yellow Pages is dropped off at our door once a year.

3. **TRAFFIC.** Choose your travel time intelligently. Be smart about when you leave and when you come back. Try to get flexibility at work to avoid congestion times.

4. **CAR DEALERSHIPS.** My friend recently wasted an entire Saturday afternoon at one. Salespeople parading around in suits making you fill out and sign a pile of forms is not my idea of a fun weekend. There is no reason to go to the showroom and test-drive the car only to be upsold on the spot. Take your time to build your dream car to your ideal specs, compare pricing, and do your research. Hours upon hours of waiting to see if the finance/lease department will approve your credit can all be done in advance. I did this recently, signed all the documents electronically, and even paid a service fee of $45 to have the car delivered right to my door without ever stepping into the dealership. I know my sales rep only through e-mail.

5. **BUREAUCRACY.** Whether you're going to renew your driver's license at the local DMV or registering to vote in a new neighborhood, changing a course at your university, or trying to get a medical record from a hospital, behemoth bureaucracies were put on earth to suck up our time and make us crazy. Their lengthy processes, endless forms, and rigid rules often force you to make repeat trips for the same request. Make sure you check out everything online before entering one of these places so that you'll know you've dotted every *i* and crossed every *t* and that you have every piece of identification they require. Once you get in, it's

hours before you're out, and the last thing you want is to have to come back the next day for a repeat visit.

6. **LINES.** Lines are everywhere, but technology exists that can help you avoid them. Ordering online can be a big time saver when it comes to stores, and other than security gauntlets, there is no reason to wait in line at the airport when you have the option of checking in remotely from your home or hotel. Avoid long security lines by registering for the Transportation Security Administration (TSA) prescreen traveler program, and if you travel internationally, avoid the customs line by getting Global Entry.

7. **AIRPORTS.** Airline delays are now the norm. Maintenance issues, oversold flights, staff furloughs, and weather issues can cause us to spend hours and hours in airports. Come equipped with everything you need to do to be productive during those lost hours. Charged laptops, kid's homework, work you've saved for a rainy day, updating your contact list, finally backing up your hard drive, organizing your files or photos—bring it all to make use of the downtime.

8. **FLY DIRECT.** Many of us will take a connecting flight if it saves us money. But go back again to the formula of calculating the value of your time. Your time is worth money. A missed connection can cost you hundreds and even thousands of dollars. Always opt for a direct flight even it costs a few hundred dollars more.

9. **CHECK IN REMOTELY.** Check in at home or at the hotel before you go to the airport and bring your boarding passes with you, either on paper or on your mobile device. Do not even think about coming to the airport without having checked in. Not only will you endure painful lines, but your seat may not be guaranteed and you could end up losing it.

10. **DON'T CHECK YOUR BAGS.** I have a simple rule on this: if you can't lift it, don't bring it. Want to bring an extra pair of shoes? Don't even think about it. Pare your wardrobe down to the bare basics so that you can avoid checking your luggage. At least 30

minutes saved every time at arrivals. Lastly, don't be a cheapskate and park your car miles from the airport. Waiting for the shuttle costs you another 30 minutes. Pay the extra $3 and count how much you've saved in personal time.

11. **OUTSOURCE YOUR CHORES.** Menial chores such as laundry and house cleaning can be outsourced to lower-paid individuals so that you can devote your time to making more revenue or being productive.

12. **SET GOALS.** Set clear goals with your personal and professional staffs. They can be huge time wasters if you don't set boundaries. Invest the time up front to communicate clear expectations.

13. **MEETINGS.** Many of us spin our wheels all day, scheduling meetings, running to meetings, and sitting through them. The majority of meetings are an utter waste of time. If there is a real need, then be sure to set the agenda in advance to fully optimize your time.

Kill the Breakfast Meeting

It's time to kill the breakfast meeting. Kill it dead. I seriously think the first breakfast meeting was convened by a bitter boss who was unhappy with family life, couldn't wait to get out of the house in the morning, and wanted to inflict pain on subordinates.

The notion of a 7 or 8 a.m. breakfast meeting is unnatural, exhausting, stressful, and completely unnecessary. First, the very anticipation of the meeting ruins a good night's sleep. Next, the way you experience your morning sets the tone for the rest of the day. If you're rushing out of bed, running out of the house with barely a shower and something to eat, skipping the morning news, and speeding through traffic, the rest of your day will feel like an uphill climb. Lastly, what could be accomplished over breakfast, with all the disruptions of wait staff and eating, that couldn't have been accomplished more effectively in the office in the afternoon or even with a brief phone call?

Most meetings are useless time wasters and accomplish nothing.

Why Meetings Suck ... Up Your Time

In a *New York Times* article titled, "They Work Long Hours, but What About Results?" Robert Pozen cautions:

> *Internal meetings can be a huge waste of time. A short meeting can be useful for discussing a controversial issue, but long meetings—beyond 60 to 90 minutes—are usually unproductive. Leaders often spend too much time reciting introductory material, and participants eventually stop paying attention.*
>
> *Try very hard to avoid meetings that you suspect will be long and unproductive. When possible, politely decline meeting invitations from your peers by pointing to your impending deadlines. If that's not an option, make clear that you can stay for only the first 60 minutes, and will then have to deal with more pressing obligations. And be hesitant to call meetings yourself; you can deal with most issues through e-mail or a quick phone call. . . .*
>
> *By emphasizing results rather than hours, I'm able to get home at 7 p.m. for dinner with my family nearly every night—except when there are true emergencies. This has greatly enhanced my family life, and has given me a secondary benefit: a fruitful mental break. I've solved some of the thorniest problems in my home office at 10 p.m.—after a refreshing few hours chatting with my wife and children.*
>
> *Focusing on results rather than hours will help you accomplish more at work and leave more time for the rest of your life. And don't be afraid to talk to your boss about these issues. To paraphrase the management guru Peter Drucker, although you don't have to like your boss, you have to manage him or her so you can have a successful career.*[25]

I've sat through my fair share of useless meetings. I have a linear mind, and often meetings swerve off the agenda and into other areas. Sometimes this is helpful, but other times it ends up wasting the time of the people around the table. Moreover, a majority of meeting organizers and participants probably will ask to reschedule, show up late, interrupt the meeting by checking e-mails or taking calls throughout, leave early, or not show up at all. Off-site meetings make for an even bigger challenge in terms of having to find the building, searching for parking, and in some buildings dealing with security screenings before finally making your way to the right conference room. I have made a rule of not accepting an invitation for a meeting unless there is a compelling reason to attend. Most conversations can be handled with a quick conference call or an e-mail exchange. When I do accept meeting invitations, I always request an agenda that concludes with assignments for next steps. Otherwise, no action will come out of the meeting, which in my opinion is the sole reason to have a meeting.

I think that the main purpose of meetings seems to make heavy-handed, top-down managers feel important. If you have to resort to such tactics, meetings should take the following format:

1. Schedule the meeting during regular business hours and limit it to one hour max.
2. Hold the meeting on-site in a nondisruptive environment. The challenge of trying to find a new place is too risky and time-costly.
3. Circulate an agenda at least one week in advance and encourage feedback to it. Bring extra copies of the agenda to the meeting.
4. At the start of the meeting, review the agenda and the time allotted for the meeting and enforce it like a drill sergeant.
5. Appoint a timekeeper to watch the clock so that the meeting does not run over.
6. During the meeting, encourage dialogue, input, and feedback. Do not create a negative environment where ideas are shot down and team members are afraid to speak.

7. Consider allowing all team members to be responsible for a portion of the agenda items.

8. At the end of the meeting, talk about next steps, communicate desired outcomes for each team member, and agree on deliverables.

Be Nice to My In-Box

Our devices are always on, buzzing, dinging, blinking, and alerting us to new messages. The frantic drumbeat of incoming information—much of it pointless—has us so stressed out that we can't even enjoy our time away from the office. Opening an in-box with 600 unread messages every day sends a serious stress flag to the brain, causing anxiety and worse.

My team knows how I feel about e-mail overload. I am constantly pleading with them to "be nice to my in-box." I even send them joking warnings when they send me too many e-mails in one day: "Cease and desist. You are an e-mail violator today!" I trust them to do their jobs; I don't need to be cc'd on everything.

E-mails on a must-see basis only is my policy. My husband feels I'm overreacting, but every time I have to open an e-mail, read it, and delete it, that's five seconds of my life I will never get back. And speaking of Richard, he is the biggest offender! He will e-mail me when I'm sitting right next to him. I will read the e-mail and say, "You know I'm sitting right here, don't you?"

Sometimes e-mail is incredibly inefficient: it takes a lot of time and keeps us from our real work and goals. Though I am not a big fan of telephones, the reality is that e-mail is asynchronous communication. Sometimes it's faster to just call someone and work things out without the intermittent back and forths.

I have a friend who recently underwent brain surgery. Fortunately, he came through it okay, but before the life-changing event, he said, he had been a slave to his e-mail. He would see the red light blinking on his BlackBerry and immediately have to check it and fire off a response. It was the first thing he did in the morning and the last thing he did before he went to bed, and he even used it in the bathroom. If he woke up in the middle of the night, he'd take a quick peek, inviting the stress of work to interrupt his sleeping patterns.

After his surgery, he decided he would allot two hours a day to read and answer all his e-mail, from 6 to 8 pm, after he'd finished his workday as an architect and before he sat down to dinner with his family. He found his days were much less stressful without the constant disruptions, and he was better able to focus on his responses when he wasn't trying to multitask while working, eating, and even driving.

Perhaps checking hundreds of e-mails a day isn't as stressful as being a social worker, an air traffic controller, or a pediatric surgeon, but the effects are still real. "Email overload is a well-documented phenomenon that has been linked to reduced productivity, inability to focus on important tasks, and even physical and emotional stress," as David Lavenda recently wrote in *Fast Company*.[26]

It is not only stressful, but it also costs companies time and money. In a *Bloomberg Businessweek* column titled, "Re: Re: Re: Confidential," Mike Rosenwald says that the "Reply All" key costs companies not only time and money but embarrassing mistakes. Rosenwald writes, "At least 15 percent of a typical office worker's day is spent on email, and 5 percent of emails received are replies to all, according to data from VoloMetrix, a Seattle start-up that tracks, minute by minute, how its clients' employees use technology at work." Rosenwald continues, "While that might sound like a small number, spread those stats over a 10,000-employee company and 'you rapidly get to a pretty big number in terms of dollar cost—in the tens of millions of dollars [per year],' says VoloMetrix founder Ryan Fuller. For worker productivity, he says, 'It's the death by a thousand cuts.'"[27]

I agree with Rosenwald: the Reply All key is a disaster. I am constantly removing those who don't need the reply off the cc line, but several times a day the Reply All string continues and I have to interject with an e-mail informing the senders that I no longer need to be on the string. Another trick I have is to put the line "NO REPLY NECESSARY" after an e-mail in which I want to inform the team of something but don't need a discussion about it. The point is to keep them in the loop so that they can take the information and file it for later use. I am always careful to not use Reply All unless absolutely necessary. I value other people's time and expect them to be nice to my in-box in return.

Holding Back the Flood

As someone who receives hundreds of e-mails a day, I feel the pain, but I do all I can to stop it. I quoted Ryan Prince's advice on e-mail management above. Here is some of my own:

First and foremost, you need to ask yourself if you've empowered your team members to do their jobs without checking in with you on every detail. If they know they have the authority to make their own decisions without repercussions, they shouldn't be bombarding you with e-mails. When I tell my team that I trust them to do their jobs and don't need to be cc'd or FYI'd, they know I really mean it.

Years ago, when I was a vice president of corporate communications, I distributed an "e-mail etiquette" memo. Most of it is pretty basic, but all of it is still pertinent. Feel free to share it with your team, friends, and family:

In an effort to address the overwhelming number of e-mails and meetings, we are recommending the following guidelines.

The goal is to reduce unnecessary e-mail, increase e-mail effectiveness, and improve the quality of e-mail correspondence. Of course, no set of rules supersedes good judgment—there are always exceptions.

- *Include signature blocks with at least your name, title, and phone number. But set your computer so the signature block only appears on the first e-mail you initiate. This reduces unnecessary questions.*

- *Do not "Reply All" unless absolutely necessary. It contributes to e-mail overload. Replying to the sender is usually sufficient.*
- *Do not send one- and two-word responses such as "thank you," "will do," "yes," "no," "got it," "on it," etc., unless necessary or asked to do so. Each time you do, you're stealing seconds of someone's life they'll never get back!*
- *Scheduling: Do not send out e-mails to try and schedule a meeting. Use the calendar option. Same for rescheduling or canceling meetings.*
- *Do not send jokes, personal items, or chain letters no matter how good you think they are!*
- *Avoid blind copying. You can always forward a message to someone after you've sent it to your primary distribution list.*
- *Keep messages concise and focused. Clearly state your expectations of the recipients.*
- *Use bullet points whenever possible. Bullets help organize thoughts and make a longer e-mail easier to read.*
- *If you're going to be out of the office and truly not checking e-mail, set up an out of office assistant and make a note of who should be contacted in your absence.*
- *Avoid all caps; it gives the impression you are shouting.*
- *Use the subject line for an accurate description of your e-mail contents. This helps you and others organize their e-mail.*
- *Know when to pick up the phone. If confusion is emerging or there's excessive back and forth, it's time to have a live conversation. E-mail has become a convenient way for people to avoid difficult discussions and can quickly devolve into a passive-aggressive form of communication. When that happens, e-mail loses its effectiveness.*
- *Avoid the urgent exclamation point unless necessary.*

- *If your e-mail requires action by someone in the same day or in a relatively short period of time, make the deadline clear or pick up the phone. Surprisingly enough, not everyone is checking their device or sitting in front of their computer all day.*
- *Think twice before hitting send. You should assume everyone will see what you have written because they very well could.*
- *Use "CC:" properly. You should address the e-mail to the intended recipients and copy those who need the e-mail as an FYI only.*
- *If an issue needs to be escalated, start by copying your own supervisor before you copy someone else's.*[28]

An additional important point that I learned from Pozen: "Avoid rereading your e-mails. I am a great believer in the OHIO principle: Only handle it once. When you read an e-mail, decide whether or not to reply to it, and, if you need to reply, do so right then and there. I have found that about 80 percent of all e-mails, whether internal or external, do not require a response. Don't let these extraneous communications clog your in-box and waste your time."[29]

Then there are those whom I call circulators of work. They are the ones who get an e-mail, and instead of just handling it, they send it on to a number of other people without providing them with clear direction or feedback, thus creating a flurry of additional e-mails. My policy for my team is that I trust you to use your best judgment and handle the situation as you see fit. There is no punishment for doing something differently; I don't need to know every little thing. Empowering those you work with to make their own decisions will greatly reduce e-mail flow.

There also those, mostly above age 40, who incessantly clog your in-box with questions that can easily be answered by Google: "Where is the restaurant?" or, "How do I get to your place?" My answer to these mundane questions is always the same: "Google is your friend."

Lastly, recognize that the more you put out, the more you'll get back. I learned an interesting tidbit when I was working with animal experts. Sometimes when training animals, doing nothing is the best way to to stop a behavior, since the animal gets no attention for it. I've see this work with people as well. I have a brother-in-law who has never responded to an e-mail once, never. Guess what my family started doing. Leaving him off the family e-mail notification! Smart man, we think! Evaluate your own e-mail volume and decide whether it is necessary.

Use Technology to Save Time

There can be no doubt that technology has sped up the pace of our lives. Most people think it has taken away our free time and downtime. We are always on and always plugged in, and someone is always waiting for an instant response. We all see the images in cartoons, advertising, and our daily lives of the family gathered around the dinner table or the TV, each with a tablet or smartphone in hand, completely engrossed in their own online worlds, together but separate. I'm thinking now of the July 23, 2012, issue of *The New Yorker* with its cover cartoon of the family on vacation at the beach, dressed in shorts, sunglasses, and sun hats, feet in the sand with waves licking about their feet, but all four of them—father, mother, daughter and son—are looking down at their devices.

When I asked digital guru Don Tapscott if technology has brought us closer together or driven us farther apart, he had a very different take on the issue: "Well, there is much we don't know about the effects of the digital revolution on relationships," he said. "But the direction is clear. Rather than asking me, why not ask the 275,000 amateur astronomers who collaborate to map the heavens on Galaxy Zoo? Or ask the 20 percent of people with Lou Gehrig's disease in the U.S. who learn from and help each other on the Patients Like Me

Network? How about the grandparents who can communicate with their grandchildren weekly rather than yearly? Or the lovers whose relationships survive long times and distances apart? Ask the students in Tunisia who came together enabled by social media to bring down a tyrant. You could ask the seven-year-old girl who was buried in the rubble in Haiti after the earthquake and whose life was saved by two youngsters who found her faint text signals on the Ushaidi network. Being alive, I guess you might say that she is closer to her family than if she were dead."[30]

For all that, few can deny that technology does sometimes drive us into our own worlds. At the same time, few of us take proper advantage of it.

We are all guilty of wasting precious hours cruising the Internet and social media sites such as Facebook and watching videos on YouTube. Isn't life busy enough without having to feel pressured to wish every high school friend you haven't communicated with in person in 15 years happy birthday or wasting time dealing with random invitations, club events, and promotions? Isn't there enough to do without having to watch the singing dog video or the walking cat video, the cutest baby posters, and more? Many of us lose hours in the abyss of social media but won't use technology to save time on mundane time-sucking chores from shopping and scheduling appointments to making dinner reservations, buying theater tickets, and avoiding lines at airports.

I'm always amused to hear people say they are balancing their checkbook or running to the hardware store, the dry cleaner, or the grocery store. Me, I hate shopping! I hate everything about it: the traffic, the parking, the lines, the loud music that's deliberately programmed to make customers move faster and buy more, the slow clerks. On the rare occasions when I'm forced to enter a department store, I march through like a drill sergeant, wary of making eye contact for fear a sales clerk will slow me down. My goal is to pick up what I need, get in, and get out in 15 minutes.

I can't remember the last time I stepped into a post office, a bank, a hardware store, or a shop. As an experiment, I tried it recently. I went to a neighborhood hardware store to pick up some wet Swiffer pads. I perused the aisles, but all I found were several different versions and sizes of the dry Swiffer. The choices were dizzying, with options for pet hair, dust, allergens, bacteria, crumbs, and small debris. Pretty much everything except the long green box that had the product that I knew would fit my handle. I approached the desk to ask the clerk where to find them. He was on the phone, and so I waited for a long while before I impatiently walked away and found someone else to help me. He looked around and couldn't find them either. He picked up his walkie-talkie, "Hey, Connie, it's Bobby in Hardware. Where are those wet Swiffer pads?" The female responded, "We're outta them. I'll put in an order." I asked when they would be here. "We get new shipments on Friday; come back then." I came back on Friday, now determined to get my wet Swiffers. I walked in, and the sales clerk, whom I was now on a first-name basis with, Bobby, said, "Oh hi, doll, let me see if they're here." As he was looking, we started chatting. He told me about his passion for baking and said he could make a killer flan and would be baking for the upcoming holiday season.

"We still don't have them," he told me at last. "Come back on Tuesday; we'll have them for sure by then, and I'll bake you a flan." This is crazy, I thought. People do this regularly. Waste hours upon hours every week on errands that can easily be done in little time online. I went home and quickly ordered two boxes of wet Swiffers from www.cvs.com. They were delivered two days later. On Tuesday, I went back to the hardware store to complete my research. "Hey, dolly, how are you today? So glad you're here, I have something for you," Bobby greeted me. "Oh great! You have my Swiffers?" I said. "No dear, not yet, maybe later today when the truck unloads, but I made you my specialty vanilla bean flan." I walked out of the hardware store, with no Swiffers in hand, but one of Bobby's homemade flans.

Practically everything you need can be ordered online, including prescription drugs and toiletries. I'm not a fan of the excessive packaging, but as much as I regret all those trees being chopped down, I do appreciate all the time I'm saving. I can place online wine orders at almost any corner wine shop in the country, and they will deliver right to my door. If I am looking for something for the home, I can order whatever I need from traditional retailers such as Pottery Barn, Crate & Barrel, and Williams-Sonoma or more modern retailers such as Design Within Reach, Unica Home, and AllModern. Amazon has everything for everyday family needs, from kids' birthday presents to books, candles, sheets, towels, and more. Even CVS delivered my Swiffers, for goodness' sake!

The Friday after Thanksgiving used to be the busiest shopping day of the year in the United States, since most Americans had the day off and spent the afternoon getting a jump on their Christmas shopping. But as of 2012, Black Friday was eclipsed by Cyber Monday, with an astounding $1.98 billion in sales, up 17 percent from 2011.[31]

The old paradigm is done; the cyber age is here to stay. Yes, technology has sped up the pace of our lives, and it can be overwhelming. The pressure of living in an instantaneous society in which everyone is expecting a response right away is real.

But a lot of that pressure can be alleviated by shifting away from the old methods of doing things. Your mother had to go to the grocery store to pick up milk and eggs. You have the luxury of getting everything delivered to you at the click of a finger. Add up how many hours a week you spend buying groceries and running chores, and you'll realize how much time you can gain.

The Internet may be old news, but it's constantly making new time-saving options available. If you haven't made the shift, now is the time to let go of your parent's habits and get rich in time.

Trade-Offs

The founder and CEO of Facebook, Mark Zuckerberg, was still in his twenties when he became a billionaire. *Forbes* contributor David Thier wrote in a recent article, "There's a Facebook account for one out of every seven people on planet earth. The social networking site has topped 1 billion users."[32] You'd think that with all this success and fame Zuckerberg would own a huge mansion with several fancy cars parked in front. But as Nitasha Tiku wrote in *New York* magazine's "Daily Intelligencer," in at least one way, "He's Just Like Us!" He finds his apartments on Craigslist. His first place was a one-bedroom that a friend described as something like a "crack den." Then he moved up to a two-bedroom. When he finally moved to a detached house, it was a modest two-story, four-bedroom rental.[33]

Focusing his time and energy on building a great company gives the hoodie-wearing 28-year-old a sense of purpose and connection to the world. Dedicating this time and energy to the care and maintenance a big house needs, from the yard care to the repairs and maintenance, scheduling and rescheduling the plumber and the electrician, and waiting around for the cable repair person, are all minor things that mount up to major obstacles and time loss when one is building a major business.

Assess all the time wasters in your life, from a too-big home to people to places and things. Start clearing them out of your life and then put technology to work for you. You will be amazed, but if you think strategically about these time-saving tips, you can free up at least 10 extra hours every week. Then go back to your list of things that make you happy and start scheduling. If golf was on your happiness list, I bet you thought it was impossible to squeeze in 10 hours of golf every week. Spending the extra time doing something that makes you happy, whatever it is, from volunteering in your child's classroom, engaging in sports, working on yourself, or taking a new class will greatly upgrade your life. Losing the time wasters that make you miserable will upgrade it too.

CHAPTER 5

THE POWER OF WE

*My style is to surround myself with really smart people
and then listen to them.*
—John Noseworthy, MD, CEO, Mayo Clinic

All of our lives, we are taught to be individual players. In elementary and middle school, high school, and college, we sit in chairs theater style and face the instructor, who once in a while asks us to raise our hands if we have the answer. Math, history, spelling, and foreign languages are all taught in an individual learning pattern. Science class exposes us to teamwork in the laboratory, not for its own sake but because of a lack of lab equipment, so that only 5 or 6 instead of 30 liquid-to-gas explosions fill the classroom.

The sports field is where most of us first experienced the true essence of collaboration or teamwork. Collaboration means engaging with others in work or life to accomplish a shared goal. Whether it was basketball, baseball, volleyball, or football, the team understood that to win the game, it had to leverage all the skills of the various positions. In basketball, the center calls the shots and leads the plays, the forwards drive the ball to the basket, and the guards excel at passing and long shots. Players are positioned, traded, and honed for their strengths as part of a bigger purpose.

But rarely do most of us carry this strategy into our personal and professional lives. Collaboration begins with self-awareness and a healthy sense of humility in accepting our weaknesses and short-comings, recognizing where our strengths lie, and accepting the fact that we need help with them. Whether we are a business in need of financing, a brand licensing its name for others to execute on, creative entrepreneurs who need a management team to implement the company vision, or even a CEO needing the team to be more productive, collaborations come in all forms.

Give Up Me in Favor of We

People often underestimate the value of collaboration. Collaboration is important in all aspects of our lives, from the way we lead and cooperate with others to the way we approach and view our personal relationships.

In a *Fast Company* article, Lydia Dishman writes, "Collaboration. It's a $1 billion industry, according to an ABI Research study on worker mobility and enterprise social collaboration. And it's projected to grow to $3.5 billion by 2016."[1] No wonder so much ink has been spilled on this business buzzword, covering everything from starting it (hint: build trust), to doing it better with social platforms, to using it as a way to achieve that holy grail of business: innovation.

Morten T. Hansen and Scott Tapp argued in the *Harvard Business Review* that another C-suite executive was needed: the CCO. A chief collaboration officer would be charged with integrating the enterprise as a company scrambles to innovate from within.[2]

Stuff the Top-Down Nonsense

It's time to let go of the top-down approach to management. Does giving orders really work better than harnessing the intellectual capacities of a team? In the *New York Times* column "Corner Office,"

Adam Bryant interviewed Sandra L. Kurtzig, chairwoman and CEO of Kenandy, a software management firm based in Redwood City, California. When he asked her about her approach to leadership, she said:

> *I think that one of the most important things in working with anybody, whether you're the boss or the person being managed, is that you have to have mutual respect. I've always been very open and down to earth. I've never taken myself very seriously. I show self-confidence, and I think that if you don't show self-confidence, no one is going to buy from you and no one's going to want to work with you.*
>
> *I'm transparent, and I ask people on a regular basis what they like about their job and what they don't like about their job. What can we be doing better? In your previous job, how did you do it? What worked better and what worked worse than what we are doing now? I'm constantly asking people for their opinions.*
>
> *A key thing is surrounding myself with people that, No. 1, I respect, and No. 2, I like. Then I ask their opinions and really listen to them. Two-way conversations are an important ingredient for building a company.*
>
> *Two-way conversations are the key to success. The most successful business leaders have learned that it's no longer a top down approach.*[3]

Lead, Baby, Lead

The top-down leadership model is outdated, old, and antiquated. Bosses wagging their finger and telling you what to do no longer works. My friend Chip Brown recently wrote a cover story for *The New York Times Magazine* about Peter Gelb, the 59-year-old general manager of the Metropolitan Opera. Gelb told him in rehearsal "My goal is to hire brilliant directors whose productions are entirely their vision, and my job is to support them and see that what they want to get done, gets done."[4]

Employees want to be valued for their skills and knowledge, and a hierarchical approach does not leverage their strengths. Instead of looking at leadership as a top-down approach in which others are given their marching orders, think about leadership as the important task of inspiring and setting a vision for the team. Think about their skills as pieces of a pie that fit together to achieve a common purpose.

"The role of a leader," Robinson emphasizes, "is to offer a compelling vision of the road ahead and to inspire people so that they'll be able to travel it successfully. Management is about organization. Leadership is about vision. Both are important. Organization without leadership breeds bureaucracy. Vision without management breeds disillusion."[5]

Tech entrepreneur Tony Hsieh says, "I like to give people a lot of freedom and then see what they are able to do. For my own life, I also value the freedom to think outside the box and do things differently."[6] Collaborators nurture new ideas, tell us when a change of course is called for, and help us accomplish our goals.

My friend Mera Rubell told me, "I came to realize that in order to achieve my own ambitions I needed the talents of others to complement my own. The challenge is to find partners that you respect and also come to love."[7] Rubell leads with a deep sense of respect for the unique qualities of the people who work with her. Bosses who inspire, mentor, and teach are going to end up with the most productive and loyal teams.

"If you have information, it is your obligation to share it with others." I once heard this powerful statement, and it stuck with me. As individuals we will be motivated to work harder when we feel valued and respected and fully-vested in our work, not when we are being treated like a cog in the system.

I never try to dictate deadlines to my team. What is the point? If they can't make the deadline, forcing them to deliver an incomplete or inferior job isn't going to make things better. I ask my team members to let me know when they think they can deliver the project. Then I make them accountable to the deadlines that they set for themselves. Then there is no excuse for missing those deadlines.

I often engage the team members in a learning process by having them make a timeline of deliverables that they can review and change as necessary. Keeping the client's timeline in mind, we work backward to devise dates and a process schedule that everyone can agree on in advance. Someone will say, "I won't be able to review it on the 16th and get it back to you on the 18th, as I'm on business travel those days, but if you can get it to me a day early, I'll turn it around before I leave." Getting everyone's buy-in on a project schedule early on will ensure both timely delivery and a happier workforce. Yes, sometimes this takes a bit longer, but getting your team members involved allows them to learn the process, be engaged, and be more accountable. Treating the people you work with respectfully and taking the time to inform and educate is an investment that continues to pay off long into the future.

A leader's job is to inspire and set a vision. Our society, our institutions, and our businesses need to embrace this new style of leadership, as it brings the largest rewards.

Serving Is the New Leading

What makes patients from around the world travel to Rochester, Minnesota, to be cared for at the Mayo Clinic? Sure, you could cite its high standards or its position atop the annual *US News & World Report* Best Hospitals list for more than two decades. But you know what inspires me? It's the clinic's outside-the-box methods and practices.

Part of the reason the Mayo Clinic's patients are so satisfied is that doctors like working there. The Mayo Clinic has been featured on *Fortune* magazine's America's 100 Best Companies to Work For list for eight years straight.

Not too long ago, I interviewed the Mayo's president and CEO, John Noseworthy, MD, who also serves as the medical director of the clinic's department of development, as a professor in its department of neurology, and as editor-in-chief of *Neurology* (the journal of the American Academy of Neurology). Teaching hospitals are notorious for their well-known senior surgeons and for providing outsized rewards to their superstars, such as the top cancer researcher or the best cardiologist or the most published oncologist. You think of hospitals as having a top-down approach with the star doctor at the top, supported by a team of nurses and technicians. But when I asked Dr. Noseworthy to describe his leadership style, he said, "Leaders at Mayo Clinic embody Robert Greenleaf's model of 'servant leadership,' in which the desire to serve supersedes the desire to lead." A leader serving others, I thought. Wow, this is clearly a much different situation.

But there you have it. The Mayo's overriding goal is to serve. "Successful leaders at Mayo mobilize the organization to best serve our patients," Noseworthy said. Mobilizing the organization means collaboration. "My style," he continued, "is to surround myself with really smart people and then listen to them, while encouraging the team to think and act boldly. Timely consensus must be followed by disciplined, successful execution of the plan."[8]

Although individual talent is important and constant learning and growth are integral, at the core of the Mayo Clinic's success is its marshaling of the entire organization's skills around that one goal.

I know that I would have thrived in such a work environment. Most of us would love to go to the office and be engaged in a learning environment. When I talked to my friend, a longtime producer at CNN, she said, "It would be a miracle for my boss to value me for my skills and commitment to the company. It would be an even bigger miracle for him to inspire us. Instead we are all afraid of him."

In a *Harvard Business Week* article, Sean Silverthorne, editor-in-chief of the Harvard Business School's *Working Knowledge*, interviewed Harvard Associate Professor Mukti Khaire about a new elective course that challenges traditional management thinking. She said, "Most CEOs have little difficulty with a top-down management style and expecting their directives to be executed. But that model wouldn't fly at Chanel (or for that matter, any creative firm). If you tell Karl (Creative Director Karl Lagerfeld) what to make, that's not going to work," Khaire says. "You don't manage the creative process, you enable it."[9]

Tim Brown of IDEO's approach to leadership is similar. He says, "I am not sure I really think of leadership as a style. I try to be the right leader for the moment. Sometimes that means trying to inspire the organization with new ideas that might challenge the status quo. Sometimes that means jumping in and helping solve a problem with a client or IDEO team." The reality is that most bosses do not sit down and help for lack of time, leadership style, or knowledge. Instead, most dictate, evaluate, measure, and observe. Brown says, "Sometimes it means stepping back and leaving room for someone else to take the lead but being there to support them."

Brown didn't understand this immediately. "It took me a while to learn that approaching every leadership moment the same way is not constructive," he admitted. "Earlier in my career I thought my job was to try to always have the best ideas and I would strive really hard to be as personally creative as I could. Now I realize that this can stifle other talented people, and that I can be far more effective helping them develop their own ideas and giving them the confidence, if they need it, to go and make their ideas happen."

The global competition to attract top talent is a race for sure. No longer are people with skills content to take the corporate job near their hometown. They are willing to live in new and exciting cities but want to be engaged with an organization that is not only great at what it does but innovative and that offers an enriched environment. Brown agrees and believes that this collaborative style is a critical asset in the global race to attract and harness talent, something that cannot be accomplished from the top down.

"This ideal of doing great work and helping others to do great work has led us to be passionate about teaching, which has been great for learning and recruiting," he says. "It has also made us comfortable with teaching our clients how to do what we do and discouraged us from being too proprietary about our knowledge. I also think this approach has allowed us to successfully compete for the best talent in places like Silicon Valley, where there are plenty of other very wealthy companies interested in hiring creative people. I believe talented people come to IDEO because they see a culture where they can learn and create impact with other talented people who they will love being around."[10]

Successful organizations don't treat their employees as merely productive staff; they treat them as individuals who are interested in learning and contributing. As Tony Hsieh advises, "Make sure that the company commits to values that match the employees' personal values, and make sure that the company has a vision that has a higher purpose beyond just profits or beating the competition."[11]

In a recent article at *Fast Company*, Erika Andersen talks about the new definition of generosity. Giving one's time, knowledge, feedback, and mentorship is the difference between being a good leader and a great one.

"We tend to think of generous people as those who share material wealth," she writes, "giving to charity, buying expensive gifts, or taking the in-laws out for dinner. In business, we think of generous leaders as those who provide a way for their people to share materially in the success of the company—through raises, profit sharing, or a bonus system. All of these things can be good, but they are only part of true generosity. Truly generous leaders share the wealth on many levels. For example, they are quick to give others credit for their good efforts and new ideas. They're also generous with their knowledge, sharing information with those who need it and teaching others around them how to do what they themselves do well. They are generous with their faith in people; they tend to assume best intent (although they are not naïve) and believe people are generally innocent until proven guilty."[12]

People want to feel valued and recognized for their contributions. When we spend a majority of our lives at work striving to make an impact, monetary rewards are nice, but a pat on the back or a few words of appreciation or recognition can have an even bigger impact.

Recently, I heard some great advice from Roger Martin, dean of the Rotman School of Management at the University of Toronto. He said that he always takes the extra time to invest in people up front, to give them all the information they need to succeed and grow. He recognizes that this takes a lot of extra time out of his very busy schedule, but he says it pays off in tremendous dividends down the road. If you don't empower those who work for you with information, train them, and develop them, you are not leading. This same principle can be applied to those in your personal life, from the people who take care of your children to those who help you with your home. Sharing, exchanging, and giving information is a powerful gesture. Can you imagine how much better, more productive, and more engaged our society would be if everyone followed this simple practice every day?

Giving those you work with the freedom to make mistakes and learn from them is paramount. If you don't, the entire organization will be frozen in its tracks with fear. Andersen goes on, "The generous leader, having provided the information necessary for success, gives people the authority and autonomy to act on that information. A leader who is fully generous shares both the power to make decisions and the responsibility for dealing with the consequences of those decisions. She shares the resources necessary for people to recover from mistakes and failure. Finally, she is generous with feedback. She takes the time to notice what her staff is doing or not doing, think about what's great and what's not, and share with them her observations."[13]

Tapscott authored several bestselling books, including *Paradigm Shift*, *Growing Up Digital,* and *Wikinomics.*

"My research suggests that peer collaboration models work better than hierarchies. Empowerment is no longer a motherboard concept. So I don't really manage people at all. I try and help them unleash their capacity."

"The new collaboration is not the traditional teamwork at all," he adds. "The difference today is that individual efforts can be harnessed on a large sale to achieve collective outcomes, like Wikipedia . . . that would have been impossible to achieve without a new generation of collaboration tools."

In a way, collaboration *is* leadership. Organizations that harness the capacity of several contributors have a competitive advantage. "The old model of the leader who comes up with a vision and sells it down is gone," Tapscott says. "Peter Senge was right years ago when he said the person at the top can't learn for the organization anymore."

If you want your organization to succeed or want to achieve success personally, you need to think of leadership as a collaboration in which you utilize people for their strengths. This approach will engage and inspire your team to work harder, be more productive, and be more involved.

Even Michael Jordan Needs a Team

Creativity is a team-based process. It requires collaboration. Jobs had Wozniak, Gates had Allen, and Lennon had McCartney. Successful creative enterprises typically have two leaders: a visionary and a strategist who can execute.

The collaboration that comes from a great team makes everyone better. Tapscott says, "I don't buy arguments that collaboration is undermining creativity. Collaboration is based on self-organization, decentralized power and knowledge and freedom of action. Collectivism is based on coercion and centralized control. Whereas communism stifled individualism, mass collaboration is based on individuals and organizations working to achieve shared outcomes through loose voluntary associations." Tapscott adds that such successful collaborations include Wikipedia and even an uprising like the Arab Spring, which was enabled to a great degree by social media.[14]

Having a set of diverse perspectives to draw on can save you from making costly mistakes. It can also give you an edge in trend spotting.

Grant McCracken, author of the *Harvard Business Review*–recommended book *Chief Culture Officer*, says that the jeans maker Levi Strauss & Co. missed out on $1 billion worth of sales when it ignored the hip-hop trend. "Culture matters for reasons good and bad," he observes. "First, it is the place to discover advantage, opportunity, and innovation. The Four Seasons, Patagonia, Starbucks, Nike, Red Bull, Target, Method Soap—each is a culture play. Each found value in culture. Each extracted value from culture."[15] He goes on to explain that a smart and culturally heterogeneous team of strategic collaborators is the key.

Don't miss out on opportunities to upgrade your business or life because of lack of collaboration. Successful collaboration comes in all shapes and forms. A wide range of contributors is readily available and wants to add value.

Who would ever think that a world-renowned architect could design tennis shoes? Zaha Hadid did just that, by using her genius for design and her mathematical grasp of shapes, Through a unique collaboration, Hadid created a limited edition collection of Lacoste shoes. Using fluid grips, which wrap around the foot, the shoes are specially designed to move with the body. But she didn't do it alone. "Teamwork has been very important to me for a long time. I've always believed in it, and that's why things are manageable," she told me. "It's very difficult to get anywhere in the profession without being meticulous, but it is important to learn how to trust others," she added. "A brilliant design still benefits from the input of others. . . . You must learn early on that you can't do everything yourself; you can do bits of it yourself, you can ask people to do things the way you want them done, but you also have to rely on their strengths and abilities."[16]

Bringing in new and different perspectives can result in hundreds of millions of dollars in new sales. Consider what happened when Procter & Gamble asked Continuum, an innovation and design practice, to think about better ways to clean floors. A team of researchers observed that most people hated mopping. First they had to sweep before they mopped and that they spent almost as much time wringing out the mops as they did running them across the floor. Few people used branded products; most considered mopping such a dirty chore that they changed their clothes first. Drawing on this new perspective, an idea for a new product emerged that would make floor cleaning much less onerous: Fast Clean, or as it became better known, the Swiffer. In the first year on the market, 11.1 million units were sold, and it continues to be one of Procter & Gamble's best-selling products, with more than $500 million in annual sales.[17] As you've read, I'm a dedicated Swiffer user myself. The research teams' collective inputs and observations are what led to this invention.

When I was VP of communications for HMSHost, collaborations were essential to our business. The world's largest provider of food, beverage, and shopping services for travelers, HMSHost operates hundreds of airport concessions around the world, from JFK International, to Reagan National, to Miami International, to London Heathrow.

It is easier for an airport to have a single large company run all its concessions than to bring in hundreds of independent operators. HMSHost collaborates with well-known brands such as Wolfgang Puck, Balducci's, and California Pizza Kitchen by licensing their names and running their operations. From the construction of the spaces to the hiring, training, and firing of the staff, HMSHost does it all in exchange for the brand and a revenue share.

Starbucks is one of HMSHost's leading brands and biggest success stories. When I worked there, there were 17 Starbucks in Chicago's O'Hare airport alone, and they brought in more than $26 million a year in revenue. HMSHost opened the first Starbucks at Seattle–Tacoma International Airport in 1991. It seemed like a big gamble at the time, and a lot of people at HMSHost were reluctant to do it. Who in their right mind, they thought, are going to pay all that money for a cup of coffee? Back then, airport coffee was uniformly terrible-tasting and was served in small white Styrofoam cups. Just a little over two decades later, there are more than 300 airport Starbucks locations, with more than 100 more in development.

I attended a meeting with the Starbucks team members in Seattle at which they were negotiating for more space. They argued that the café environment was an important part of their brand proposition and that the spaces we were putting them in weren't large enough to do them justice. Our contract was coming close to its end, and we knew how important their brand was to our bottom line—and so did they. They said to us, "When we first signed on with you, you were dealing with Michael Jordan in high school. At our second contract negotiation you were dealing with Michael Jordan in college. Now at our third negotiation, you are dealing with Michael Jordan—PERIOD."

Collaboration is key in everything. We knew we couldn't re-create a brand that delivered the quality, name recognition, and taste Starbucks had perfected. They knew how vast our footprint was in airports around the world. Although Starbucks had expertise in running stores on the streets, the airport environment was a vastly different beast. For one thing, the stores were open 365 days a year. Second, employees had to travel much farther than they did to work at a typical neighborhood Starbucks and had to deal with airport security rules and regulations. Just delivering product and inventory posed special logistic challenges. The landlord relationship was also different. Both businesses recognized their strengths and their weaknesses, which in the end made this collaboration equally successful. In the end, we gave them more space in better locations with more foot traffic. The additional square footage was used for retail opportunities, such as baskets of food, souvenir mugs, and carry-on items, and so it was a win-win.

Let Go of Your Inner Control Freak

It's hard to believe, but the software giant Microsoft did not foster an environment of collaboration within its own organization until recently. According to a *Bloomberg Businessweek* article, "About every six weeks, a small group of Microsoft executives gathers at a Seattle restaurant to talk strategy. The location varies, but the cast of characters tends to stay the same: Don Mattrick, the head of the division that produces the Xbox, will be there sitting alongside Qi Lu, the head of search and advertising, as well as top executives from the mobile team. . . . It may seem strange, but meeting to discuss the melding of different product lines did not take place in years past. The environment in Microsoft's executive suite resembled something out of *Game of Thrones*, with division heads poaching talent from one another and thwarting attempts from other groups to collaborate on products." The article went on to say that, "The dinners led to changes like the integration of Microsoft's Bing search system in the company's Xbox console and a Windows smartphone working as an Xbox remote control."[18]

However, this new concept apparently was not appealing to everyone. Microsoft's new collaborative approach is the alleged reason longtime Windows chief Steven Sinofsky, who was described as "an abrasive loner," stepped down after 23 years. Oddly, Sinofsky looked at the different divisions within the organization as rivals.

This kind of reactive, defensive thinking is alien to true entrepreneurs. When a successful entrepreneur meets someone with a great talent, he doesn't worry about the competitive challenge she poses; instead, he grooms her as a potential member of his team or a potential collaborator, eager to leverage whatever value she can add.

I didn't understand the value of collaboration at first. Early in my career, I felt that others slowed me down. I used to be a control freak like Sinofsky; I thought I could do everything better myself. I could work faster and more efficiently, I thought, if I didn't have to engage the team, be interrupted by others, wait for their feedback, and attend group meetings. When I became CEO of the Creative Class Group, I realized that I didn't have all the answers, skills, or expertise. Although I was good at marketing and communications, I was weak in research and data analysis. I needed other experts to form the foundation. You have to surround yourself with partners who complement your strengths and compensate for your weaknesses. I realized that the different perspectives and skill sets that the team members bring to bear contribute value to all of our projects.

I soon concluded that collaboration is the key to getting more done faster, better, and more efficiently. When I approach my team members with an idea and ask them to explore it, I never accept the answer, "We can't do that, and this is why." I encourage them to come back and say, "Yes, we can, but here's what we need to do it right," or, "While what you asked for is not feasible, here are three other alternatives." Squelchers are of no value to anyone. An environment that recognizes and fosters team inputs leads to new and better ways of doing things.

Sitting Idle? Try Collaborative Consumption

Consider the new business collaboration model based on idle capacity. Zipcar, plus dozens of innovative start-ups such as City CarShare, PhillyCarShare, I-Go, and CommunAuto, are car-sharing programs that realized that cars sit idle 95 percent of the time. Why not use a collaborative approach for consumers to share that idle capacity, gaining greater economic returns? Zipcar's approach to collaborative consumption has grown into such a robust business model that Avis Budget Group recently acquired it for $500 million. Buzzcar takes the

Zipcar model one step further. Instead of using rental cars in a share program, it allows citizens to have their idle cars used by others in the network. Zipcar cofounder and Buzzcar CEO Robin Chase spoke at an event we produced recently called StartUp Miami in partnership with the Knight Foundation and *The Atlantic*. When Richard interviewed her on a panel, she explained that "peer-to-peer car sharing makes better economic sense." Several others have caught onto the trend that a collaborative approach to idle capacity is a great business strategy. There are even books on this business model, including *What's Mine Is Yours: The Rise of Collaborative Consumption* by Rachel Botsman and Roo Rogers and *The Mesh: Why the Future of Business Is Sharing* by Lisa Gansky. Collaboration not only leverages the skills of a team, but in its new forms it can even minimize waste.

Technology Amplifies

Some argue that the collaborative model combined with technology leads to yet more innovations than the "closed loop" model by tapping and harnessing the creative inputs and intelligence of the greater community versus the team. Such insights led to crowdsourcing. Crowdsourcing allows organizations to attract a very large, unknown network of outside contributors to amplify the innovation process. Traditional collaboration allows you to execute on set goals and objectives. Crowdsourced collaboration can open you up to brand-new ideas and discoveries that are still untapped.

Crowdsourced collaboration surfaces new ideas and gets people excited about them, while creating new connections, initiatives, and opportunities that traditional methods of collaboration can then execute upon.

Frito-Lay has been using this approach since 2006 for its über-successful "Crash the Super Bowl" campaign for its Doritos brand. Consumers are invited to create 30-second spots and submit them for cash prizes, a chance to have them run during the Super Bowl, and in 2013, the opportunity to work with Michael Bay on a movie. Not only do hundreds of millions of viewers see the finalists at the Super Bowl, but the submissions draw countless eyeballs on YouTube and Facebook." This is the best amplification of our brand narrative," Jeff Klein, the senior marketing director of Frito-Lay, said. "We just continue to be blown away by the creativity of Doritos fans." And it sounds likely that Doritos will run the "Crash" initiative again next year.[19]

Hackaway

Hackathons take crowdsourcing one step further by convening experts. The are all the rage, and companies such as American Express are offering large awards and incentives for the valuable information and insights that come out of these collaborative sessions. A hackathon is typically a daylong event in which computer programmers, developers, designers, and coders collaborate intensively on a software project in an attempt to get to the root of a problem. *Hack* is a fun term that refers to exploring programming, and *athon* refers to a marathon session. Hackathons have become increasingly popular. Facebook recently hosted a hackathon in partnership with the Bill and Melinda Gates Foundation to kick off the $2.5 million investment fund for the College Knowledge Challenge. Typically they start in the morning and go well into the evening and are fueled by heavily caffeinated sugary drinks, such as Red Bull. They harness the collaborative efforts of users worldwide; the exchange of ideas leads to innovation, problem solving, and new insights.

The world of fashion is getting into this model of collaboration, attempting to bridge the gap between fashion and technology. Decoded Fashion and the Council of Fashion Designers of America hosted a hackathon over a 24-hour period with a deadline of the last day of New York Fashion Week.

The event drew over 600 participants, half of whom were women, as well as support from fashion designers, media, and techies.

Stephanie Winston Wolkoff, a former *Vogue* editor and the founding fashion director of Lincoln Center, told the *New York Times*: "People on the tech side think very differently about fashion. It's not just about brands, it's about publishing and distribution and manufacturing. And when you say fashion, people think clothing, but it's more than that. It's the business of clothing."[20]

Even Edison Had a Wing Man

Whether you have a small business, work in an organization, or are evaluating your personal goals, you can benefit immensely by having the right strategic partners. The first step is to identify the areas in which you need help; only then can you look for the right partner. Investing the time up front to clarify your goals is key.

Slightly more than a decade ago, the Italian luxury fashion house Bottega Veneta went into bankruptcy and was acquired by PPR, formally the Gucci Group. Fashion maven Tom Ford's first step was to bring in the German designer Tomas Maier as creative director. Maier had trained in Paris and made his name at Hermès; his mission was to strip out the tawdry excess that had diluted Bottega Veneta's brand, restoring its focus on craftsmanship and understated elegance. Maier not only brought the company back to solvency, but he made it a watchword for contemporary functionality and timeless design.

I asked Maier what qualities he looks for in his collaborators. "Integrity, expertise, an appreciation for tradition, and a genuine interest in working with other people," he said. "I also look for a strong aesthetic point of view, because I enjoy working with people who bring a compelling perspective to the table."[21]

In business, in science, and even in the arts, the romantic legend of the lone genius is as often as not just that: a legend. Just think about some of these historical partnerships. The incandescent light bulb was the product of a business collaboration between Thomas Edison and J. P. Morgan and the Vanderbilts. Edison was the genius entrepreneur who perfected the 50-year-old concept and turned it into a viable consumer product, but he needed financial backing before he could launch it in the marketplace. He called his laboratory an invention factory.

HP began as a partnership between two electrical engineering grads from Stanford, Bill Hewlett and David Packard. They started working together from a rented garage with an investment of less than $1,000.

The famous ice cream company Ben & Jerry's Homemade was founded in 1978 by Ben Cohen and Jerry Greenfield, who shared a social conscience. Now their Chunky Monkey and Cherry Garcia flavors are enjoyed around the world.

Google was a collaboration between Larry Page and Sergey Brin. The two met at Stanford and soon dropped out to focus on making the world's number one Internet search engine.

Look at songwriters and musicians: the Gershwin brothers, Mick Jagger and Keith Richards, Jimmy Page and Robert Plant, Bono and the Edge—the list goes on and on.

No One Can Do It All

We need collaborators to reach our personal goals too. Go back to Chapter 1 and look at your vision statement for the future. Dig deep and do a self-analysis, come to terms with where you are in your life, and reconcile it with where you want to be. Assess your shortcomings and then think about how a collaborator can help you reach your goals.

There's so much I want to do. Every week I have a new crazy idea: write a children's book, open a restaurant, produce and direct a documentary film, create a cool app. I want to launch a magazine and start an online retailer, a pop-up shop, a food truck, and more. Every week, I add something new to my list even though my days are already jam-packed. I've always had lists of things I want to do and accomplish. I wanted to write a family cookbook for quite some time. My mother and aunts are amazing cooks, but none of my siblings knew how to make any of their delicious family recipes. Not too long ago, I found myself with 14 hours to kill on a flight to Korea, and so I wrote the introduction. Knowing my impatience with regimented detail, I realized there was no way I was going to be able to take the time and trouble to see the project all the way through myself. I never measure anything and can barely understand the plethora of Arabic spice names. My family is Jordanian, and Jordanian cooking is complicated; the dishes take hours to prepare and include ingredients from all over the world. Moreover, my mother and aunts do not have one single recipe written down.

One day, it dawned on me to collaborate with my sister Ruba. She loves cooking, has the patience of a saint, and lives near our mother and all our aunts. Moreover, she is a third grade teacher and has her summers off, which gave her the time she needed to commit to the work. She enthusiastically accepted my offer to collaborate and agreed to a timeline that would allow us to give the book to all our family members for the holidays. We seriously underestimated how much time and work it would take and the difficulties of self-publishing, but one week before Christmas our stocking stuffer was ready: *Simply Jordanian: Middle Eastern Meals Made Easy*.

There is no way I could have made that happen without first accepting my shortcomings and then finding a collaborator who could complement my skills. My collaborator could not only execute her responsibilities, but was personally invested in the project and had the same vision. She sat down with my mother and aunts and extracted the recipes from them, she test cooked and set up photo shoots for every recipe, while I managed the production, design, edit, and copy. Now our family recipes will live on for future generations.

How to Harness the Power of We

As much as we hate to admit, we can't do it all ourselves, and so collaborations are essential. They allow several benefits, including the following:

- They provide better deliverables by using people for their strengths to compensate for your weaknesses.
- They bring more resources to the table.
- They allow for idea exchange.
- They expand your work into other areas.
- They introduce new insights and discoveries.

Key Steps for Collaboration

1. First identify the need for the partnership. Understand your strengths and weaknesses and write them down.
2. Put feelers out. The right partner is crucial in helping you grow, but the wrong partner can eat up time and resources. Ask friends, family, and colleagues for possible leads.
3. Evaluate the partner's capabilities and strengths. Finding a partner with the right skills is essential, but finding someone with a genuine passion for the project is even better.
4. Assess the working relationship; you have to like working together.
5. Set up an initial project with a limited time period to test the relationship.
6. Keep evaluating along the way. Sometimes one collaborator isn't enough.

Target is a great example of an organization that leverages collaborations. The funny thing is that when you walk into a Target store, the first things you see are hot dog and pretzel stands. The clerks wear red polyester vests. It's a convenient place to to stock up on candles, light bulbs, back-to-school supplies, sporting supplies, birthday party gifts for kids, and other household essentials. This giant cost-cutting retailer is just like a Walmart or Kmart, right?

Not at all. At first glance they might seem similar, but on thorough examination they couldn't be more different. Target is one of the first big box retailers to set itself apart from the competition through its advertising and branding campaigns and even more so through its collaborations. Target's partners in fashion and design have dramatically raised its profile, setting it above and apart from its competitors.

Target first launched its now-legendary design initiative more than 20 years ago, in 1999, with the architect and prolific designer Michael Graves, who created everything from unique toilet brushes to brooms and dustpans for the store. This relationship has now come to an end. But its lessons were not lost on other retailers such as H&M, which is now doing very much the same thing for fashion that Target did for housewares, offering inexpensive collections to its customers' by such high-profile designers as Stella McCartney, Marni, and Versace.

Target's designer collaborations also extend into fashion with a dress collection from Jason Wu, the 20-something designer who created Michelle Obama's inaugural ball gown, as well as Missoni, Zac Posen, and Alexander McQueen, who have each made limited-edition collections available at affordable prices.

Think about collaborations as more than just ways to compensate for your weaknesses—they are bigger than the sum of their parts, and as such they can help you or your organization to advance.

Diversity, Collaboration, and Creativity

Diversity is the key to a successful collaboration. Bringing together a creative mix of backgrounds sparks new innovations and discoveries.

When I asked Dr. Noseworthy about the Mayo Clinic's take on diversity, he said, "Bringing together great minds from a spectrum of backgrounds has always been crucial to our mission. Our diversity allows us to accelerate innovation and solve problems faster. Ultimately, it fuels the medical discoveries that lead to better care for our patients and people around the world.

"To drive innovation to meet their changing needs, we nurture an environment in which our physicians, scientists, and staff can use their unique backgrounds and perspectives to tackle important problems. Collectively, their diverse perspectives enhance our productivity and help us better meet the needs of our increasingly diverse patients.

"Yet as a goal or strategy, diversity is not enough. Inclusion, or creating a workplace where each member of our staff feels valued and empowered, is crucial."[22]

Think about what happens when five people of similar background, age, sexuality, race, religion, education, and profession sit around a table to offer their perspectives on a new initiative. It is likely that they will reach consensus very quickly. Then think about having five completely diverse people sit around the same table, discussing the same thing. Instead of five 30-year-old executives who went to the same university and grew up in the same neighborhood, imagine that there are five people who vary greatly in ages, from young to old, who are black and white, French and Turkish, gay and straight, Jewish, Christian, Islamic, Buddhist, and atheist. I imagine that the conversation would be much more interesting, heated, engaged, and eye-opening. When different perspectives interact, you're much more likely to learn something new.

Mario Batali was recently interviewed in the *New York Times* column "Corner Office." The headline read, "In Mario Batali's Kitchen, You Will Refrain from Shouting." "One of the most important things," he said, "is realizing you're not the most important or the most intelligent person in the room at all times." Surprisingly, Batali told me he'd learned this important life lesson by listening to my husband talk passionately about cities when they were college students together at

Rutgers. "Understanding that is a crucial component of the kind of self-deprecation that makes someone really good at understanding other people, especially when they're faced with their own limitations and they come to you for help. It's about being able to empathize and understand and communicate, even under stress, in a way that helps them solve a problem, as opposed to becoming part of the problem. The first day that a chef believes that he or she knows everything is the first day for the rest of their life that they will be a jerk, because you can't know everything about our field."[23]

Collaboration in work and in life is about listening, lending a hand, and learning when to step in and when to step back. When I asked Tim Brown of IDEO what he looked for in his team members, he answered in detail. "From a skills perspective, we look for depth and diversity," he said. "Sometimes this is described as T-shaped: people who have depth of 'craft' in a discipline such as design, business, engineering, or the social sciences, but who also have a breadth of perspective and an insatiable appetite to cross disciplines and collaborate. In terms of traits, we look for people with empathy (because it is hard to design for others if you are not interested in understanding them), with creative imagination, with a drive to make ideas real rather than merely speculating about them, and, finally, with storytelling skills, because new ideas rely on great storytelling to get out into the world successfully."[24]

Collaboration rests on the premise that you believe you can learn by listening to others, that everyone on your team has something to contribute. Give this experiment a try. Approach someone you would never think to approach about a problem or initiative you have at work that you are trying to sort through. Ask your mother, for instance, or someone from outside the industry. Ask someone from a different country; ask an eight-year-old. Jot down their answers and see if you learned anything. See if you gained a new perspective on the situation by getting a broad range of inputs.

In their book *Becoming a Life Change Artist*, Fred Mandell and

Kathleen Jordan help readers connect with their own creativity and build on their innate talents to create a more fulfilled and satisfying life by examining the creative processes of great artists such as Henri Matisse, Vincent van Gogh, Leonardo da Vinci, Willem de Kooning, Frida Kahlo, and Georgia O'Keeffe, among others.

Their list of four important outcomes of personal collaboration, I believe, provides an excellent summary on the benefits of collaboration:

- **BRIDGE TO NEW NETWORKS.** Collaboration with others helps bridge us into new networks that facilitate change.
- **BETTER DECISIONS.** As powerful and inventive as our minds are, they work within the boundaries of our own backyards, but when we collaborate with others, we extend our boundaries. We see how others have arranged their gardens. We benefit from their perspective and creativity. Collaboration is a source of fresh ideas which in turn get us to better solutions.
- **EMOTIONAL SUPPORT.** Life change has its good days and bad days. Change even has its very painful days. Sometimes we have the sense that time is moving much too slowly, and others times we feel that events are getting the better of us. Collaborating with others provides not only practical support in figuring out how to navigate change but the emotional support to remain afloat during the tough times.
- **ACCOUNTABILITY.** Sometimes support for personal change comes in the form of being accountable to others for things we say we will do but let slip. Change never follows a straight line, but true collaborative partners will call us on those slips.[25]

Your Crib Notes

- Start by realizing that you can't do it all on your own.
- Recognize your strengths and call out your weaknesses.

- Find partners who complement your strengths and compensate for your weaknesses.
- Throw out everything you learned in business school about management; the top-down leadership style is outdated.
- Collaboration is the new leadership approach.
- Don't be a dictator. Lead by serving.
- Collaboration is the key to getting more done faster, better, and more efficiently.
- A great collaboration is a convergence of diverse inputs.
- Hey, know-it-all, don't be a jerk and assume you're the smartest guy or gal in the room. Surround yourself with smart people and learn by listening.

CHAPTER 6

BIG RISKS = BIG REWARDS

Never was anything great achieved without danger.
—Niccolò Machiavelli

Some Risks Are Just Cray Cray

I had so much energy when I was 18 years old that I ran out of productive ways to release it, and so one morning I decided I was going to get a tattoo and go skydiving. I went with two of my friends to get the tattoo. Benny had a strange "figurative" character etched onto his left calf, which he regretted four years later, so he covered it up with another tattoo, an equally odd, large black rectangle. Sara, as she puts it, went with "a sun on my right shoulder—a few years later I covered it with something bigger and dumber, and I still have it because it costs thousands of dollars to get it burned off at Dr. Tattoff." I also wanted the tattoo on the back of my right shoulder. It was a small daisy that peeked out when I wore a sundress. I spent $180 to get it. Ten years later, I too regretted it and wanted it removed; $2,000 out of pocket and five painful laser sessions later, I realized that perhaps this was a risk that had not paid off.

Later that week, I did a little bit of research and found a skydiving facility just an hour's drive from my house. It cost $90 and included a five-hour training course. After I passed the course, I would be allowed to take the jump. An instructor would be there to guide me all along the way; the rush and excitement of the feeling afterward would be like no other buzz, or so they said.

My two best friends and one of my sisters came along for the ride, but they were smart enough to join me only as observers. We arrived and walked past the field of small aircraft and into the office, where photos of skydivers were displayed on the walls alongside certificates of safety and "accreditation." I checked in and was separated from my friends to start the training course.

After signing about a hundred waivers of liability, we watched a video, checked out the packs with the parachutes, and practiced rolling on impact. The idea was to hit the ground shoulder first. We geared up in a military-style army green jumpsuit and big plastic goggles. Then my six training mates—all of them young men—and I walked out to the plane. By then, I was starting to feel really nervous.

Off we went, with our packs firmly secured to our backs. As the plane began to climb, the instructor gave us the earpieces through which the coaches would tell us which way to steer our chutes. When we reached the altitude for the jump, he asked for a volunteer to go first. I couldn't stand the suspense any longer, and so I raised my hand.

The plane had no door, and so I could hardly hear what he was saying over the motor and the wind. He motioned me over to the hatchway and told me to reach out and grip the wing with both hands. I leaned over and took a firm grip. Then he told me to hold on tight and drop my legs outside the plane. This was news to me, as it was not what they had taught us in the course! But it was so loud that I didn't ask any questions; I just did what he said. Holding on with all the might in my 10 fingers, I looked up at him. With his funny goggles on and his cheeks vibrating with the force of the wind, he motioned and yelled for me to scoot hand over hand to the very tip of the wing. The goal was to get as far away as possible from the aircraft and its propellers at the time of release. There I was, hanging onto an airplane wing, thousands of feet in the air, with the wind gusting at my dangling body. I felt like James Bond, Ethan Hunt, and Jason Bourne wrapped up in one. This was certifiably insane! What was I doing?

"At the count of three," he yelled, "release both hands and lean backward." Oh, sweet effing Jesus, I thought. "One, two, three! *Release!*" I prayed my parachute would auto release as they had promised. And just a few seconds later, with a sudden jerk and flap in the wind, it did. I was cruising! Now all I had to do was pull on a string to my left or my right according to the directions of my instructor, whose voice was supposed to be emanating from my earpiece; however, all I could hear was static.

Uh-oh, I thought, as the static continued and the trees and houses below me grew larger. I'm going to have to do the landing myself.

I had no idea what I should be looking for, but almost before I knew it, there was a clump of big trees right in front of me and there was nowhere else to steer. I landed at full force and speed, smack dab in the middle of the trees, with my parachute stuck in the branches. My body missed a huge tree to my left by five inches and another to my right by even less. Wow, I thought as my suspended chute held me swaying between the two trunks. That was a close one.

My friends and sister, who were watching from afar, later told me, "We thought for sure you were dead!"

That was when I learned to assess risks, both negative and positive. As I waited for the rescue vehicle to come untangle me, I realized that the free fall buzz had not been worth risking my life for.

Maximize Opportunity, Open Doors

Life already is a risky business. Every day we explore new territories, every day we take risks, whether we realize it or not. The goal of life is to maximize opportunities and open doors, something that can't be done without taking some chances. For most of us taking risks means danger, as we are afraid of uncertainty; we don't hold a crystal ball with the answers and can't predict what today or tomorrow will bring.

Art enthusiast Mera Rubell told me that she approaches risk by realizing that each day is itself a miracle: "The risk is being alive. No winner wins all the time, and no loser loses all the time. I believe that you must keep your own scorecard—it's too dangerous to let others do the judging."[1]

Many of us derive vicarious pleasure from risk taking whether we're watching an action-packed *Mission Impossible* movie with Tom Cruise, viewing a contentious sporting match, or reading a thriller. We like the high intensity, the rush of energy and excitement, when we see someone else take terrible chances. But when it comes to ourselves, we are content to sit on the sidelines, afraid to risk our reputations, our money, our relationships, or physical injury. However, we have to realize that embracing uncertainty can open doors and be the way to an upgraded life.

Not long ago, I listened to a BBC story about artisanal food producers in Brooklyn. There was a chemist who built a soda business that sells gourmet beverages to high-end bars, a maker of exotic teas who financed his start-up with a small inheritance from his grandfather and promptly landed a contract with Whole Foods, and more. Many of them introduced their products in stalls at the Brooklyn Flea, a weekly market in downtown Brooklyn that features locally made craft beers and artisanal foods as well as antiques and vintage clothes. As these tiny companies gain traction, many of them have moved into an old Pfizer factory near the Brooklyn Navy Yard, a 660,000-square-foot space where thousands once worked.

One of those companies is People's Pops, which was founded by Joel Horowitz, Nathalie Jordi, and David Carrell with an initial investment of $1,000 each. They make gourmet frozen pops and shaved ices that are flavored with local, sustainably grown fruits and herbs. The syrups are cooked in small batches and infused with basil, lemongrass, mint, and a variety of other flavors; the sugar is organic. The exotic flavors include peach-habanero, watermelon-ginger, cantaloupe-jasmine, apple-lavender, raspberry rosewater, rhubarb-chai, and strawberry lemongrass with sauvignon blanc.

With 25 employees, People's Pops makes and sells some 10,000 pops a week through its four retail establishments, wholesale customers, and catering operation. As ambitious as its owners are, however, they have no plans to grow to such a size that their product ceases to be literally artisanal: prepared by individuals who are attentive to the individual qualities of the ingredients, who recognize that fruits are more or less sweet at different times in the growing season and know how to compensate by changing the amount of sugar or the cooking time.

All three of the partners worked other jobs while they were launching the company; none of them had a great deal of experience. They had a steep learning curve, one of the founders noted, and they learned some of their most valuable lessons by making mistakes. One of the partners chimed in at that point, saying, "Making mistakes has been the most important thing we've done."[2] You could put those words on a plaque and hang it on the wall of many successful businesses.

I have an old friend who took extravagant risks and experienced both success and failure along the way. After forging an international reputation for herself in the fashion and advertising worlds, she took a leap and produced and directed a documentary film that won major awards and got spectacular reviews. "I couldn't believe the film was an amazing success, and I was thrilled," she told me. But the glow didn't last long. After the 2008 financial meltdown, her business, like thousands of others, was suddenly teetering on the brink of bankruptcy.

"I was going full speed ahead, and it all came to a screeching halt. No more were there big budgets for fashion shoots, advertising shoots, or seed capital for new films. No more were there big travel budgets to jet set around," she recalled. "I was advised to declare bankruptcy. I had to fire all my employees and assistants. I had to take a loan out and sublease my office space or the business was going to die. I was on Craigslist every day looking for people and businesses to share my office space with and pick up some of the rent. I realized then at that time, if you are going to follow dreams, you have to surrender to change, part of the excitement is not knowing what is going to happen, but a true entrepreneur must remain strong enough to shift and change routes."

The same strength of will that enabled her to build her business kept my friend going during her sojourn; the same confidence and courage allowed her to confront her problems and learn from them. "What do you do when you have nothing? I shifted and downsized and become self-sufficient," she recalled. "That's a hard thing after 12 years; you have to answer the phone and do everything yourself; you go into survival mode. My personality was, what do I have to do to survive and focus? I learned some valuable lessons during this time. I learned that a company can't grow and be authentic if the visionary is out of the business. I had neglected the company for a year away on shooting the film. While I had a great team, I had to feed it with a vision and inspiration. I also learned of the trade-offs I made and was able to accept risk for those gains even in turbulent times."

As successful as she had been, as many doors as her name could open, in many ways she had to start over from scratch.

"I had to put my all my energy, focus, and spirit back in my business or it was going to fail," she told me. "I was f*cking scared shitless that I built this company, and I felt like I had no traditional skills to go work for someone. I still felt that I didn't fit the mold of a job. My friends thought I could easily get a job at an ad agency or that I should find a headhunter and look for a job. But even with all my travels and real-world experience in one of the biggest industries in the United States, I couldn't even think how to sell myself in a job interview and that there was no job I could do. I couldn't see it in a job. I couldn't imagine it."

"For me, a person who started a business and who became successful just by unleashing my inner passion and creativity, it didn't seem like that could translate to a job." But my friend did come back, and she is a much stronger person for it.

Assessing and accepting risk takes a lot of out you emotionally; it causes fear and confusion. Physically, it can lead to stress and fatigue. But it's part and parcel of upgrading your life: we have to calculate what's at stake and what's the potential reward and be careful to not overinflate it but at the same time not be so timid that we throw important opportunities away.

The Motown Lowdown

My sisters and I wrote an advice column for the *Detroit News* for 10 years in which we took readers' questions about love, life, and careers. It ran on the front page of the features section. It was internationally syndicated and was even picked up in broadcast format. My sisters and I became regular contributors to the local Fox News station, which at the time was one of the top 10 media markets in the United States.

How did we get this column? I met the editor of the paper at a fashion event at the Fox Theater. He asked me what I did, and I asked him what he did. When he told me he was the editor of the *Detroit News*, I quickly teased, "I want my own column." He said, "Oh, really. On what?" Just then my three sisters walked up, and I introduced them to him, quipping, "We want a column like *Sex in the City*. There are four of us, so we could bring four different outlooks on life."

My sisters and I are all close in age, but we all have very opposing viewpoints and personalities. One of us will say yes, one of us will say no way, the oldest says compromise, and the other sister says you should look deeper to find your answer. I had no idea what I was talking about, and my sisters—who at the time were a third grade teacher, a former corporate exec turned stay-at-home mom, and a speech pathologist—had no writing background and no advice experience, never mind any special knowledge of the ways of sex in our city. He smiled and asked for my card, and we went our separate ways.

The next Monday, I received an e-mail from the editor saying he'd love to meet me to talk more about my idea. I didn't think we could venture out in this new arena, and so I deleted the e-mail and tried to forget about the conversation. But he was determined and sent a few more e-mails, which I also ignored. Maybe I feared the unknown, or maybe I thought it was too much of a stretch. I shared the information with my sisters, and they too thought it was absurd. To publicly risk our reputations in a field we had no experience in was a huge risk.

Then, a week later, I was sitting at my desk in my office when the phone rang and the caller ID read "The Detroit News." I thought it was a reporter looking for help with a story, and so I picked up the phone. It was the editor's secretary. She told me that he was serious about the column and wanted to set up a lunch to talk about it. After I hung up the phone, I called my sisters. We finally agreed that I should at least explore what he had to say and report back.

The lunch went terrifically. He explained that newspapers were trying to attract younger readers and this column—four sisters with opposing viewpoints doling out advice—might be just the ticket. Readers would write in and ask us questions, and all four of us would give our takes. He asked us to work up two sample columns.

I was still very nervous but starting to get excited about this new opportunity. I convened my sisters. They were enthusiastic too but were much more worried than I was. "If Dad finds out we're doing a *sex* column," Ruba said, "he's going to go nuts!" Leena responded, "Well, let's just do it and see how it goes. Maybe he won't even notice."

"Are you kidding? He reads the paper *every* day!" Reham retorted. She was right. He was like clockwork. He returned home from work every day around 5 p.m. He sat down for dinner with the family, helped us with our homework, and then he kicked up his feet with the daily newspaper. How was he going to miss his four daughters' faces plastered on the front page of the Features section? As American as my sisters and I were, my Jordanian parents, though quite modern in their thinking, liked to hold onto some of our traditional cultural values. We decided to let them know only after the column was a go.

The two test columns went well, and we were offered the job. But then the newspaper decided to introduce its newest columnists with a major full-page splash feature. The best way for their readers to get to know us, they decided, was to interview us and photograph us in our parents' kitchen with our mother.

Uh oh. We were busted; we could not keep it a secret anymore. It was time to break the news to our parents.

We told our father it would be about work and life, conveniently leaving out relationships, which in his mind translated directly to sex and was thus out of the question. He thought it sounded interesting. Our profile ran on the front page of the section with a full-page spread, and we were off.

We received all sorts of questions, letters, and feedback. We were asked to host local events such as the International Auto Show, cultural celebrations, red carpet events, black tie affairs, food festivals, and fashion shows and were even paid appearance fees!

We published a compilation of our best columns in a book. The first big buy was from the airport retailer Paradies, which took a thousand copies. Soon afterward we became regulars on the Fox News affiliate with our own spot. Although we were still uncomfortable, we pushed ourselves outside our comfort zones and helped each other. We were having a lot of fun.

One day, *Inside Edition* called me. They'd heard of the "Four Sisters" and wanted to run a feature on us. They came to Detroit and spent two days following us around and interviewing each of us. Then I received a call from a producer at CBS's *The Early Show* who wanted to shoot the "Four Sisters" outside on the plaza in New York, taking questions from viewers. We were scheduled for the following weekend. They offered to pay for all of our travel in exchange for a first, which meant they wanted to be the first national show to feature us. We agreed and asked *Inside Edition* to hold its tape until the following week. When Jane Pauley found out about us, she wanted us on set.

We were thrilled. All of our risk taking, hard work, and efforts were finally going to be recognized. Though we had feared the worst, my father was very proud, my mom was excited, and my younger brothers were mortified. My brother said his boss and colleagues used a photo of the four of us as their screen saver just to torment him.

The next day, Hurricane Katrina hit. The devastation and shock shook the nation. Needless to say, all feature stories were put on hold indefinitely; it was all Katrina news all the time for months: the devastation, the human-interest stories, the relief efforts, the political fallout.

Months went by, and we never felt it was the right time to follow up. Also, we were quite busy with other things. All of us were still juggling full-time jobs and our families. I had just moved to Washington, D.C., and was building a new life; my sisters were having children and changing careers.

Two years later a new kind of sister sensation premiered when *Keeping Up with the Kardashians* hit the airwaves. The Los Angeles–based Armenian sisters had replaced the Detroit-based Jordanian sisters. I often tease my sisters that it took both a catastrophic hurricane and a sex tape to catapult the Armenian sisters to fame.

The column would have never happened if we hadn't just gone for it and pushed ourselves outside our comfort zones. We risked venturing into not one but two areas we had no experience in: column writing and advice giving. We risked our reputations, we risked our parents' approval, and we sacrificed our free time by picking up another two jobs with the newspaper and television. We risked (and experienced) disappointment, too, when we couldn't take our success all the way to national fame. But for all those risks, we not only had fun and learned a lot, but we had experiences that we would have never otherwise had.

It's surprising to me how few organizations encourage risk taking. We are taught to set goals, achieve measurable results, and assess success. But we are rarely encouraged to push the boundaries of new ideas and pioneering thoughts.

Most organizations do not foster a culture of risk and outside-the-box thinking. Risk is not something that is embraced at the workplace. People keep their heads down. They're afraid to take risks as it may lead to failure, and that's not rewarded. They want to keep their jobs.

That hurts them more than they know. When I asked Tim Brown about IDEO's culture, he said, "At IDEO we think our culture has been the single most important contributor to our success. Traditional creative organizations can be quite hierarchical, but this is a hard idea to scale, especially if you want to work on a diverse range of projects. We have tried to create an organizational culture where every individual is comfortable taking risks and exploring new ideas, but where they are also fixated on helping improve the quality of each other's ideas."[3]

Taking this idea one step further, Mario Batali says risk taking is essential. When I asked him what it takes to be a successful entrepreneur, he said, "It seems to be smart people who are not afraid to be creative and are not averse to independent thinking or risk."[4]

I caught up with my friend, the über–event planner David Stark. Stark advises us to break the rules. He has staged innovative and memorable events for a host of high-wattage celebrity clients such as Beyoncé Knowles and Martha Stewart, top corporations such as Target and Condé Nast, and high-visibility fund-raising galas for the nation's most prominent not-for-profit organizations, including the Whitney Museum of American Art and the Metropolitan Opera. Stark is a frequent guest on E! News, the *Today Show*, and *The View*. His work on décor, party planning, and gardening has been featured in the *New York Times, ELLE Décor, House Beautiful,*and many other publications.

Whether it is using reels of archived film to chicly replace traditional flower centerpieces for the Film Society gala in Lincoln Center, or making a 5-foot-long, 150-pound birthday cake in the shape of a yellow cab that doubles as a party sculpture and dessert, or using paint swatches from the hardware store for curtains, it's his creative genius combined with his risk-taking spirit that transforms even the most mundane spaces into an environment that dazzles and delights.

I caught up with Stark between events, and we talked about risk. "You have to remember," he said to me, "I am very lucky to work with clients whose world outlook is all about innovation and risk taking. This propels their events to the vanguard of experiential marketing."

Risk taking isn't the same thing as heedlessness as I learned early on the hard way. Successful businesspeople and creative artists aren't reckless; they don't spend their days jumping out of airplanes. They may be fearless, but they're focused at all times.

"The push of the artist to break new ground is so central to my core," Stark added, "that I don't see it as risk-taking at all. It's just what I do. On the other hand, the business side of the company is solid and run as a sound corporation would be run. That is often unusual for a creative business. But that foundation and structure, married to the creative process (which is all about risk), is what makes us successful, I believe."[5]

The same goes for life. Moving to a new city, falling in love, buying a house, starting a new job, launching a business, having a child—all of them are built on unknowns. But if their potential return is more than a half-day buzz, go for it. The worse that can happen is failure, and we're all bound to fail sometimes.

CHAPTER 7

FAIL TO SUCCEED

Fail early, fail often!
—Peter Diamandis

Failure Paralysis

Why aren't you living the life you want to live? What's holding you back from your upgrade? For most people, it is simple fear of failure, which paralyzes them, preventing them from unleashing their full potential and moving forward.

We are brought up as children to get good grades, get on the right team, and score the winning goal. If we fail the class, we won't get into a good school; if we don't get into a good school, we won't get a good job; and if we don't get a good job, we'll be living at home with our mom and dad for the rest of our lives or living on the streets, and everyone will know we're a failure. There is nothing great about failing a class or losing the statewide football championship. We set up children from a very early age to believe that only success is rewarded, especially when it comes to school. This, however, is very unlike the way we learn.

Ken Robinson observes that you can't learn or create anything new unless you first open yourself up to the possibility of being wrong. We learn through trial and error, by making mistakes and analyzing them. That is how scholarship works, as well as science: you put your idea out there, you test it, and you make your data available to other people so that they can test it too. You have to have thick skin; being challenged and criticized is an integral part of the game.

Sara Blakely is the outrageously successful entrepreneur who founded the undergarment company Spanx. She is the world's youngest self-made female billionaire and has been included in the Time 100, *Time* magazine's annual list of the 100 most influential people in the world. In his profile of her in *The Startup Playbook*, David Kidder relates that "when she was a little girl, her father would ask her, 'What did you fail at today?' He made it clear that failure was an indication that you tried something. It was a good thing. That's a profound idea, and it speaks against many of the assumptions of our success-based culture."

We need to rethink how we approach failure. "If you celebrate a child's gift rather than her effort, you do her a disservice," Kidder continues. "In exactly the same way, it does no good to celebrate an entrepreneur's idea. The important thing is being able to execute on it."[1]

Don Tapscott says, "I fail at something every day and it is true that one learns more from failures. Besides, how boring it would be if all that happened was success? We are trained not to take chances, not to fail and to play it safe. When was the last time you were rewarded in a performance review for failing to reach your goals?"[2]

On the BBC radio show about the artisanal food makers in Brooklyn that I wrote about in Chapter 6, the reporter, Peter Day, quoted a saying that's well known in Silicon Valley: "Failure is something everyone has to have on their CV."[3] This powerful statement is a testament to the innovative thinking of the region.

Pony Up! Place More Bets

I am always surprised when entrepreneurs tell me that they've staked everything on one big idea.

"Just one proposal?" I ask.

"Yes, but it's a big one," they respond.

Yeah, good luck with that, I think. My rule is to never let an opportunity pass you by. Early in your career, try lots of things. Most of them are bound to fail, and so you might as well cast your net as widely as you can.

Peter Sims, the entrepreneur and bestselling author of *Little Bets: How Breakthrough Ideas Emerge from Small Discoveries*, advises us to place lots of small bets. It's just a numbers game, after all; in the end one of them is bound to succeed.

Recently, I was stuck on a 14-hour flight to Shanghai. Unable to sleep, I flipped through the media channels to try to find a lighthearted movie. My five- and seven-year-old nieces are big Katy Perry fans, and so I decided to watch *Part of Me,* a Brian Grazer documentary that chronicles her rise from teenage gospel prodigy to modern-day pop icon. I was glad I did.

The movie is a tribute to Perry's ability to rebound and learn from failure. I learned that when Perry finally landed a major deal with Columbia Records, she couldn't have been more excited. But though she worked and worked with them, she couldn't get it right. She said they wanted her to be more like Ashley Simpson and Avril Lavigne than herself; when they heard what she'd been recording, they complained: "That's not the right way. That's not what people want to hear." Finally, after giving it her all, a frustrated and deflated Perry made the difficult decision to leave Columbia Records. Everyone thought she was insane to leave a major record label, but she did.

Then Perry persuaded Capitol Records to take a chance on her music after her failure at Columbia. When she released her first hit single with Capitol, "I Kissed a Girl," the song hit number one on the charts and stayed there for seven weeks. And that was just the beginning. "I'm just kind of like holding on to the rocket for dear life, hoping that I don't get bucked off," she told Barbra Walters.[4]

Most people see sports stars or singers and actors rise to fame and fortune and don't realize how much time and effort they invested before finally making it. It took Perry years of singing to small crowds in churches and bars before she got a record label to sign her. Then it took another five years to get a record out. When she finally did, it had five hit singles on it, outpacing Madonna and John Lennon and earning her a Michael Jackson–like level of superstardom. But there were lots of closed doors, naysayers, and rejections along the way.

Success in life often comes after failure, after being turned down but not giving up. Mark Cuban has started several businesses and invests in start-ups in his role on ABC's *Shark Tank*. Cuban's advice to me was, "You need to be brutally honest with yourself. You can't be a dreamer. You have to be able to focus on doing the work to prepare and execute on your ideas rather than dreaming about what might happen. And you can't be afraid of failing. It's amazing to me that some people who have no problem jumping out of an airplane cower at the idea of starting a business because they might fail."[5]

I often have several projects and proposals out at once, knowing that the majority won't work out because of budget constraints, timing, or other business issues. I go down every avenue that presents itself and knock on every door. The worst that can happen, I think, is that I'll fail or be rejected, and in that case I'll just start over again.

Rethink Failure

Most of us need to reset our definition of failure. Too many of us view it as something we haven't been able to accomplish, a goal not met; worse, we view it as a disaster, a catastrophe, or a fiasco, a shameful black mark that we can never erase. Singer Nelly Furtado told me, "Failure is very important, as it is inevitable in life. Incredible growth, self-realization and reflection come from failure."[6] We need to create a new definition of failure.

Graffiti artist Kenny Scharf made a splash in the New York art scene in the 1980s with his roommate and collaborator Keith Haring; he has been a figure to contend with ever since. He has received commissions from the likes of Mercedes-Benz, Absolut, Kiehl's, Mattel's Barbie, and the Brooklyn Children's Hospital and has even been featured on *The Simpsons*. After having dinner with this ultrasuccessful pop culture icon, I asked him to share his thoughts about failure. He has an interesting take on it: he says it doesn't exist.

"There's no such thing as failure," he told me. "It's all part of the learning process."[7] I agree wholeheartedly with this notion. We need to retrain ourselves to view failure as an educational and growth experience, not a catastrophic event.

It's not just creative people or artists who believe this. The Partnership for 21st Century Skills is a consortium of business, education, and policy leaders focused on K–12 education; its founders include the U.S. Department of Education, AOL Time Warner Foundation, Apple Computer, Cisco Systems, Dell Computer Corporation, and Microsoft Corporation. They've helped shaped curricula online and in the classroom and equipped students with skills and training to prepare them for the twenty-first-century workforce. Their view on failure is as follows: "View failure as an opportunity to learn; understand that creativity and innovation is a long-term, cyclical process of small successes and frequent mistakes."

Robinson advises us to just get over it. He says, "I once asked a scientist who'd won the Nobel Prize for chemistry how many of his experiments failed. He said most of them. But failure, he said, isn't really the right word. Science is about finding out what doesn't work in the expectation of discovering what does. Trial and error is at the heart of all creative processes. If we want to promote creativity and innovation we have to honor and accept mistakes, false starts and dead ends. As Sir Winston Churchill once said, 'Success is the ability to go from one failure to another with no loss of enthusiasm.' Booker T. Washington put it this way: 'I have learnt that success is to be measured in life not so much by the position one has reached as by the obstacles one has overcome while trying to succeed.' So it should be."[8]

Far too many of us waste too much effort and emotional energy dwelling on past failures instead of pushing forward. Our internal monologues can hold us back. People make excuses, saying they don't have enough time, money, or connections. A harder truth is that they may be as afraid of success as they are of failure. Andre Agassi told me, "Failure is lonely, success is lonelier."

But then he went on to say, "Don't think about it. Don't dwell on it. Don't treat it as anything more than a blip, which is the same way you should treat early failure. Success and failure are so often the result of outside factors, things beyond our control, so you need to keep your mind on the few things you can control. Learn to love the process, the work, and disconnect your ego from the results. The earlier you learn this, the more peaceful you'll be, and peace, not success, is the goal."

"How do I handle failure?" he concluded. "Same way I tackle success. By treating it as the illusion it is."[9]

Fail Fast

Learn the art of failing fast. Most successful people rebound quickly and incorporate everything they learned from being knocked down. Mario Batali is one of those people. He has several successful restaurants, a kitchen product line, a chain of stores, and a syndicated show on ABC, *The Chew*. He says, "Even at 51 years old, I do not look back and regret anything I have tried. I regret only the things I have not."[10]

I walked away from high school with no idea about what I wanted to do. I took my first job when I was 15 as a hostess in a café in a high-end mall near my house. Some of my sisters worked there too. It didn't take me long to realize that the wait staff made a heck of a lot more money than the hostesses. A year into the job, I asked to be promoted to waitress. Legally I was not allowed; the restaurant served wine, and you had to be 18 to pour. But I was a hard worker and mature for my age, and the owner liked my sisters, and so he allowed me to straddle a role between hostessing and waitressing.

The café was flanked by a Neiman Marcus and a Saks Fifth Avenue. When I learned from the patrons that Saks employees were given a 30 percent discount on clothes, I made my move and took a sales job in the men's department. I had to work a full week before I could afford one garment, but the discount kept me motivated to work more, to pitch in for overtime and work the fashion shows on the weekends for an even bigger paycheck that I foolishly used to buy more clothes.

Between that first job as a hostess and my position as CEO of the Creative Class Group, I held 13 other career positions. I was a barista in a coffee shop and a volunteer in a hospital. I did ad sales at a classical radio station and worked in public relations and marketing for a cultural lifestyle magazine. As I've mentioned, my sisters and I had an advice column. From airports and live entertainment productions, I dived into several different industries to figure out what I wanted to do. But along the way, there were a lot of things I applied for and didn't get. I *really* wanted a job at MTV in New York and wanted to attend business school at the Sorbonne in Paris. When I received the two rejection letters, my dreams were shattered. But not for long.

As someone wise once said, "What do you do when your dreams don't come true? Find a new dream."

I've taken that advice to heart ever since. When one door closed, I saw it as an opportunity to knock on another.

Creative thinker Mera Rubell told me, "Examining failure objectively can lead to many worthwhile lessons. I believe that success can only be achieved when we recognize failure as a spark for change—only then can we hope to realize our life's ambitions."[11]

Persistence Pays

Carter Kustera is a New York–based artist whose paintings and draw-ings have been featured in books and galleries around the world; he has been included in the Venice Biennale more than once. He told me a long story about his ultimately successful foray into the world of big business that I want to share with you. It hits every note I've just been sounding, and, better yet, it has a happy ending.

"Failure and persistence," he began, "are mainstays for anyone who wants to achieve something in particular in life. This is not limited to creative people, only creative people often attempt many more things that have never been done before and so they meet more obstacles, backlash and resistance. I have had many of these mo-ments in my life and career but as I and many others have learned, the longer you stick with something, the greater chance you have of succeeding."

At a critical point in his career, when it seemed like the gallery world was cooling to his work, he decided to change directions. "I came up with a very simple product idea. I ended up creating a self-empowering little product called the 'I Love Me' mirror." So when you looked into the mirror, the phrase gave lookers a warm, happy feeling.

At first he sandblasted that phrase on a mirror as a joke, but after a friend saw it, she asked if she could give it to a friend who was going through a hard time as a gift. "Right then I knew I had something," he continues, "but how could I ever make something like this on a large scale and get it out into the world?

"First I enlisted the help of a lawyer to begin a lengthy process of trademarking the phrase 'I Love Me.' That in itself was an act of persistence; many filings were made to secure the trademark. Then the next thing was to shop a prototype around, to find a manufacturer and/or a retail outlet. I had no idea what I was doing. I only knew that I had what I thought was a good idea. As the Internet wasn't what it is now, I would look through the phone book for manufacturers. I would cold call or send letters, asking to take meetings to discuss my product. Many companies never contacted me back, and all the ones that did grant me a meeting were baffled by my concept.

"Most meetings would be in an office with an older man who was never really listening to me. They would hold up my mirror and say, 'I don't get it.'"

Even when that didn't work, he still fought on. "From the time I thought of the idea to the time I finally got my break was 5 years and 50 meetings later," he told me. His break came when Bed Bath & Beyond liked his product. "I ended up producing a successful line of home decor and refrigerator magnet mirrors as well as other products. What I learned was that if you want something bad enough you will find a way to make it happen."

Getting rejected over and over again somehow gives some people the fuel to work harder. Tim Ferris, author of *The 4-Hour Workweek,* said his manuscript was turned down by 26 out of 27 publishers.[12] The book has now been translated into 35 languages and made the *New York Times, Wall Street Journal,* and *BusinessWeek* bestseller lists. He's been featured in countless media interviews and is a popular guest lecturer on entrepreneurship at Princeton University. His publisher recently reissued his book in a revised edition.

Kustera's product earns him hundreds of thousands of dollars in royalties now, but it took countless attempts to get there. Failure is sometimes the beginning, not the end, of the road.

Yet still, many of us won't dive into something new for fear of failure. A good friend of mine is a second-grade teacher; she's had the same job for 15 years. She's terrific at what she does, and the kids love her. She likes her schedule and enjoys her vacations and summers off. For the last four years, however, she has expressed interest in moving on and doing something else. I encouraged her to apply for jobs in the for-profit educational industry, such as one I showed her after quickly searching an online job board. It was a position as senior consulting executive for Kaplan, the education company. She looked at me like I was crazy. "How could I ever do that?" she said. "I don't have any business experience!"

"Sure 'business experience' may help," I counseled her. "But you have years of on the ground education experience. Why not just apply and see what happens?"

I urged her to submit her résumé to that job and to 20 or so similar ones, but she never did. I often wonder why.

Why was I fearless in applying for multiple jobs, none of which I had industry experience for, while my best friend refuses to try new things? I am not smarter than she is; I am not better educated. In fact, she got better grades in high school and college. I used to copy her answers in the high school French class we took together. Why, then, did I push forward while she hung back?

What is the worst that can happen when you apply for a job online? Either you don't hear back or you get mailed a rejection letter. Well, I've had plenty of those. I place my money on a lot of different bets, always hoping that one will come through.

Although several inspirational leaders agreed to be interviewed for my *Huffington Post* column and this book, there were several others who ignored or rejected my offers. Some of them include President Barack Obama, First Lady Michelle Obama, President Bill Clinton, former Secretary of State Hillary Clinton, and basketball star LeBron James. There were the musicians Bono, Jack White, and Dave Grohl; the fashion designers Miuccia Prada and Rodarte; the comedian Larry David; the actors Meryl Streep and George Clooney; the filmmaker Wes Anderson; the news journalist Anderson Cooper; and *Vogue* publisher Anna Wintour. Although some people might view this as a failure, I recall being excited by the sheer effort of trying.

From: FN-WHO-FirstLadyPress

Date: Friday, February 1, 2013 4:38 PM

To: Rana <rana@creativeclass.com>

Subject: RE: Feature Profile of the First Lady on Women in Leadership in the Huffington Post

Dear Rana,

Thank you for your patience as we reviewed your request. Unfortunately, the First Lady's schedule is extremely tight and we are unable to accommodate your request.

Thank you for this gracious offer to include the First Lady in your plans and, also, thank you for understanding.

Sincerely,

Press Office of the First Lady

I remember when my colleague asked me frantically why his cell phone was ringing with the caller ID "U.S. State Department, Secretary Clinton."

We had worked with the U.S. State Department a few years earlier but not with Secretary Clinton's office. "I don't know! Just answer it fast!" I said.

He did. "Yes, this is Steven. Yes, I work with Rana."

He paused to listen, "Sure thing. I will let her know. And thank you for calling."

"What? What did they say?" I said.

"They were calling to thank you for offering to feature Secretary Clinton in your column but said that she was too busy at this time to participate," he explained.

We were both cracking up. "How did she get my cell number? That's so cool that she called at least," Steven said.

I said, "They're the U.S. State Department; I'm sure they have their ways. And yes, that's very cool!"

Remember my other friend, the one who called me for advice when she was wondering if she should consider applying for a job with a higher salary but a less flexible schedule than the one she had? She was in decision-making mode before there was a decision for her to make. There was no offer on the table; she hadn't even had a job interview. She just saw a listing for a position that she might or might not have been interested in, and already she was thinking herself into a state of paralysis. First, apply for the job, I urged her. If they want you, you can always negotiate for more flexibility. Too many of us talk ourselves out of potential opportunities when it's really the fear of failure that holds us back.

Bulldoze Through It

- Understand what your underlying fear is. Will you be judged? Humiliated publicly? Are you afraid of next steps? Do you risk financial security? Afraid of success? Determining the fear is the first step to removing the obstacles.
- Try visioning exercises in which you envision what failure is and what success looks like and then determine the end result.
- Assess the damage of the end result. You didn't get the job. You didn't get into the school of your choice. The girl or guy you like rejected you. You were demoted at work for reckless risk taking. Was it really that bad? Did you learn something new or grow from the experience?
- Assess the value of success against its dangers. You landed the job and a raise. You were admitted into the top school, and now you have to deliver. Tossing the outcome around in your mind will help you overcome the obstacle.
- Now dive right in and go for it!

If you or anyone you know has opened a restaurant, you know how much time and resources and investment it entails. According to statistics from the Small Business Administration, about a third of small businesses fail within year 1 and close to half fail by year 5. It is a highly risky proposition. And restaurants, with a failure rate between 60 and 80 percent in the first three years, represent even bigger risks.

My husband and I worked with Jean-Georges Vongerichten, one of the world's most innovative chefs, in our roles as cultural curators for Starwood's global hotel brand, Le Méridien. His 30-plus restaurants in far-flung locations such as Bora Bora, Paris, Doha, Mexico City, Vancouver, and Shanghai have earned him a galaxy of Michelin stars and other accolades; he is the James Beard Award–winning author of a number of bestselling cookbooks and a familiar face on television.

But Vongerichten's amazing talents in the kitchen are aligned with a genius for business—and not just for the big picture but for the nitty-gritty details that turn high concepts into profitable undertakings. He oversees every aspect of his restaurants and product lines, from concept to menu development, from the architectural design of the spaces to the hiring and training of his team.

I put a question to him: "Opening a new restaurant takes a big investment; how do you approach risk?" His answer made him sound like the poster boy for the Nike ad campaigns. "When it comes to a new restaurant or venture I am fearless," he said. "I just do it."[13]

My good friend Frank Toskan, the cofounder of MAC Cosmetics, has a different take on failure. He opened some 300 MAC stores worldwide in just 15 years and was recently honored by the International AIDS Conference for the $250 million MAC has raised to date for AIDS research. MAC took several risks in its branding campaigns. It set the bar high for its humanitarian and cause-related work, standing up for animal rights, encouraging recycling, helping children, and more. It featured gay, lesbian, and drag queen celebrities (such as Elton John, k.d. lang, and RuPaul) as brand ambassadors in the 1980s, when few companies did so.

I was keenly interested in interviewing my friend to learn more about one of the world's most recognizable cosmetic brands—one that has done so much to show how risk taking and pioneering new ways can also be good for business. After much cajoling, he agreed to sit down for his first in-person interview in more than 15 years.

As fascinating as the story of his fearlessness and MAC's meteoric rise might have been, what moved me the most were his thoughts on failure. "It was never an option for me," he said. "I never gave it any thought." Even though everyone around him was worried about it, he faced it head on. "My accountant was constantly urging me to sell the company because he thought we were always on the verge of bankruptcy," he recalled. "But my parents mortgaged their house for me. I *had* to make it work; there was no way I was going to fail and leave them homeless."[14]

Although successful entrepreneurs and leaders have to have the resilience to tackle failure, they also can't be afraid to quit midstream and change course.

Know When to Walk Away

Many of us are programmed to finish what we start, whether it is a class, a sports team, a hobby, or college. College, we are constantly told, is a sure ticket to wealth and success. But Steve Jobs set off a firestorm when he said that dropping out of Reed College was the best thing he ever did.

In a *New York Times* article, Alex Williams charted a new trend: "The idea that a college diploma is an all-but-mandatory ticket to a successful career is showing fissures. Feeling squeezed by a sagging job market and mounting student debt, a groundswell of university-age heretics are pledging allegiance to new groups like UnCollege, dedicated to 'hacking' higher education. Inspired by billionaire role models, and empowered by online college courses, they consider themselves a D.I.Y. vanguard, committed to changing the perception of dropping out from a personal failure to a sensible option, at least for a certain breed of risk-embracing maverick."

Look at Facebook founder Mark Zuckerberg, who dropped out of college in 2010. Williams writes of UnCollege's members, "None were sheepish about their lack of a diploma. Rather, they were proud of their real-life lessons on the job."

The founders of Twitter, Apple, and Tumblr also dropped out of college, as did Bill Gates and Michael Dell. Of course many of them were already well on the way to their first billions by the time they left school; they weren't exactly slackers.

Williams writes that, "Ambitious young people who consider dropping out of college a smart option have a different set of role models from those in the 1960s, who were basically stuck with the acid-guru Timothy Leary and his 'turn on, tune in, drop out' ramblings. Nowadays, popular culture is portraying dropouts as self-made zillionaires whose decision to spurn the 'safe' route (academic conformity) is akin to lighting out for the territories to strike gold."[15]

FIND YOUR NIRVANA

Dave Grohl, one of my favorite musicians, gave the keynote address this year at the South by Southwest Music Festival in Austin. I had every Nirvana album, starting from one of their first releases, Bleach, released in 1989 through Sub Pop. My friends and I saw them play at St. Andrews Hall, a tiny theater in Detroit when hardly anyone else had heard of them. Grohl told the SXSW audience that his life had been forever changed when he saw the legendary Dead Kennedys perform at the Rock Against Reagan event at the Lincoln Memorial in Washington, D.C., on Independence Day. He describes the experience:

"Helicopters buzzed overhead, shining spotlights into the crowd as policeman on horses beat their way through the punks with their billy clubs. It was right out of *Apocalypse Now*. This was my Woodstock. This was my Altamont. This was rock and roll, no matter what T-shirt you wore or what haircut you had. This was f*cking *real*. I burned inside. I was possessed and empowered and inspired and enraged and so in love with life and so in love with music that it had the power to incite a fucking riot, or an emotion, or to start a revolution, or just to save a young boy's life."

So what did he do? He dropped out of high school and hit the road. He describes the experience. "I starved. My hands bled. If I slept, I slept on floors. I slept on stages. I slept on the fucking floors under the fucking stages. And I loved every minute of it. Because I was free. And I wanted to incite a riot, or an emotion, or a revolution, or to save someone's life by inspiring them to pick up an instrument just like I did as a kid. I wanted to be someone's Edgar Winter. I wanted to be someone's Naked Raygun. I wanted to be someone's Bad Brains or Beatles. Because *that* was the reward, *that* was the intention. We played *that* type of music, so we were left alone. There was no career opportunity. There was no hall of fame. There were no trophies. There was no A&R credit card–buying Benihana dinners. Our reward was knowing that we had done all of this all on our own, and that it was real."

Trusting your gut and your instinct to walk away for a bigger calling even when the societal peer pressure to stay the course or being broke and desolate is overwhelming is a difficult decision and sometimes feels like failure, but it can lead to greater rewards.

"But . . . inevitably it wasn't long before I found myself stranded in Hollywood without a cent to my name and no way home, crashed out in a Laurel Canyon bungalow with a bunch of female mud wrestlers. And, that's when I heard the 5 words that changed my life forever:

"Have you heard of Nirvana?"[16]

Grohl's passion and energy are what ultimately led him to find his path. But what if you don't have such a burning desire, or if it's no longer leading you in the right direction? How do you know when it's time to walk away? The singer Nelly Furtado told me, "If the momentum is lost, the chemistry soured, or the relationship broken beyond repair, I usually walk away. If you are not having fun anymore, it's simply not worth it."[17]

I have a hard time walking away from a project I've invested time, money, and resources in, not because of pride or shame, but because I like to see the end results of my work; I have an almost irresistible desire to see any project through from beginning to end. But when a relationship is so soured that you are turning into a person you wouldn't want to spend time with, that's when you know you have to walk away.

Life would be painfully boring if it were too easy. Most risk takers like to try new things just for the growth experience and are not afraid to cut their losses in something even after having invested hundreds of thousands of dollars, as witnessed by statements like these:

Chef and restaurateur, Jean-Georges Vongerichten: "After 40 years of being in the industry, I can really feel and sense when it is time to walk away."[18]

Designer Tomas Maier: "Learning to walk away from something that isn't working is one of the hardest things to do. I'm a perfectionist and I will shut down a project when I realize the result won't meet my standards. I can't tell you when I know this, though—of course, it always feels like it's too late. At that point, I just move on. Maybe I'll come to the idea another time, maybe not. But I don't dwell on it."[19]

Whether your reputation is at stake or your standards aren't being met, these are difficult decisions to make. But architect Peter Marino puts it more bluntly. When I asked him when it's time to walk away from a project, he told me: "When either the client is totally unreceptive to my ideas, or he/she stops paying!"[20]

How to Avoid Failure

Now that we've established the case for rethinking failure to upgrade your life, there are some key things you can do to ensure success. Businesses, managers, and people who rest on their laurels and never change, never adapt, and never adjust their path are doomed. You don't have to be.

We all love Twinkies; we grew up eating them, taking them in our lunch bags to school, and once in a while splurging on them as adults. But now they've become an American tradition from a bygone era. The CEO of the Hostess brand, Gregory Rayburn, was interviewed in *Bloomberg Businessweek*. He said, "I made the decision to liquidate Hostess last night. . . . A number of factors have contributed to this. Hostess is 93 percent unionized, and it's been formed by a number of acquisitions over the decades; a lot of old rules were grandfathered into contracts from companies that no longer exist."[21]

"There were all these crazy work rules," he said of the Teamsters. "Like one driver can only drive cake and the other can only drive bread."

The company was locked into an antiquated way of doing things that made it impossible for it to change course to remain profitable, dooming it to obsolescence.

This story about Twinkies, a childhood favorite, is a great example of the lessons I've tried to highlight in this book. If you are not constantly growing, learning, and adapting, whether in business or in personal development, you too will become obsolete. Just as new scientific findings and medical breakthroughs take a big investment in time with constant tweaking, learning, and discovery, a path to a better life doesn't come easily. Success does not happen overnight, and change is often scary and tumultuous. But if you stop and dedicate some time to thinking about these simple strategies and act on them, you could be living a better, more fulfilled, and more purposeful life.

CHAPTER 8

YOUR TIME TO UPGRADE IS NOW

The best way to predict the future is to create it.
—Peter Drucker

When my husband and I moved from Washington, D.C., to Toronto, we had a party and invited our oldest and dearest friends to meet our new friends. After a long evening of drinking, a high school friend sat down and told me she'd had an amazing time. She had met one of my friends, who, she said, "was the better version of me!"

"What do you mean by that?" I asked.

"She is me exactly, but she has a better life! She has the life I always dreamed of. We are both married to similar guys, and she has three kids, who are all about the same age as my kids. But she is doing all these cool things with them and traveling and learning foreign languages and taking tennis lessons, going snorkeling, and oh, she even hired a chef to give her and her girlfriends cooking lessons one night a week."

She went on: "We're the same age, but she's in great shape, she loves her job, her husband is also into fitness. She and her family are spending the summer in Nantucket, and they did a house swap so they could live in Provence for a year!"

I was surprised to hear her comments. "Well, you're in the same bracket financially, and you both have similar careers. Why don't you do those things?" I asked.

"I don't know, but I just saw her and was listening to her in awe, thinking that's how I envision my life! She is me, only better!"

I tried to reason with her, saying that for her it wasn't about the resources or the time. Both women were in the same socioeconomic class. It's about envisioning the life you want to live and making it happen. But within just a few minutes, she rattled off a bunch of reasons—excuses, really—why she couldn't do any of these things. "We're just so busy, and with school and the sports and the therapy and the house, and now I have to help my mom with her back pain. . . . I know, I know, I'm going to do it one day," she responded as she settled into her last glass of wine for the evening.

We are still great friends, but nothing has changed. My good friend lets the minutiae of life set the pace. Her upgraded life will stay on hold as long as she keeps making excuses.

Most of us were somehow brainwashed into thinking that life had to be work and that if we weren't working, we were goofing off. Yes, we all need to make money to support our families, but there are choices and trade-offs that we can make in our everyday lives: bigger homes and bigger cars and more stuff to fill them with or more adventures and better experiences. We can spend time doing things we don't have to do out of sheer obligation and guilt or indulge in things that make us happy.

Whether we are fathers, mothers, managers, leaders, employees, or entrepreneurs, we can choose how we want to approach the world. We can accept the status quo and encumber ourselves with the old rules that were thrust upon us, or we can take chances and risks to think differently and creatively to introduce new and better ways of doing things.

My sister-in-law Christina took the latter approach recently and is quite happy with her decision. She is a 33-year-old assistant principal of a middle school and seven months pregnant. When I asked her how she was feeling, she said, "Good, no morning sickness, but it's really difficult for me to sit at my desk for hours a day. I get very uncomfortable and toward the end of the day, my back aches a lot." I told her about the exercise ball as a chair trend. Christina responded, "That's interesting, but I'd be worried that if a teacher, a parent, or even a student walked in, they'd think I was goofing off."

I was surprised by her answer. "Why do you say that?" I asked. "You're the school administrator and a leader. Shouldn't you be pioneering better and healthier ways of working?"

"They would think it's unprofessional," she responded.

I couldn't get her words out of my head. It finally sunk in; I finally understood what she was up against. Our old systems have burdened us with an environment that does not encourage risk taking; it's primed us to view even changes for the better as "unprofessional." We need to work collectively to change that.

I followed up our talk with an e-mail. "Hey, Baby Fiz," I wrote. (Our family often teases her and me for being the big party fizzlers, the first to sneak off to bed, hence the nickname.) "I still think you should try the exercise ball, and here are all the reasons why." I listed the statistics about its health benefits, urging her just to take a chance and break out of the old mold. "As a young leader of the school, it's your obligation to pioneer new and better ways of working," I concluded. I checked in with her a few weeks later, and guess what? She's adopted the exercise ball approach! I was thrilled, not only for her health and well-being, but for her having the courage to take a stand.

I hadn't understood that it was peoples' judgments that she feared, not breaking out of the mold itself. Yes, she has to explain herself when parents and her colleagues pop into her office, but she doesn't regret her decision. She shares the information with them and talks about the health benefits. She approaches it as a way to inform and educate others. If we approach our lives and work with a fresh perspective on how to continually improve, it can be more fulfilling and rewarding.

Whether it is the simple act of introducing a new, odd-looking office chair in a staid environment, Hard Candy pushing the boundaries of traditional fashion by introducing a nail polish with crazy colors and wacky names, Mayor Bloomberg taking a stand for pedestrians by closing streets to cars and banning smoking, or Zappos' CEO Tony Hsieh's belief that happiness can be delivered outside the norms of corporate culture, any of us can break the old rules and structures that have been imposed on us.

It's time to take back our freedom, to be ourselves, and to follow our dreams and passions, whether it's at school, at the office, or in our homes. I've had to throw out everything I learned in business school, and you should too. The collaborative approach to leadership is much more effective than any top-down, finger-wagging boss could ever hope to be. Workforces are much more productive when every individual approaches his or her work as a growth and learning experience.

We all need to think strategically about time. Time is something we can never get back but that most of us keep giving away. By simply knocking out the time wasters in your work and life and spending more of your time on the things you are passionate about, that you enjoy and grow from, you can immeasurably upgrade your life.

Whether you realize it or not, the majority of us are still riding through life in coach class, in a state of managed dissatisfaction, scared to take risks and afraid of failing. As we are forced to walk through the first-class cabin, our gazes linger on the privileged few in their oversized seats with all that extra legroom. While we are making our tortuous way down the crowded aisle, hoping that there's still room in the overheads for our luggage, the first-class passengers are sipping champagne and snacking on warm nuts while flipping through magazines; perhaps they're booting up their laptops or having a last tap on their smartphones.

Must be nice, you think as you squeeze into your cramped middle seat near the toilets. Well, why shouldn't that be you? You don't have enough money? The truth is, we all have enough resources at our disposal to upgrade our lives. Small changes such as consolidating your credit card points can get you a first-class seat. Small changes in work and in life can lift you from a state of managed dissatisfaction to an enjoyable ride and greater happiness and fulfillment. Why should upgrades be reserved for a privileged few?

Most of us think it's wise to save our points for a major trip sometime in the future. Wrong! Your time is now. Before you know it, some major changes will happen—the company will declare bankruptcy or merge, and your points will vanish—the same way your life will pass you by while you wait for the right time or for more resources. Our time is finite; be sure you're living your upgraded life today, not tomorrow!

We've heard from a wide array of people, from a graffiti artist and rocket scientist to a Grammy Award-winning musician, star athlete, famous fashion designer, tech billionaire, celebrity chef, leading politician, world renowned architect, television host, eminent neurologist, and global CEOs. What could they possibly have in common? Seven key ingredients for an upgraded life. Their lessons are simple, but they can help propel you to live your life to its fullest potential. Small changes add up; together, they can create a major overhaul in your life.

When I polled my friends and colleagues about how their lives would be different if they had millions of dollars, some important facts were revealed. It's not about having more time and money; it's about using what you already have at your disposal, organizing your resources to make them work for the life you want to lead.

With just a few simple tweaks, we can all improve our lives and make each day more enjoyable.

If you've been taking notes along the way, terrific. If you haven't, here are the most important takeaways. Feel free to use this list as your personal and professional guide and share it with your friends, family, and colleagues. Check it often to upgrade your life.

Envision your future
- Your life doesn't have to suck; stop settling for a state of managed dissatisfaction.
- Envision the type of life you'd like to lead and write it down.
- Stop making lame excuses; knock out the obstacles that are keeping you from your upgraded life.
- Getting your physical environment right is the foundation for everything.

What's your passion?
- If you can't find your passion, get on board with someone else's.
- If you don't have a passion, that's okay--just focus your time on the things that make you happy.
- Buy experiences, not things.

Get creative
- Be different; think creatively.
- Creativity thrives in a YES environment.
- Embrace diversity as a key driver of creativity.
- Constant change and innovation are the keys to success.
- Build recess time into your daily life; we all need a playground to recharge our thinking.

Design your time
- There are only three things to do with your time: have fun, be productive, and give back. Fill up those three buckets!
- Ditch the *no* people in your life; more fun awaits you on the side of *yes!*
- Your time is your most important possession; guard it fiercely.

- Get control over your own schedule now.
- Identify the time wasters in your life and get rid of them.

The power of we
- Seriously, you cannot do it all; collaborate with others.
- Stop being a dictator; lead by serving.
- If we stop learning, we stop growing, and no one likes boring people.
- Surround yourself with smart people and listen to them.
- Don't be an information hoarder. If you have information, it's your obligation to share it.
- There all sorts of collaborative models: personal, professional, and technological; find what works for you.

Big risks = big rewards
- Growth, learning, and discovery happen when you leave your comfort zone.
- If you don't constantly innovate, you will be left behind.
- Don't be crazy, but take some risks!
- New ideas, discoveries, and opportunities seldom come without risks.

Fail to succeed
- Fail fast and fail often.
- Forget everything you learned in school; it's okay to fail.
- Embrace failure as part of the learning process.
- Failure is sometimes just the beginning, not the end.

NOTES

INTRODUCTION

1. Raymond, Joan, "Frequent Flier: On Adventure's Trail, Some Endings Bring a Blush," *New York Times*, January 10, 2011 (http://www.nytimes.com/2011/01/11/business/11flier.html).

CHAPTER 1

1. Florida, Rana, interview with Mario Batali in "Your Start-Up Life," *Huffington Post*, February 16, 2012 (http://www.huffingtonpost.com/rana-florida/your-startup-life-advice-_b_1262396.html).

2. Robison, Jennifer, "Happiness Is Love—and $75,000,"*Gallup Business Journal*, November 17, 2011 (http://businessjournal.gallup.com/content/150671/happiness-is-love-and-75k.aspx).

3. Florida, Rana, "Your Start-Up Life: World's 100 Most Powerful Women: Zaha Hadid on the Struggle to Succeed," *Huffington Post*, May 31, 2012 (http://www.huffingtonpost.com/rana-florida/zaha-hadid_b_1553959.html).

4. Florida, Rana, "Your Start-Up Life: With Governor O'Malley: Never Give Up and Keep Moving Forward," *Huffington Post*, June 14, 2012 (http://www.huffingtonpost.com/rana-florida/martin-omalley-maryland_b_1591690.html).

5. Florida, Rana, "Your Start-Up Life: Advice from a CNN Anchor on How to Make Money," Ali Velshi interview in *Huffington Post*, March 1, 2012 (http://www.huffingtonpost.com/rana-florida/ali-velshi-cnn_b_1293355.html).

6. Brody, Jane E., "When Daily Stress Gets in the Way of Life," *New York Times*, December 10, 2012 (http://well.blogs.nytimes.com/2012/12/10/dont-let-stress-get-in-the-way-of-life).

7. http://www.fastcodesign.com/1672137/forget-the-mission-statement-whats-your-mission-question?utm_source=twitter.

8. Rubin, Gretchen, *The Happiness Project* (HarperCollins, 2009), p. 30.

9. Lohr, Steve, "Taking a Stand for Office Ergonomics," *New York Times*, December 1, 2012 (http://www.nytimes.com/2012/12/02/business/stand-up-desks-gaining-favor-in-the-workplace.html).

10. Berger, Shoshana, "Get a Standing Desk," *Wired*, October 7, 2012 (http://www.wired.com/wiredscience/2012/10/mf-standing-desk).

11. Jackson, Susy, "To Stand or Sit at Work: An Auto-Analytics Experiment," *Harvard Business Review*, January 2, 2013.

12. Florida, Rana, "Your Start-Up Life: Take It All in Stride: The Good, the Bad, and the Ugly," *Huffington Post*, August 9, 2012 (http://www.huffingtonpost.com/rana-florida/chicago-richard-daley_b_1742034.html).

13. http://www.nytimes.com/2013/03/10/opinion/sunday/living-with-less-a-lot-less.html?pagewanted=2&_r=2

14. MacNeill, Kara, "Why I'm Not Giving Presents This Christmas," December 12, 2012 blog post in *Huffington Post* (http://www.huffingtonpost.ca/kara-macneill/giving-to-charity-christmas_b_2324693.html).

15. http://www.nytimes.com/2013/03/10/opinion/sunday/living-with-less-a-lot-less.html?pagewanted=2&_r=2.

16. Florida, Rana, "Your Start-Up Life: Fail to Succeed," interview with Sir Ken Robinson in *Huffington Post*, February 5, 2013 (http://www.huffingtonpost.com/rana-florida/your-start-up-life-fail-t_b_2586288.html).

17. Florida, "Fail to Succeed."

18. Florida, Rana, "Your Start-Up Life: Find Leaders Better Than You," interview with Jamie Drummond in *Huffington Post*, September 6, 2012 (http://www.huffingtonpost.com/rana-florida/jamie-drummond-one-campaign_b_1822128.html).

19. Florida, "Fail to Succeed."

20. Florida, Rana, "Your Start-Up Life: With the Woman Who Remade New York, *Huffington Post*, February 18, 2013 (http://www.huffingtonpost.com/rana-florida/your-start-up-life-with-t_b_2713412.html).

CHAPTER 2

1. Florida, Richard, "The World Is Spiky," *The Atlantic,* October 2005 (http://www.theatlantic.com/past/docs/images/issues/200510/world_is_spiky.pdf).

2. Florida, Rana, "Your Start-Up Life: Rocket Man on Making the Impossible Possible," interview with Peter Diamandis in *Huffington Post*, August 23, 2012 (http://www.huffingtonpost.com/rana-florida/your-startup-life-advice-_2_b_1812728.html).

3. Florida, Rana, "Your Start-Up Life: Dan Pink on Why 'Passion' Doesn't Matter," *Huffington Post*, April 5, 2012 (http://www.huffingtonpost.com/ rana-florida/dan-pink_b_1389898.html).

4. Nemy, Enid, "Exchanging Standard Careers for Dreams," *New York Times*, August 7, 1981 (http://www.nytimes.com/1981/08/07/style/exchanging -standard-careers-for-dreams.html).

5. Linkner, Josh, "27 Lessons from 27 Years," Dan Gilbert aphorisms, posted December 9, 2012 (http://joshlinkner.com/2012/12/).

6. Florida, Rana, "Your Start-Up Life: Find What You Love to Do," interview with Wayne Pacelle in *Huffington Post*, July 26, 2012 (http://www.huffingtonpost .com/rana-florida/wayne-pacelle-humane-society_b_1699655.html).

7. Florida, Rana, "Your Start-Up Life: With Andre Agassi: Playing Big," *Huffington Post*, September 10, 2012 (http://www.huffingtonpost.com/rana-florida/ your-startup-life-with-an_b_1866970.html).

CHAPTER 3

1. Wang, Shirley S., "Ted2011: Smiling Makes the World Go Round," *Wall Street Journal Health Blog*, March 1, 2011 (http://blogs.wsj.com/health/2011/03/01/ ted2011-smiling-makes-the-world-go-round/).

2. Robinson, Sir Ken, "Do Schools Kill Creativity?" http://blogs.wsj.com/ health/2011/03/01/ted2011-smiling-makes-the-world-go-round/.

3. Robinson, "Do Schools Kill Creativity?"

4. Bartel, Marvin, "Stereotypes and Divergent Thinking" (blog post). (http:// people.goshen.edu/~marvinpb/11–13–01/Effects-of-Stereotypes.html).

5. Florida, "Fail to Succeed."

6. Linkner, "27 Lessons from 27 Years."

7. Linkner, "27 Lessons from 27 Years."

8. Pace, Julie, "Obama, Chris Christie Tour Damage Left by Hurricane Sandy in New Jersey," *Huffington Post*, October 31, 2012 (http://www.huffingtonpost. com/2012/10/31/obama-chris-christie-_n_2050017.html).

9. Florida, "Rocket Man."

10. Bergland, Christopher, "The Athlete's Way," *Psychology Today*, February 8, 2012 (http://www.psychologytoday.com/blog/the-athletes-way/201202/ the-neuroscience-imagination).

11. Schwartz, Tony, "Relax! You'll Be More Productive, *New York Times*, February 9, 2013. (http://www.nytimes.com/2013/02/10/opinion/sunday/relax -you'll-be-more-productive.html)

12. Bergland, "The Athletes' Way."

13. Reynolds, Gretchen, "Easing Brain Fatigue with a Walk in the Park," Phys Ed blog, *New York Times*, March 27, 2013 (http://well.blogs.nytimes. com/2013/03/27/easing-brain-fatigue-with-a-walk-in-the-park/).

14. http://well.blogs.nytimes.com/2013/03/27/easing-brain-fatigue-with-a-walk -in-the-park/?smid=tw-share).

15. Stewart, James B., "Looking for a Lesson in Google's Perks," *New York Times,* March 15, 2013 (http://www.nytimes.com/2013/03/16/business/at -google-a-place-to-work-and-play.html?pagewanted=all&_r=0).

16. http://www.nytimes.com/2013/03/16/business/at-google-a-place-to-work -and-play.html?_r=0.

17. Florida, Rana, "Your Start-Up Life: Tory Burch on Making Fashion Her Business," *Huffington Post,* May 3, 2012 (http://www.huffingtonpost.com/ rana-florida/tory-burch_b_1461153.html).

18. Marcus, Gary, "Happy New Year: Pick Up a New Skill," *New Yorker,* January 1, 2013 (http://www.newyorker.com/online/blogs/newsdesk/2013/01/ new-skills-for-a-new-year.html).

19. Rubin, Gretchen, *The Happiness Project,* p. 67.

20. Florida, Rana, "Your Start-Up Life: How a Focus on Quality Took a Company from Bankruptcy to Profit," interview with Tomas Maier in *Huffington Post,* October 3, 2012. (http://www.huffingtonpost.com/rana-florida/bottega -veneta-tomas-maier_b_1892081.html).

21. Florida, Rana, "Your Start-Up Life: Design Your Thinking," interview with Tim Brown in *Huffington Post,* August 16, 2012 (http://www.huffingtonpost. com/rana-florida/your-startup-life-design-_b_1742074.html).

22. Florida, Rana, "Your Start-Up Life: Espresso King Ricardo Illy on La Dolce Vita," *Huffington Post*, March 22, 2012 (http://www.huffingtonpost.com/ rana-florida/ricardo-illy_b_1325444.html).

23. Florida, Rana, "World's 100 Most Powerful Women."

24. Florida, Rana, "Your Start-Up Life: The Business of Art," interview with Mera Rubell in *Huffington Post,* December 3, 2012 (http://www.huffingtonpost. com/rana-florida/your-start-up-life-the-bu_b_2204897.html).

25. Florida, Rana, "Your Start-Up Life: Spreading Positivity with Nelly Furtado," *Huffington Post,* December 10, 2012 (http://www.huffingtonpost.com/rana -florida/your-start-up-life-spread_b_2258198.html).

26. Florida, Rana, "Your Start-Up Life: Mark Cuban on Business as the 'Ultimate Sport,'" *Huffington Post,* March 8, 2012 (http://www.huffingtonpost.com/ rana-florida/mark-cuban_b_1295048.html).

27. Tischler, Linda, "5 Tips for Forging a Creative Partnership," *Fast Company* (http://www.fastcodesign.com/1671372/5-tips-for-forging-a-lasting -creative-partnership).

28. Bruce Nussbaum, personal e-mail to the author.

29. Pozen, Robert C., "They Work Long Hours, but What About the Results?" *New York Times,* October 6, 2012 (http://www.nytimes.com/2012/10/07/ business/measure-results-not-hours-to-improve-work-efficiency.html).

30. *Mad Men*, season 5, episode 1, "A Little Kiss," aired March 25, 2012.

31. Interview with Chrystia Freeland, *Elle*, October 2012.

32. Florida, Rana, "Your Start-Up Life: Designing the Perfect Office," interview with Bruce Kuwabara in *Huffington Post,* June 7, 2012 (http://www.huffingtonpost.com/rana-florida/office-design-creativity_b_1574702.html).

33. Florida, "Fail to Succeed."

34. *Forbes,* "Billionaires Issue," March 26, 2012.

35. Smith, Chris, "Open City," *New York Magazine,* September 26, 2012.

CHAPTER 4

1. O'Brien, Keith, "How to Make Time Expand," *Boston Globe*, September 9, 2012 (http://www.bostonglobe.com/ideas/2012/09/08/how-make-time-expand/26nkSfyQPEetCXXoFeZEZM/story.html).

2. Christensen, Clayton M., *How Will You Measure Your Life?* (New York: HarperBusiness, 2012), p. 73.

3. Florida, Rana, "Playing Big."

4. Florida, Rana, "Your Start-Up Life: Advice on Life, Work, and Play," interview with Tony Hsieh in *Huffington Post,* February 23, 2012 (http://www.huffingtonpost.com/rana-florida/your-startup-life-advice-_1_b_1289248.html).

5. Florida, "Why 'Passion' Doesn't Matter."

6. Johnson, Luke, "Beware the Boss with the Messianic Complex," *Financial Times,* September 11, 2012, p. 63.

7. Jobs, Steven, commencement address, Stanford University, delivered June 12, 2005; transcript available at http://news.stanford.edu/news/2005/june15/jobs-061505.html.

8. Ferriss, Tim, *The 4-Hour Workweek* (Harmony, 2007), p. 321.

9. Wilson, H. James, "You, by the Numbers," *Harvard Business Review,* September, 2012 (http://hbr.org/2012/09/you-by-the-numbers).

10. Wolf, Gary, "Know Thyself: Tracking Every Facet of Life, from Sleep to Mood to Pain," *Wired*, June 22, 2009 (http://www.wired.com/medtech/health/magazine/17-07/lbnp_knowthyself).

11. "Self Tracking: Becoming Your Own Big Brother," *Talk of the Nation*, National Public Radio, January 15, 2013 (http://www.npr.org/2013/01/15/169432736/self-tracking-becoming-your-own-big-brother).

12. Trebay, Guy, "Guess Who Isn't Coming to Dinner," *New York Times,* November 28, 2012 (http://www.nytimes.com/2012/11/29/fashion/saving-the-endangered-dinner-party.html?pagewanted=all&_r=0).

13. Florida, "Espresso King Ricardo Illy."

14. Florida, "Take it All in Stride."

15. Patrick, Josh, "Do You Listen to Your Employees?", You're the Boss Blog,

New York Times, March 7, 2013 (http://boss.blogs.nytimes.com/2013/03/07/do-you-listen-to-your-employees/).

16. Fried, Jason, "Be More Productive: Take Time Off," *New York Times*, August 18, 2012.

17. Schwartz, "Relax! You'll Be More Productive."

18. Linkner, "27 Lessons from 27 Years."

19. Stillman, Jessica, "Sheryl Sandberg Leaves Work at 5:30: Why Can't You?" *Inc.com*, April 9, 2012 (http://www.inc.com/jessica-stillman/facebook-sheryl-sandberg-can-leave-early-why-arent-you.html).

20. Entis, Laura, "The Case for a 25-Hour Work Week (This is Not a Joke)," *Inc.com*, February 4, 2013 (http://www.inc.com/laura-entis/25-hour-work-week-an-argument-for-redistributing-working-hours.html).

21. Florida, Richard, "The World's Worst Commutes," blog post at *The Atlantic*, July 1, 2010 (http://www.theatlantic.com/international/archive/2010/07/the-worlds-worst-commutes/59062/).

22. Goudreau, Jenna, "Back to the Stone Age? New Yahoo CEO Marissa Mayer Bans Working from Home," *Forbes*, February 25, 2013 (http://www.forbes.com/sites/jennagoudreau/2013/02/25/back-to-the-stone-age-new-yahoo-ceo-marissa-mayer-bans-working-from-home/).

23. Guynn, Jessica, "Yahoo CEO Marissa Mayer Causes Uproar with Telecommuting Ban," *Los Angeles Times*, February 26, 2013 (http://www.latimes.com/business/la-fi-yahoo-telecommuting-20130226,0,5913345.story).

24. Florida, Rana, "Your Start-Up Life: Do Team-Building Retreats Ever Work?" *Huffington Post*, June 28, 2012 (http://www.huffingtonpost.com/rana-florida/your-startup-life-team-bu_b_1630316.html).

25. Pozen, "They Work Long Hours."

26. Lavenda, David, "Email Is Crushing Us: Can Activity Streams Free Us?" *Fast Company*, March 22, 2012 (http://www.fastcompany.com/1825915/email-crushing-us-can-activity-streams-free-us).

27. Rosenwald, Mike, "Eradicating 'Reply All,'" *Bloomberg Businessweek*, November 21, 2012 (http://www.businessweek.com/articles/2012-11-21/eradicating-reply-all).

28. Florida, Rana, "Your Start-Up Life: Help, I'm Drowning in E-Mail," *Huffington Post*, March 29, 2012 (http://www.huffingtonpost.com/rana-florida/manage-email_b_1378010.html).

29. Pozen, "They Work Long Hours."

30. Florida, Rana, "Your Start-Up Life: Don't Manage, Lead," interview with Don Tapscott in *Huffington Post*, November 20, 2012 (http://www.huffingtonpost.com/rana-florida/don-tapscott-business-advice_b_2158269.html).

31. Gaffney, Tamara, "Cyber Monday Sales Climb to New Heights," *Digital Marketing Blog*, November 26, 2012 (http://blogs.adobe.com/digitalmarketing/analytics/predictive-analytics/cyber-monday-2012).

32. Thier, David, "Facebook Has a Billion Users and a Revenue Question," *Forbes,* October 4, 2012 (http://www.forbes.com/sites/davidthier/2012/10/04/facebook-has-a-billion-users-and-a-revenue-question).

33. Tiku, Nitasha, "Mark Zuckerberg: He's Just Like Us!" *New York Magazine* "Daily Intelligencer," September 13, 2010 (http://nymag.com/daily/intelligencer/2010/09/mark_zuckerberg_hes_just_like.html).

CHAPTER 5
1. Dishman, Lydia, "Why Your Company Needs a Chief Collaboration Officer," *Fast Company,* May 6, 2012 (http://www.fastcompany.com/1836468/why-your-company-needs-chief-collaboration-officer).

2. Hansen, Morten T., and Scott Tapp, "Who Should Be Your Chief Collaboration Officer?" *Harvard Business Review* Blog Network, October 11, 2010 (http://blogs.hbr.org/cs/2010/10/who_should_be_your_chief_colla.html).

3. Bryant, Adam, "Don't Chase Everything That Shines: Interview with Sandra L. Kurtzig," *New York Times,* December 1, 2012 (http://www.nytimes.com/2012/12/02/business/sandra-kurtzig-of-kenandy-on-keeping-companies-focused.html).

4. Brown, Chip, "The Epic Ups and Downs of Peter Gelb," *New York Times Magazine,* March 21, 2013 (http://www.nytimes.com/2013/03/24/magazine/the-epic-ups-and-downs-of-peter-gelb.html?pagewanted=all&_r=0).

5. Florida, "Fail to Succeed."

6. Florida, "Advice on Life, Work, and Play."

7. Florida, "The Business of Art."

8. Florida, Rana, "Your Start-Up Life: Why Serving Is the New Leading," interview with John Noseworthy, MD, in *Huffington Post,* July 12, 2012 (http://www.huffingtonpost.com/rana-florida/your-startup-life-why-ser_b_1652112.html).

9. Silverthorne, Sean, "Culture Changers: Managing High-Impact Entrepreneurs," *Working Knowledge,* January 7, 2013 (http://hbswk.hbs.edu/item/7157.html).

10. Florida, "Design Your Thinking."

11. Florida, "Advice on Life, Work, and Play."

12. Andersen, Erika, "Don't Be a Power Hog: How Sharing Information, Time and Authority Makes You a Better Leader," *Fast Company,* November 19, 2012 (http://www.fastcompany.com/3003033/dont-be-power-hog-how-sharing-information-time-and-authority-makes-you-better-leader).

13. Andersen, "Don't Be a Power Hog."

14. Florida, "Don't Manage, Lead."

15. McCracken, Grant, *Chief Culture Officer* (New York: Basic Books, 2009), p. 2.

16. Florida, "World's 100 Most Powerful Women, op cit.

17. "Swiffer: A Game Changing Home Product," Continuum Advanced Systems (http://continuuminnovation.com/work/swiffer).

18. Vance, Ashley, and Dina Bass, "Why Steven Sinofsky Really Left Microsoft," *Bloomberg Businessweek,* November 15, 2012 (http://www.businessweek.com/articles/2012-11-12/microsoft-shows-its-windows-chief-the-door).

19. Heine, Christopher, "Frito Lay Likes the Data from 'Crash the Superbowl,'" *Adweek,* February 7, 2013 (http://www.adweek.com/news/technology/frito-lay-likes-data-doritos-crash-super-bowl-147127).

20. Oliver, Simone S., "Decoded Fashion and CFDA Host Fasion Hackathon," *New York Times*, February 22, 2013 (http://runway.blogs.nytimes.com/2013/02/22/decoded-fashion-and-cfda-host-fashion-hackathon/).

21. Florida, "How a Focus on Quality."

22. Florida, "Why Serving Is the New Leading."

23. Bryant, Adam, "In Mario Batali's Kitchen, You'll Refrain from Shouting," *New York Times,* August 25, 2012 (http://www.nytimes.com/2012/08/26/business/in-mario-batalis-kitchen-please-refrain-from-shouting.html).

24. Florida, "Design Your Thinking."

25. Mandell, Fred, and Kathleen Jordan, *Becoming a Life Change Artist* (New York: Avery, 2010), p. 216.

CHAPTER 6

1. Florida, "The Business of Art."

2. Day, Peter, "Brooklyn Start-Ups," BBC World Service, November 25, 2012 (http://www.bbc.co.uk/programmes/p010n7tz).

3. Florida, "Design Your Thinking."

4. Florida, Rana, interview with Mario Batali, *Huffington Post.*

5. Florida, Rana, "Your Start-Up Life: Break the Rules, but Do So *Brilliantly,*" interview with David Stark in *Huffington Post,* December 27, 2012 (http://www.huffingtonpost.com/rana-florida/your-start-up-life-break_b_2323368.html).

CHAPTER 7

1. Kidder, David, *The Startup Playbook* (Chronicle, 2013), p. 32; http://qz.com/65713/how-spanx-came-to-be-a-girl-was-allowed-to-sit-and-think/.

2. Florida, "Don't Manage, Lead."

3. Day, Peter, "Brooklyn Start-Ups."

4. Interview with Barbara Walters, "Most Fascinating People of 2011," ABC, December, 14 2011.

5. Florida, "Mark Cuban on Business."

6. Florida, "Spreading Positivity with Nelly Furtado."

7. Florida, Rana, "Your Start-Up Life: Artist Doesn't Believe in Failure," interview with Kenny Scharf in *Huffington Post*, August 2, 2012 (http://www.huffingtonpost.com/rana-florida/your-startup-life-artist-_b_1695822.html).

8. Florida, "Fail to Succeed."

9. Florida, "Playing Big."

10. Florida, interview with Mario Batali, *Huffington Post*.

11. Florida, "The Business of Art."

12. Pfeffer, Jeffrey, "What You Can Learn from Tim Ferriss About Power," *Harvard Business Review* Blog Network, March 29, 2011 (http://blogs.hbr.org/cs/2011/03/power_comes_to_those_willing_t.html).

13. Florida, Rana, "Your Start-Up Life: Jean-Georges's Ingredients for Success," interview with Jean-Georges Vongerichten in *Huffington Post*, October 24, 2012 (http://www.huffingtonpost.com/rana-florida/your-startup-life-jeansge_b_1998455.html).

14. Florida, Rana, "Your Start-Up Life: Why Diversity and Freedom Are Good for Business," interview with Frank Toscan in *Huffington Post*, September 26, 2012 (http://www.huffingtonpost.com/rana-florida/mac-cosmetics-frank-toskan_b_1905808.html).

15. Williams, Alex, "Saying No to College," *New York Times*, November 30, 2012 (http://www.nytimes.com/2012/12/02/fashion/saying-no-to-college.html).

16. Grohl, Dave, "Dave Grohl's SSXW Keynote Speech: The Full Text," *Rolling Stone*, March 15, 2013 (http://www.rollingstone.com/music/news/dave-grohls-sxsw-keynote-speech-the-complete-text-20130315#ixzz2PVXlTj6m).

17. Florida, "Spreading Positivity."

18. Florida, "Jean-Georges's Ingredients for Success."

19. Florida, "How a Focus on Quality."

20. Florida, Rana, "Your Start-Up Life: The Fashion of Business," *Huffington Post*, September 20, 2012 (http://www.huffingtonpost.com/rana-florida/peter-marino-design_b_1876996.html).

21. "Gregory Rayburn on the Dimming of Twinkies," *Bloomberg Businessweek*, November 21, 2012 (http://www.businessweek.com/articles/2012-11-21/gregory-rayburn-on-the-dimming-of-twinkies).

INDEX

ABOUT THE AUTHOR

Rana Florida is the CEO of the Creative Class Group, managing new business development, marketing, consulting, research, and global operations. CCG is a boutique advisory services firm composed of leading next-generation researchers, academics, and strategists. Its clients include BMW, Starwood, IBM, Philips, Pinewood Studios, Zappos, and Johnson & Johnson, to name just a few.

Rana has more than two decades of experience in corporate strategy, communications, marketing, and branding. She previously directed global strategic communications for HMSHost, one of the world's largest airport developers, where she led all marketing, advertising, and communication efforts.

Rana is a business advice columnist for the *Huffington Post* and an editor on design and lifestyle for HGTV and Food TV. Rana was an internationally syndicated advice columnist in major daily newspapers for almost a decade and a regular Fox News (WJBK) contributor. Her platform as a smart and trusted interviewer led to multiple conversations with celebrities, businesspeople, and all-around creatives such as

Andre Agassi, Nelly Furtado, Tony Hsieh, Tory Burch, Mark Cuban, Sir Ken Robinson, Mario Batali, Dan Pink, and Maryland Governor Martin O'Malley, among others. *Upgrade* springs from these interviews and the breadth of Rana's business experience.

She recently wrote for and was featured in the business section of the *New York Times* and has appeared as a business advice contributor on the *Today Show*.

Rana holds a bachelor of arts in communications and an MBA in marketing and management. When she's not stuck at an airport, she lives with her husband in Toronto, Miami, and New York City.